THE
BROWNS
BLUES

Also by Terry Pluto

TERRY PLUTO

THE BROWNS BLUES

Two Decades of UTTER FRUSTRATION:
Why Everything KEPT GOING WRONG for the CLEVELAND BROWNS

GRAY & COMPANY, PUBLISHERS
CLEVELAND

Gray & Company, Publishers
www.grayco.com

ISBN 978-1-59851-100-0
Printed in the United States of America
1

To Mary Kelly and all who love the Browns
even if they don't know why

Contents

THE
BROWNS
BLUES

Browns Key Front-Office Personnel by Season

1999
Owner: Al Lerner
CEO: Carmen Policy
Exec. VP: Dwight Clark
Head coach: Chris Palmer
Record: 2-14

2000
Owner: Al Lerner
CEO: Carmen Policy
Exec. VP: Dwight Clark
Head coach: Chris Palmer
Record: 3-13

2001
Owner: Al Lerner
CEO: Carmen Policy
Exec. VP: Dwight Clark
Head coach: Butch Davis
Record: 7-9

2002
Owner: Al Lerner*
Owner: Randy Lerner*
CEO: Carmen Policy
GM and head coach: Butch Davis
Record: 9-7 (wild-card playoff game loss, 36-33, to Pittsburgh Steelers)
* Oct. 23: Al Lerner dies. His son, Randy Lerner, takes over.

2003
Owner: Randy Lerner
CEO: Carmen Policy
GM and head coach: Butch Davis
Record: 5-11

2004
Owner: Randy Lerner
President and CEO: John Collins
GM and head coach: Butch Davis*
Interim head coach: Terry Robiskie*
Record: 4-12
* Nov. 30: Davis resigns, replaced by interim head coach Robiskie.

2005
Owner: Randy Lerner
President and CEO: John Collins
GM: Phil Savage
Head coach: Romeo Crennel
Record: 6-10

2006
Owner: Randy Lerner
GM: Phil Savage
Head coach: Romeo Crennel
Record: 4-12

2007
Owner: Randy Lerner
GM: Phil Savage
Head coach: Romeo Crennel
Record: 10-6

2008
Owner: Randy Lerner
GM: Phil Savage
Head coach: Romeo Crennel
Record: 4-12

2009
Owner: Randy Lerner
President: Mike Holmgren*
GM: George Kokinis**
Head coach: Eric Mangini
Record: 5-11
* Dec. 21: Holmgren becomes Browns president.
** Nov. 2: Kokinis fired.

2010
Owner: Randy Lerner
President: Mike Holmgren
GM: Tom Heckert
Head coach: Eric Mangini
Record: 5-11

2011
Owner: Randy Lerner
President: Mike Holmgren
GM: Tom Heckert
Head coach: Pat Shurmur
Record: 4-12

2012
Owner: Randy Lerner*
Owner: Jimmy and Dee Haslam*
President: Mike Holmgren
CEO: Joe Banner*
GM: Tom Heckert
Head coach: Pat Shurmur
Record: 5-11
* Oct. 25: Jimmy and Dee Haslam purchase Browns from Lerner, hire Banner to be CEO.

2013
Owner: Jimmy and Dee Haslam
CEO: Joe Banner
GM: Mike Lombardi
Head coach: Rob Chudzinski
Record: 4-12

2014
Owner: Jimmy and Dee Haslam
GM: Ray Farmer
Head coach: Mike Pettine
Record: 7-9

2015
Owner: Jimmy and Dee Haslam
GM: Ray Farmer
Head coach: Mike Pettine
Record: 3-13

2016
Owner: Jimmy and Dee Haslam
Exec. VP: Sashi Brown
Head coach: Hue Jackson
Record: 1-15

2017
Owner: Jimmy and Dee Haslam
Exec. VP: Sashi Brown*
GM: John Dorsey*
Head coach: Hue Jackson
Record: 0-16
* Dec, 7: Brown fired, Dorsey hired.

About Writing This Book

Will the Browns ever get it right?

Over and over again, fans ask me that question.

Who can blame them?

From the return of the franchise in 1999 through the end of the winless 2017 season, the Browns had the overall worst record in the NFL.

It was two winning seasons. One playoff appearance. Zero playoff victories.

And more ulcers than any fan base should have to endure.

The focus of this book is what went wrong with the Browns. In writing about that, I stayed away from conspiracy theories and gutter gossip. What I wrote are things that I'm absolutely sure happened—or at least that people who were actually there believe happened.

Some people talked on background. Others for the record. Because I have been covering the Browns since 1999 as a columnist for the Akron Beacon Journal and The Plain Dealer, I was able to know virtually all the general managers and coaches. At some point, I had one-on-one interviews with most of them.

Some of the material for the book comes from those talks. Other material comes from reading transcripts and stories I wrote from key press conferences over the years.

What did they say on draft night? What did they say when this coach was fired?

Simply reading those comments is revealing of the state of mind of those running the Browns at those key moments.

The fans are a huge part of the story. Why do they still care about this team? Without them, there are no Browns.

The Browns have been a dysfunctional football family for decades. Because the franchise moved to Baltimore after the 1995 season, the fans have abandonment issues. Because the NFL had the team return so quickly in 1999—the fastest start-up for an expansion franchise since 1976—the fans have trust issues. So many front office people and coaches have come through with so many ideas and promises. The results have been more losing, more frustration, more changes . . .

And more of the same dreadful football on Sunday.

Browns fans are conflicted. They want to believe, but they are afraid of being let down again. Yet they come back, often with fear and trepidation.

That's why I included their voices in this book. After all, they are the best part of the franchise.

Introduction

"It's hard to believe it's been that bad."

Stop the pain!

That has been the problem for the Cleveland Browns since the franchise returned in 1999.

That's because the franchise was reborn in pain ...

Lots and lots of pain.

It's the pain of betrayal, the old Browns moving from Cleveland to Baltimore after the 1995 season. That remains one of the most outrageously unfair franchise shifts in all of sports history. I documented that in my book *False Start*, published in 2004.

Not much has changed since then.

In fact, it's been worse.

In some ways, it's been much, much worse. It's been no playoffs since 2002 worse.

It's the pain of the last winning season being 2007, that 10-6 record only the second winning season since the team returned in 1999.

Think about this ...

In 2001, the Browns were 7-9. It was only the third season since the Browns returned. That year showed promise.

In 2002, the Browns were 9-7 and made the playoffs. That's major, major progress in the fourth year of an expansion franchise.

But since then ...

Pain!

False Start explained how the 1999 Browns had the quickest startup time of an NFL franchise since 1970. The book talked a lot about the decisions of Art Modell and Al Lerner. I'm not going to dwell on those issues again in this book.

Instead, I'll try to figure out what happened since . . . and why.

Why did so many good people fail?

I repeat: Why did so many good people fail while trying to fix the Cleveland Browns? And many of the executives and coaches who passed through here were talented people.

"The Browns are kind of like a train," said Phil Savage, the team's general manager from 2005 to 2008.

Savage is one of those people. His drafting helped Ozzie Newsome build a Super Bowl winning team in . . . Baltimore.

Talk about the pain!

So what was Savage talking about when he brought up a train?

"The Browns have had a lot of good cars . . . good people," said Savage. "But it's like they could never get them lined up the right way. There were a lot of good cars, but they never could get them in the proper order on the right track."

For example, I believe Eric Mangini could have been an effective coach with Savage as his general manager.

But owner Randy Lerner fired Savage after the 2008 season—along with coach Romeo Crennel. He hired Mangini to replace Savage *and* Crennel. He turned the franchise over to a guy who had been a former New York Jets coach, but had never run the front office.

Savage and Crennel survived the longest in Cleveland—together for four years.

Coach Butch Davis lasted 3½ seasons.

Chris Palmer, Mangini, Pat Shurmur and Mike Pettine lasted two years. Rob Chudzinski was fired after a single season.

I believe Chudzinski is an excellent offensive coordinator. He proved that with the Browns in 2007, when they were 10-6.

How about Savage as general manager, Mangini coaching? And Chudzinski calling the plays for the offense. Toss in Crennel as defensive coordinator, a job he has done well for several franchises.

Now that train could be headed in the right direction.

Instead, the Browns have been a train wreck.

I had two long interviews with Joe Banner, CEO of the Browns in 2013. He came to town with an excellent reputation as a salary cap expert who also was a strong big-picture NFL executive.

He had one year.

At one point, Banner said, "It's hard to believe it's been that bad in Cleveland."

It is . . .

And it isn't . . .

It goes back to Stopping The Pain.

Each new front office/coach combination inherits the failures of the previous regimes. It also is covered with the frustration of the fans, all the failures turning many of them cynical.

Browns fans are like an abused sports family. Anyone who marries into them has to deal with all the broken promises, failed plans, changing quarterbacks, botched drafts and the Browns consistently losing on any given Sunday.

Most of all, it's the pain!

Before the 2017 season opened, I asked Jimmy Haslam if the owner had any real understanding of the pain experienced by Browns fans when he bought the team in August of 2012.

"Dee (his wife) and I had no clue," said Haslam. "No clue at all. Do we realize it and share the pain now? Absolutely. Dee says this better than I do: 'We share that pain and share the responsibility for helping ease the pain.'"

The pain is deep from a gaping wound infected with a sense of rejection.

For all the talk of The Fumble, The Drive, Red Right 88 and the other mileposts of Browns heartbreak, the biggest is The Move.

The Browns never should have moved. The NFL knows it. The fans know it. Everyone with any sense of justice who happens to live outside of Baltimore County should admit it. The Browns got a raw deal. Those in Baltimore believe they finally received some justice because their team (the old Baltimore Colts) moved to Indianapolis in 1984. They figured the Browns showing up for the 1996 season was retribution finally being paid.

The pain of The Move created a sense of mistrust from the fans.

When Haslam bought the Browns, I received a lot of emails from fans convinced he'd move the franchise to Knoxville—Haslam's home town. The fact that the NFL would never approve a move to Knoxville didn't matter. The NFL already has a team in Nashville (the Tennessee Titans). That franchise is a mere 180 miles from Knoxville. The reason the Titans are called "Tennessee" and not Nashville is because the franchise represents the entire state.

No matter.

Browns fans never thought their team would move to Baltimore. And the NFL has a reckless and terrible reputation of ripping franchises out of one city and moving them to another without any sense of fairness or concern of damage to the old city and fans.

Not only have Browns fans been traumatized by what has happened to their team, they understandably have major trust issues.

An older group of Browns fans never trusted Art Modell because he fired Paul Brown, the coach and football godfather of the franchise.

Some Browns fans didn't trust the Lerner family because Al Lerner helped Modell move the franchise to Baltimore. And they didn't trust Randy Lerner, who seemed like an accidental owner after his father died. While the Lerner family at least had deep Cleveland roots, the Haslams do not.

I don't believe the Haslams want to move the team. I doubt the NFL would allow it.

But as Bishop Joey Johnson of Akron's House of the Lord often says: "When your heart is broke, your head don't work right."

Johnson intentionally mauls the grammar to make his point: So many things lose focus when we are in pain.

And too often, Browns fans have screamed, "Just stop the pain!"

That usually meant, "CHANGE THE QUARTERBACK! FIRE THE COACH! BLOW UP THE FRONT OFFICE!"

In some ways, it's their hearts screaming: "WHY DO I LOVE THIS TEAM WHEN IT HURTS SO MUCH! PLEASE STOP THE PAIN!"

Owners often responded by firing people . . . quickly . . . painfully . . . and too soon.

The desire to stop the pain has led to even more pain.

And that's a big reason the Browns have had so many problems since they returned in 1999.

It Started With Tim Couch, but Don't Blame Him

"You feel like you're letting people down."

We knew nothing.

That's what I was thinking when I was writing this book.

When Tim Couch was the first draft pick of the Cleveland Browns' expansion franchise in 1999, did anyone believe the Browns would be the NFL's worst franchise over the next 19 years? Or that Couch would be the first of 28 different starting quarterbacks for the Browns heading into 2018?

Think back to 1995, when the Browns moved to Baltimore. They were not a franchise where quarterbacks went to die.

Brian Sipe was the starter from 1976 to 1983, winning the MVP award in 1980.

Bernie Kosar took over as the starter in the middle of the 1985 season, and held the job until he was cut in the middle of the 1993 season.

Vinny Testaverde was the primary starter after Kosar left until the team moved.

Sipe . . . Kosar . . . Testaverde.

That's not exactly Cody Kessler . . . Kevin Hogan ... DeShone Kizer. Or Colt McCoy . . . Brandon Weeden . . . Johnny Manziel.

In the name of Otto Graham, the Browns actually had respectable-to-good quarterback play for a long time.

Then came 1999 when the Browns returned, but their ability to find a quarterback seemed lost in the franchise move to Baltimore in 1996. The Browns had the first pick in the 1999 draft.

Looking back, they would have been better off trading the choice to New Orleans. The Saints were run by Mike Ditka, and he offered his entire draft for that pick—and the right to draft running back Ricky Williams.

The Browns turned it down, because they wanted to start fresh with a new quarterback—Couch.

The Saints eventually traded with Washington for the right to draft Williams.

In the 1999 draft, New Orleans gave up picks in the first, third, fourth, fifth, sixth and seventh rounds. The Saints also traded their first- and third-round picks in the 2000 draft for the No. 5 overall selection in the 1999 draft.

Considering the inept way the Browns were drafting in those early years, who knows what they would have done with those picks.

* * *

It's hard to remember the hype around Couch in 1999.

He was from Hyden, Kentucky, a town about 125 miles southwest of Lexington. Not only was he the best high school football player in the state, he was considered perhaps the best basketball player.

He was considered the top high school quarterback recruit in the country when he enrolled at Kentucky in 1996. He was going to one of the worst football programs in the SEC. He was playing in a basketball crazy state for a school that considered football a minor diversion until the ball started bouncing.

He played little as a freshman under coach Bill Curry. Couch was ready to transfer when Curry was fired, replaced by Hal Mumme. One of the first things the new coach did was tell Couch that the offense would be centered around him. Mumme brought in what is now called the spread offense. Back then, it was a "run-and-shoot."

The quarterback is usually in the shotgun position. No huddle. No variance of a snap count. It's a quick "1-2-3-hike," and lots of short and medium passes. The playbook is limited, the quarterback is in control.

"I rarely got hit at Kentucky," Couch said. "Everything was quick." The previous three seasons before Couch/Mumme took over, Kentucky had records of 1-10, 4-7 and 4-7.

With Couch starting, Kentucky was fun to watch, lots of high-scoring games. The team improved to 5-6 and then 7-5.

In his last season (1998) at Kentucky, the 6-foot-4 Couch was 400-of-553 passing (72 percent), throwing 36 touchdown passes compared to 15 interceptions. He made lots of All-American teams, shattered most of Kentucky's school passing records. In six games of his 1998 season, Couch heaved at least 50 passes.

While a 7-5 record and a loss to Penn State in the Outback Bowl is modest compared to football powers such as Ohio State and Alabama, it was a huge step forward for Kentucky. It made the already popular Couch even more revered in his home state.

*   *   *

The Browns' new front office of CEO Carmen Policy and general manager Dwight Clark wanted a quarterback in the draft. Having a major say in the selection was Chris Palmer, a former offensive coordinator and quarterback coach for several franchises. This was Palmer's first chance to be a head coach.

Palmer rejected Donovan McNabb, a highly rated Syracuse quarterback. Palmer said he had heard some things about McNabb at Syracuse that bothered him.

Palmer was sold on Couch. At 6-foot-4, 227 pounds, he looked the part of an NFL quarterback. The Browns liked the fact that Couch went into a difficult football situation in Kentucky and became a star. The new Browns quarterback in 1999 was destined to face a lot of obstacles.

Looking back at the 1999 draft, there were five quarterbacks taken in the first 12 picks:

1. Kentucky's Couch went to the Browns.
2. Syracuse's McNabb went to Philadelphia.
3. Oregon's Akili Smith went to Cincinnati.
11. Central Florida's Daunte Culpepper went to Minnesota.
12. UCLA's Cade McNown went to Chicago.

Looking back, it was a disastrous draft for quarterbacks.

McNabb was terrific for Philadelphia. He was the Eagles' first pick, they had him rated higher than Couch. He made six Pro Bowls and reached the 2004 Super Bowl.

Culpepper made three Pro Bowls. He also had some very rough seasons. His career record was 41-59.

Smith was bust in Cincinnati, a 3-14 record as a starter in four seasons.

McNown was 3-12 as a starter in two seasons.

"It came down to Akili Smith and Couch," said Todd Stewart, who was the Browns director of public relations in 1999.

Now the athletic director at Western Kentucky, Stewart has stayed in touch with Couch over the years. He also has a clear memory of the thinking of the front office heading into that draft.

"It's the first year of a new franchise and we need to start with a quarterback," said Stewart. "That was the approach. If we could get a franchise quarterback for an expansion franchise, we'd be locked in for years with a guy to play the most important position on the field."

Stewart said the Browns did have Ricky Williams to Berea for a visit, but the running back was never under serious consideration. It was more of a smoke screen, a way to make other teams believe the Browns might not take a quarterback.

It's odd how NFL teams do that with the first pick. Even when they are sure who they will select—and no one else can draft in front of them—they still like to cover the decision with the haze of mystery.

"We thought Tim had the ability to lead an expansion franchise," said Stewart. "He could have gone to any major college football school in the country, but he decided to stay in his home state and help Kentucky build a program. That impressed the front office. He was a high-profile guy from the moment he stepped on campus. He was used to living under a lot of pressure."

So playing for a bad team in a state where he was a huge celebrity— that correlated to what he'd face in Cleveland.

As for Akili Smith, he had a much different background.

He was a seventh-round pick in the Major League Baseball draft in 1993 by the Pittsburgh Pirates. He signed at the age of 17. He played three seasons in the low minors, batting only .176 with four homers in 62 games as an outfielder. He then went to Grossmont Community College for two years, playing quarterback.

That led to Smith playing two seasons at Oregon, where he became a hot prospect as a senior. He had a strong arm and some athleticism, but the Browns didn't see him as ready to face the challenge of an expansion team. He went No. 3 to Bengals, where he never could establish himself as a starter.

*   *   *

The new Browns gave Couch the star treatment.

This was before the rookie salary cap, which didn't come into place until 2011. It was an era when first-round picks often missed parts of training camps with ugly contract disputes. CEO Carmen Policy decided he'd reach a contract agreement with Couch's agent before the draft—or the Browns would not pick him.

"I wanted to play for the Browns," said Couch. "I liked the idea of going to a new team, starting something."

Of course, Couch had no idea what it would mean to be a young quarterback on an expansion team. Browns fans had no idea what expansion football would be like.

No one had a clue.

The Browns signed Couch to a 7-year, $48 million deal. About $12 million was guaranteed.

Before taking an NFL snap, Couch had one of the league's most lucrative contracts in 1999. He signed on the morning of the draft. He told his agent he didn't want to miss any of training camp.

Couch was at the draft in New York to go up on stage when his name was called as the Browns' first pick. Browns owner Al Lerner had his private jet waiting. After the first round, Couch flew from New York to Cleveland where he met with the media.

*   *   *

From the rebirth of the franchise, the Browns had one plan for their quarterbacks—and quickly changed it.

The front office signed veteran Ty Detmer. He was a little like Josh

McCown, a respected quarterback who spent more time as a backup than as a starter. But he could do a decent job. Policy thought it was wise to let Detmer take the physical pounding and the losing that was inevitable for many expansion quarterbacks.

Palmer had other ideas.

The Browns opened the season with the Pittsburgh Steelers. It was the first game of an expansion franchise.

The Browns lost 43-0, which should not have been a surprise. The team was ill-equipped to deal with the NFL after having less than a full year to assemble a roster, a coaching staff and a front office.

The Browns had two first downs. That's right, *two!*

The Browns had nine total yards rushing. That's right, *nine* in nine carries!

The Browns' longest passing play from scrimmage was 19 yards to Leslie Shepherd. They ended up with 52 total yards passing. (Only 31 net, because Detmer and Couch got sacked three times.)

They were behind 36-0 early in the fourth quarter when Couch replaced Detmer. His first pass was intercepted.

The next week, Palmer decided to start Couch.

"I thought I was going to sit behind Ty for most of the year," said Couch. "They pulled the plug on that pretty quick."

And the front office of Carmen Policy and Dwight Clark nearly blew a gasket. They were shocked by Palmer's decision. But they stood by their coach.

I had a private conversation about it with Palmer, and he said everyone knew Detmer "was a just a backup. He's a good backup quarterback, but that's all he'll ever be."

His theory was Couch was drafted to be the starting quarterback, so just throw him in there.

"You learn more by playing," Palmer said. "You learn how to prepare for games better. You learn how to deal with the speed of the game. You can't duplicate game conditions in practice."

Palmer also knew the Browns were not going to win many games, so he thought they should begin to develop Couch.

So what did Couch learn in his first pro start?

He was sacked seven times, once for a safety. He lost a fumble and was harassed by the Tennessee defense all afternoon in a 26-9 loss to the Titans.

Couch started 14 games that season. The Browns had a 2-12 record with him as a rookie under center. He threw 15 touchdown passes compared to 13 interceptions, completing 56 percent of his passes.

For a first-year quarterback on a first-year expansion NFL team, those numbers are very respectable.

But he was sacked a league-high 56 times.

"At the time, I thought it was great getting a chance to start right away," said Couch. "As a player, you want to be out there competing."

But it was a horrible idea.

Kentucky coach Hal Mumme's spread offense was great for college, but didn't prepare Couch for the NFL. Not only was Couch learning the pro game, he was dealing for the first time with taking snaps under center rather than everything in the shotgun. He never had a complicated playbook until he was given one by Palmer.

I recall Palmer telling me the playbook was a big challenge for Couch because the pro-style offense was so new to him. A quarterback must not only know the plays. He also must be confident enough to call them and make sure all his teammates are in the right spots before the ball is snapped. It's a daunting task for most rookie quarterbacks.

"Looking back, it probably wasn't the best thing for me," said Couch. "If you are going to put a rookie quarterback in a situation like that, you need some pieces around him. You need to protect him on the line. You need some talented receivers and running backs. We didn't have many of those things—we were just getting started as a franchise. It was tough."

*   *   *

A year before Couch (1998), Peyton Manning had been the first pick of the NFL draft. The Tennessee quarterback went to Indianapolis, where Stewart was working in the public relations department before he came to the Browns in 1999.

"When Tim was a young player, I had friends and media people ask me to compare him to Peyton," said Stewart. "The Colts were 3-13 (in

1997), the year before Peyton was drafted. That wasn't good. But the Browns had NO record, NO team before Tim came to them. Look at the 1998 Colts roster. They had Marshall Faulk (1,319 yards rushing). They had an elite receiver in Marvin Harrison. They had Tarik Glenn, who was growing into a franchise left tackle."

Stewart becomes very passionate discussing the obstacles faced by Couch.

"While Peyton was handing the ball to Faulk, Tim was giving it to Terry Kirby," he said. "While Peyton was throwing to Marvin Harrison, Tim was throwing to Kevin Johnson, another rookie. The Browns line was really make-shift. It was nothing close to the supporting cast Peyton had with the Colts. I was there, I saw it in both places."

Stewart said Peyton Manning started from Day One with the Colts, where general manager Bill Polian subscribed to the Palmer theory.

"This is our guy, we're going to throw him in there," said Stewart, recalling Polian's approach. "Yes, he will be overwhelmed at times, but he's going to improve and use the experience to his benefit."

Manning was 3-13 in his rookie season as a starter. He threw 26 touchdown passes and 28 interceptions, completing 57 percent of his passes.

A big difference was Manning being sacked only 22 times, compared to 56 for Couch.

"He didn't take anything close to the physical beating Tim sustained," said Stewart.

*   *   *

Nothing prepared Couch for that first season.

"There were sacks," he said. "Lots and lots of sacks. Some of the sacks were on me because I was a young quarterback, not getting rid of the ball fast enough. Some was because of protection problems. Some was because we didn't have a lot of talent, being an expansion team."

While the physical bruises were painful, the hardest part was mental.

"There were points in that first year where I lost my confidence," he said. "I was the No. 1 pick in the draft and had never dealt with failure before. In high school, I became the No. 1 college recruit in the country. I was the SEC Player of the Year, first team All-American and a finalist for the Heisman Trophy. Then I got to the NFL and I'm losing games. I'm not putting up numbers. I didn't feel like I was playing up to my capabilities."

He paused, thinking.

"The hardest part was being the first overall pick and the face of the new franchise and not winning games," he said. "You feel the pressure every week. It weighs on you, all the losses. They just pile up."

His voice trailed off as he collected his thoughts.

"It takes a toll on you, being sacked so much," he said. "You feel like you don't have time to let plays develop downfield. You rush things. You speed up your reads. When a guy starts to pop open deep, you try to get rid of the ball quick before you get hit. Or you try to run (for a first down) and you get hit. A lot of things go through your mind."

Couch desperately wanted to succeed. He took his position as the face of the new franchise seriously.

"At times, you feel like you're letting people down with all the losing," he said.

Couch mentioned the Browns being in the same division with Baltimore, Pittsburgh and Cincinnati.

"Some of those teams had rugged defenses," he said. "The rules didn't protect the quarterbacks like they do now. They would just tee off on you."

*   *   *

Some fans still remember the day Couch cried after a game.

It was October 6, 2002.

Couch left the game with a concussion. He heard the fans cheering as he departed from the field, being replaced by Kelly Holcomb at quarterback.

In a 26-21 loss to the Ravens in Cleveland, Couch was trying to recover a fumble in the end zone after being hit by several Baltimore defenders. He took a helmet-to-helmet hit but stayed in. Later, he was hit hard and had to leave the game.

"I've been in this city for four years now and I've laid it on the line,"

Couch told the media after the game. "For them to turn on me and boo me, it's a joke . . . I'm lying there in the end zone hurt and they're cheering."

Stewart still blames himself for allowing Couch to talk to the media after the game.

"Tim had the desire to always answer the call and be responsible to the demands of being a quarterback," said Stewart. "I suggested he wait until the next day. He had a concussion. But he wanted to talk. He didn't want it to look like he was running from a tough situation by dodging the media."

As Stewart explained, we know so much more now about concussions and their impact than we did in 2002. He would never be allowed to talk to the media if that happened today.

"I was director of media relations," said Stewart. "I should have made the decision for Tim, even though we didn't know for sure he had a concussion. That diagnosis came later. He became emotional talking to the media, and that became a big deal—and it was my fault."

Stewart recalled hearing Couch say, "Home games are hard because of the fans."

Stewart realized what a mistake he made.

"I just hated that moment," he said. "I still blame myself for that."

Within a few days, Couch had received more than 5,000 letters and emails from fans supporting him. He returned to action and had the best season of his career.

"Tim always wanted to do the right thing," said Stewart. "He was such a true professional. I remember the day we decided to start Kelly Holcomb to open the 2003 season. Most veteran quarterbacks who lost the job would not have stayed and talked to the media. But Tim insisted he'd do it, he considered it part of the job."

* * *

Heading into the 2018 season, the last quarterback to lead the Browns to the playoffs was Couch.

"That's why I always say everything was not horrible in Cleveland," Couch said. "In many ways, I'm proud of what we accomplished the last few years."

The Browns were 2-14 in his rookie season. They were 3-13 in his second year, but he played only seven games that season due to a broken thumb on his throwing hand that required surgery.

In 2001, Couch played all 16 games. The Browns were 7-9. He also was sacked 51 times, second most in the NFL.

Then came 2002 when the Browns finished 9-7. Couch suffered a broken leg in the 24-16 victory over Atlanta that clinched a playoff spot. When the Browns faced Pittsburgh in the post-season, Couch was out with the fracture and Kelly Holcomb started.

That was a symbol of his career with the Browns—Couch watching a playoff game with his leg in a cast after he sacrificed so much for the young franchise to finally reach the post-season.

In 2001–02, the Browns were 16-16 and Couch had a 15-15 record as a starter.

"I thought if you put me on the right team, I could have been a good quarterback in the NFL," he said. "A lot of guys are that way. You put them in the right situation, they stay healthy and have good coaching and players around them—they can be successful."

*   *   *

By 2003, all the injuries were wearing down Couch.

He had multiple concussions. He had a broken thumb. A broken leg. Some broken ribs.

"I don't know how many concussions I had," he said. "I know there were one or two in high school. I had a couple in college. I don't even remember the concussion from the Baltimore game. The last thing I remember was a snap going over my head and I'm going into the end zone to get the ball. I don't remember anything else."

Couch dealt with tendinitis in his throwing elbow. That probably led to shoulder problems in 2003 as he changed his throwing motion a bit to deal with the pain.

The Browns cut Couch after the 2003 season. He signed with Green Bay.

"I was taking a ton of reps in training camp," he said. "I woke up one morning and I could hardly move my arm. I couldn't get the sheets off me. I went to the doctor and it turned out had I had a torn rotator cuff, a torn labrum and a torn bicep. They had to repair my whole shoulder. I came back from that, then I tore the rotator cuff again. After that second operation, I had no velocity . . . I wasn't accurate . . . nothing."

Couch never played in another regular season game after the 2003 season. He was 26 years old.

He later had a tryout with Jacksonville and was cut.

"I remember thinking how I wasn't even close to the player I was early in my career," he said. "My confidence was shot."

Once in a while, Couch wonders what it would have been like to "be a quarterback like Ben (Roethlisberger) who went to Pittsburgh where they had an established team with a good defense. But it's just frustrating to do that."

The remarkable part of this story is when I talked to Couch during the 2017 season, he said, "I'm a Browns fan. I watch every game."

I started to laugh and asked, "Why would you be a Browns fan after all you've been through?'

"I love the Browns," he said. "They will always be my team. When I run into Browns fans, they are so great to me."

Couch lives in Lexington, Kentucky, where he is involved in several businesses. In 2018, the Browns hired him to be a color analyst for their preseason games.

"I'm proud of what I accomplished there," he said. "I wish I could have stayed healthier and played longer. I thought I'd play 10 to 12 years and be the kind of quarterback who really helped the franchise grow. But I've always been grateful to the Browns for giving me a chance to play in the NFL and live out a dream. I think as the years have passed, most people realize that when I was healthy, I was a pretty decent player. I just wish it could have been better for the fans."

He paused.

"I poured my heart and soul into that organization," he said. "I gave it all I had. I loved being with the Cleveland Browns."

* * *

I spent a lot of time writing about Couch because it set the stage for what Browns fans have watched since.

The team drafts a quarterback. The plan is for the rookie to sit and a journeyman veteran to start. But soon, the plan is abandoned. The rookie isn't ready. The sacks, injuries and losses pile up.

Couch mentioned Palmer was a rookie head coach. His top receiver (Kevin Johnson) was a rookie.

"And I was a rookie," he said. "We had a lot of people new to their jobs."

It showed.

That is another theme with the Browns—inexperienced coaches dealing with inexperienced players in a losing environment where the mantra becomes, "Play the rookie . . . play the rookie."

Then they play the rookie quarterback . . . who looks like most rookie quarterbacks.

It's as if the franchise has never learned much from Tim Couch or any other of the quarterbacks rushed into action and given little chance of success.

Spergon Wynn and Tom Brady

---

*"His own team passed on
Tom Brady several times."*

When I called Spergon Wynn, he thought I wanted to talk about Tom Brady.

"I'm one of the Brady Six," he said.

Wynn meant he was one of six quarterbacks picked in the 2000 draft before Brady went to New England. That wasn't the reason for the call, although Wynn being in the group is fascinating. The future Hall of Famer Brady was the 199th pick in the 2000 draft. Wynn was No. 183 from Southwest Texas State, which played in what was called the NCAA Division 1-AA level in 2000.

"His own team passed on Tom Brady several times," said Wynn.

He's so right. Not only was Brady picked in the sixth round by the Patriots, he was their SECOND selection in the sixth round.

With the No. 187 pick, the Patriots selected Antwan Harris, a defensive back from Virginia. They took Brady later in the sixth round. That made Brady the SEVENTH player picked by New England in that draft.

"Some people remember me because my name (Spergon) is so different," he said. "And because of the Brady Six."

* * *

In the 2000 draft, the Browns had nine chances to draft Tom Brady.

Here is a list of players the Browns picked instead of Brady: Court-ney Brown, Dennis Northcutt, Travis Prentice, JaJuan Dawson, Lewis Sanders, Aaron Shea, Anthony Malbrough, Lamar Chapman and then Wynn.

Of course, all but the Patriots have their own 2000 draft list minus Brady.

ESPN's Mel Kiper had Chad Pennington as the top quarterback in that draft. He was the first quarterback picked – No. 18 by the Jets.

Kiper also had a special "sleeper" quarterback. Not Mr. Brady. It was Joe Hamilton, a quarterback from Georgia Tech. Hamilton was a seventh-round pick by Tampa Bay. He played in one regular season game.

"It just shows you how everyone is sort of guessing when it comes to the draft," said Wynn.

Wynn began his career at Minnesota in the Big Ten. He played only two games in 1996, throwing eight passes. The Minnesota coaching staff wanted to convert Wynn into a tight end. He wanted to remain at quarterback.

Wynn transferred to Southwest Texas State (now Texas State) in San Marcos. He played for the NCAA Division 1-AA school for two seasons.

In 1999, he had modest stats of 14 TDs vs. 13 interceptions, com-pleting 50 percent of his passes (161-of-322) for a team that was 3-8.

In today's NFL, those stats would have anyone with even a remote interest in draft analytics screaming: "Don't pick the guy! If you like him, bring him to camp as an undrafted free agent."

The warning signs:

1. Completing only 50 percent of his passes. If he could only com-plete half of his throws at what was then the NCAA 1-AA level, how would that improve in the NFL?

2. The 14 TDs to 13 interceptions is a sign he was turnover-prone.

3. He played only two years. His quarterback experience was limited.

So how did Wynn appear on the NFL draft radar?

He was 6-foot-3, 230 pounds. He had an extremely strong arm.

"I worked out for some teams," he said. "Truth is, I worked out better than I played. I was at the NFL Combine and I probably had the strongest arm there."

During the draft, Wynn stayed in his apartment near the college campus. He didn't watch it on TV.

"That was too hard," he said. "I even stayed alone, just in case I didn't get picked."

In the sixth round, his phone rang. He was listening to some music, wondering if anyone would call his name.

"I saw it was a 216 area code," he said. "My agent said if anyone called, pick up the phone. I did. It was Coach (Chris) Palmer asking me if I wanted to be a Cleveland Brown . . . I said . . . SURE!"

Palmer told him to turn on the TV because he'd soon hear his name called by the Browns.

"We considered him a project," recalled Palmer. "He had raw talent. He was a very good kid, very bright. The idea was to work with him for a few years and develop him."

*   *   *

It seems the Browns' plans for rookie quarterbacks never match reality. The team talks patience but ends up consumed with desperation.

It could be injuries. Or losing. Often, it's both.

"Put the kid in there," say many of the fans and members of the media.

And at some point in their rookie seasons, that's exactly what happens. They play the kid. It rarely works out well.

When Wynn joined the Browns, he realized it was a brand new ballgame—and a rather intimidating one.

"It was a big jump from Southwest Texas to the NFL," he said. "I had so much to learn in terms of preparation. But I also thought I'd have time to acclimate to the pro game."

He thought wrong.

In the preseason, quarterback Ty Detmer suffered a torn Achilles. He was out for the 2000 season before it began.

Tim Couch started the first seven games, then suffered a broken thumb in practice and was out for the rest of the season.

The Browns didn't want to start Wynn, knowing he wasn't close to ready.

They signed veteran Doug Pederson to replace Detmer. He took over for Couch as the starter and the plan was for him to finish the season.

But in Game 13, Pederson suffered a rib injury. He was replaced by Wynn.

"I was excited, but I really wasn't prepared to play," he said.

Wynn started the next week in Jacksonville, a 48-0 loss. Wynn completed only 5-of-16 passes for 17 total yards. He was sacked five times and knocked out of the game with a knee injury.

The Plain Dealer's Tony Grossi wrote:

"Using Spergon Wynn almost the entire game—even after he barely escaped a serious knee injury in the second quarter—the Browns achieved two first downs on offense . . . They did not cross midfield. After their first possession, they never advanced past their own 35-yard line. Chris Gardocki punted a franchise record 12 times."

This game was brutally unfair to Wynn. Nothing in his background prepared him to play on a terrible second-year expansion team.

As Wynn told the media after the game, "I didn't expect this. They were doing some things we hadn't seen on film. It's like a war out there. You can't call time out every time they do something you don't expect."

He became the fourth different quarterback to start for the Browns since 1999 . . . and that Jacksonville game was his last appearance with the Browns.

But here's something to consider—Wynn started an NFL game before Brady did with the Patriots.

In his rookie season of 2000, Brady played in one regular season game. He threw three passes. He sat behind veteran Drew Bledsoe. He didn't start until September 30, 2001. That happened only because Bledsoe was injured.

Yes, you can find a lesson in that bit of history.

*   *   *

Tom Brady was a backup for his first two years at Michigan, then started the next two seasons. He completed 62 percent of his passes, with 30 TDs compared to 17 interceptions. He was a good athlete, drafted in the 18th round in 1995 by the Montreal Expos. He was a left-handed hitting catcher.

At Michigan, Brady had a 20-5 record as a starter.

Ernie Accorsi was a superb general manager. He drafted John Elway, Eli Manning and Bernie Kosar.

He told ESPN he had this memory of Brady from some scouting tapes:

"He was very careful with his passes, very accurate, no interceptions. I wondered if his arm would be strong enough. He was listed at 6-foot-5 and 195 pounds—and he didn't look good. He looked kind of emaciated with no muscle definition."

Accorsi was with the New York Giants at the time. His views probably matched that of most teams.

Spergon Wynn *looked* far more like an NFL quarterback than Tom Brady. So did several other members of the "Brady Six."

Accorsi added that Brady threw four touchdown passes in the Orange Bowl against Alabama. He was playing for a Big Ten school.

"We all were asleep," Accorsi told ESPN.

Here are the members of the "Brady Six" besides Wynn:

1. Chad Pennington (Marshall), the No. 18 overall pick in the draft by the Jets. He made 81 starts and had a 44-37 record.

2. Giovanni Carmazzi (Hofstra) was a third round pick (No. 65) by San Francisco. He never played in a regular season NFL game.

3. Chris Redman (Louisville) was a third round pick (No. 75) by Baltimore. He started 12 games and had a 4-8 record.

4. Tee Martin (Tennessee) was a fifth round pick (No. 163) by Pittsburgh. He threw only 16 regular season passes in three NFL games.

5. Marc Bulger (West Virginia) was a sixth round pick (No. 168) by New Orleans. He made two Pro Bowls. He started 95 games and played eight seasons.

So Wynn actually played in more NFL games than Carmazzi and Martin.

I asked Chris Palmer if he remembered anything about Brady for the draft.

"I just don't," he said.

Like most teams, the Browns didn't consider Brady to be draft-worthy.

*   *   *

When I interviewed Wynn in 2017, he was 39 years old, a husband and father of two boys. He lives in Houston where he is a broker for natural gas and energy products for Amerex Energy Services.

"I knew I'd need a career after football," he said. "I'm from Houston. Oil and gas are big in Houston, along with the medical field. I picked oil and gas."

Wynn should be brought into NFL camps to talk to young players about life after football.

"It goes by so fast," he said. "Especially for me."

Wynn doesn't even remember his Browns signing bonus, other than "it wasn't much. And I signed a minimum contract."

That was for $193,000.

He was with the Browns for the 2000 season. He was traded to Minnesota right before the 2001 season.

"I can't remember who I was traded for," he said.

The answer is no one.

Running back Travis Prentice, Wynn and a seventh round pick were traded to Minnesota for a fifth round pick. He spent a season with the Vikings.

Wynn's NFL career covered two years, three starts and 152 passes—one for a touchdown, seven for interceptions.

Then came three more years playing in Canada.

"I knew I had to prepare for something after football," he said.

While he was playing football, he finished his undergraduate degree from what is now Texas State. Then he got a job in the energy business, earning his MBA degree in the process. He went to work, making a good life for his family. He didn't think playing some pro football gave him a free pass for life.

"Most people don't know I played pro football," said Wynn.

Wynn understands why.

"It was so brief," he said. "But there has been this weird notoriety because of the Brady Six and my name is different. Some people recognize it."

Wynn is glad to talk football, but doesn't watch a lot of it.

His current career is demanding and intense.

"And it always seems I'm driving the kids somewhere or picking them up," he said.

Wynn has his No. 13 Cleveland Browns jersey framed.

"Where is it?" I asked.

"In my garage," he said.

"Your garage?" I asked.

"It's really like a workout room," he said. "I have it on the wall. I have a Browns helmet from that year signed by the guys (from the 2000 team)."

Wynn talks about those days as if they were a lifetime ago. He still keeps in touch with Tim Couch.

"I wish I could have played longer and picked the brains of guys some more," he said. "But I'm glad I got the chance to play pro football. I enjoyed it."

Here Comes Butch Davis!

"The coaching piece is in place."

On the day Butch Davis was hired by the Browns, Al Lerner said something that now seems outrageous—pure foolishness.

But on January 30, 2001, the Browns owner might have had a good reason to dream.

Davis came to town with excellent coaching credentials. He had revived the University of Miami football program, finishing second in the country with an 11-1 record in 2000. Rounding out the resume were six years coaching in the NFL. He began as a defensive line coach with Dallas, then spent two seasons as the Cowboys defensive coordinator.

Davis was a Jimmy Johnson disciple. Johnson had a 1-15 Dallas team in 1989 and ended up winning two Super Bowl rings in 1992 and 1993. A member of those coaching staffs, Davis wore one of those glittering rings to the press conference.

Let's face it, this was Cleveland. No Browns team has ever gone to the Super Bowl. The reflection off that ring was an almost blinding light of hope for Browns fans who'd spent so long living on the dark side of the football moon. Even before the franchise moved to Baltimore after the 1995 season, it seemed as if Cleveland fans had been haunted and tormented by the football gods.

Butch Davis was more than a football coach. He's a recruiter and a salesman. He preaches hope. He talks about "the heart." Davis often said his players don't just work hard, "They spill their guts all over the field."

The first time I interviewed Davis, I was shocked by how much he knew about me. Either he did his homework, or someone else did it for him—and he memorized key facts. He knew how long I had worked in Northeast Ohio. He knew that I worked in jail ministry. He knew I wrote a lot of books.

I kept thinking, "No wonder this guy was such a good recruiter at Miami."

And no wonder Policy and Lerner fell in love with him. Davis has the ability to make you think you are the most important person in the world to him when he's talking to you, 1-on-1. He had a powerful, positive personality.

That was part of what the Browns were buying on the day they hired Davis.

That's why Lerner said: "The coaching piece is in place."

That was not a ridiculous comment. More than a few in the local media compared the hiring of Davis to that of Paul Brown, who is still the football Godfather of the Browns.

Davis looked very, very good—and not just because of the Super Bowl ring. He rebuilt Miami after Sports Illustrated in 1995 called for the program to be shut down because it was so corrupt. At one point, Davis was playing with 20 fewer scholarships than most teams because of the NCAA sanctions he inherited. He was there for six years. The scandals ended. His graduation rate was a very solid 65 percent. He was praised not only for winning, but doing it the right way.

*   *   *

The Browns first considered hiring Davis before the 1999 season.

Davis made it clear to me that he was never offered the job. But Browns CEO Carmen Policy said on the day of the press conference that he wanted Davis to be the Browns' first coach. Davis knew he had the Hurricanes on the verge of winning big and was not about to leave.

He also knew what most people in the NFL knew—and what Chris

Palmer, the coach the Browns did hire before the 1999 season, once told me.

"Ideally, you don't want to be the first guy who coaches an expansion team," said Palmer. "You want to be the second guy."

Why?

"Because the first guy will probably be fired in a few years," said Palmer. "That's how it usually goes. The second guy comes in and the team now has some high draft picks and some structure in place. You're not starting from scratch."

Palmer was right on every point.

In *False Start*, I wrote about how he was hired nine months before the first game. He had no secretary. I met him for an interview during one of his first days on the job. He had a legal pad on his desk. He had media guides from every NFL team. He was looking through the guides, checking the biographies of various coaches who had been fired.

Remember, this was January 22, 1999, before the Internet was very widely used. That's how Palmer was gathering information for his first coaching staff.

Palmer took me to the weight room. It was an empty room with one barbell on the floor.

In 1999, Butch Davis was very wise to stay in Miami. And Brian Billick was smart to turn down a chance to coach the Browns, taking the Baltimore job instead. All he did there was win a Super Bowl.

Before hiring Palmer, Policy mentioned the name of Mike Holmgren. That's right, Mike Holmgren! It was at a November 1998 Cleveland City Club banquet when the subject of head coaches came up. There was a problem. Holmgren was coaching Green Bay and still under contract to the Packers. The NFL fined Policy $10,000 for tampering.

No matter, Holmgren was not about to come to Cleveland to coach in 1999.

In 1999, Policy wanted to hire a coach with an offensive background. It was partly a reaction to the Bill Belichick regime. Remember, this was 1999. Belichick was vilified when the Browns moved in 1995. He was fired before coaching a game in Baltimore, and had joined the New York Jets as an assistant. No one saw Belichick as a future head coach. In fact, his name was poison at the time, Policy refusing to even interview some of the assistants associated with Belichick. He thought it would be too hard to sell Belichick associates to the public.

I can't list all the names of coaches Policy could have hired in 1999. But some of them are Marvin Lewis, Bill Callahan, John Fox, Jim Haslett and Nick Saban. It would not have mattered.

The first coach was going to take the hit for the second coach.

It's interesting that Policy turned down a chance to even interview Andy Reid, who had been Holmgren's quarterback coach in Green Bay. He wasn't a coordinator. Holmgren called the plays with the Packers. So it was hard to know if Reid was prepared to be a head coach.

But Philadelphia liked Reid. The Eagles liked Reid a lot. Tom Modrak was director of football operations. The other man who really wanted Reid in Philadelphia was Joe Banner, the Eagles vice president.

That's right . . . that Joe Banner, the Browns CEO in 2013.

Would it have made a difference if the Browns hired Reid over Palmer? Would they have drafted Donovan McNabb over Tim Couch? Who knows?

Palmer did not like McNabb. The Browns didn't even interview the Syracuse quarterback. Palmer had some friends with Syracuse and he didn't like what he heard about McNabb. Nor did he like what he saw on tape.

Banner told me the Eagles had McNabb rated over Couch. So maybe the Browns would have opened the 1999 season with Reid as coach, McNabb as the quarterback. But somehow, I doubt the results would have been anything close to the success Reid/McNabb had in Philadelphia. The Eagles were yearly contenders. McNabb went to six Pro Bowls. He led his team to five NFC championship games and one Super Bowl. Reid has become one of the NFL's most respected coaches.

But I doubt any of that would have happened here.

*   *   *

The hiring of Davis before the 2001 season was protracted and painful, especially to Chris Palmer.

Palmer sat around for three weeks after the 2000 season, knowing he was about to be fired. He still had three years and $3 million left on his contract. He watched video of college prospects. He made some plans for next season.

He knew it was futile.

One of the last things he did was write a report recommending the Browns draft running back LaDainian Tomlinson in the first round.

"I worked on the draft until my last day on the job," said Palmer. "We needed a running back. I thought Tomlinson would be a star."

Meanwhile, the Browns were courting Davis.

Davis said in January of 2001, "about four days after we had beaten Florida State in the Sugar Bowl, I met with Mr. Lerner and Carmen Policy in West Palm Beach."

Lerner had a home in West Palm Beach.

"I wanted to think about it for a day, talk to my wife," said Davis. "Then I called back to say I was still committed to Miami and the program we were building."

At that point, the agent for Davis was negotiating a new contract to stay with Miami. He also told his players he planned to stay.

Davis said about two weeks later, he received another call from the Browns. His contract situation with Miami was stalled. The Browns were offering him a 5-year, $15 million deal. It was far above what he was being offered by Miami. There also were some issues with Miami about buy-out clauses and other things.

"I couldn't turn down a life-changing offer for my family," said Davis. "So I accepted the offer."

Meanwhile, the Miami players felt betrayed. Palmer was unhappy because word of his firing leaked to the media before he was officially told.

But in the end, Palmer knew he would be fired after the season. And he was indeed fired.

Davis knew he was being enticed by the NFL and an extremely rich owner, and it was too lucrative for him to resist.

As for Lerner and Policy, they were convinced they had the right coach. This time, Davis was their first choice. That was not the case when they hired Palmer after several others turned down the job.

*   *   *

Besides praising Davis at that introductory press conference, what did Lerner say that was so surprising in the rear-view mirror of time?

"The coaching piece is now in place," said the owner. "We've talked about having a quarterback in place. And a defensive end . . . so here we go."

The quarterback? Tim Couch.

The defensive end? Courtney Brown.

On that late January afternoon of 2001, that sounded like a stretch . . . but not delusional.

Couch had played only seven games in 2000. He broke his thumb in practice. After throwing a pass, his hand hit the helmet of a team-mate as he released the ball. He needed surgery and was done for the season. At this point, Couch was only 23. He'd played behind an awful offensive line. He had thrown 22 touchdown passes compared to 22 interceptions in 22 games, completing 59 percent of his passes.

Those numbers weren't bad for a young quarterback in an expansion situation.

He had been sacked an NFL-high 56 times in 1999. But it was only 10 times in 2000 when the broken thumb limited him to seven games. So Couch was not completely battered physically as he would be a few years later.

As a rookie, Brown had a big game with three sacks against Pittsburgh when the Browns won, 23-20. Couch was the quarterback in that game.

Injuries had yet to hit Brown. He played every game as a rookie. Not sure he was going to be a star, but he had a chance to be a good NFL player for a long time.

That's how it looked as Davis was hired.

Davis was not focused on the roster.

"Before I was hired, I didn't look at any tape of the team," he said in 2001. "I didn't even look at the media guide. I knew 8-to-10 players. That was it."

So why take the job?

"Because it was one of only 32 head coaching jobs in the NFL," he said. "I really like Al Lerner and Carmen Policy. I knew Mr. Lerner had all the resources to be a great owner. Carmen had run teams that went to the Super Bowl. He had been on the big stage. I know they knew the fans loved football in Cleveland."

That's how Davis was thinking when he was hired. Listening to him, it was clear no one had more confidence in Butch Davis than Butch Davis.

As I wrote on the day he was hired: "If you're Butch Davis, you don't worry much about what happened before you arrived. You just figure you'll find a way to fix it. You have done it before, you'll do it again . . . You don't think about the 5-27 record in the first two seasons. In fact, if you're Butch Davis, you consider that a positive. The miserable team won five games in two years? How can I do any worse than that? Nowhere to go but up."

There Goes Butch Davis

"Mr. Lerner dying changed everything,"

Butch Davis and Eric Mangini have something in common besides having coached the Browns.

OK, they coached the Browns when Randy Lerner was the owner.

But there is something else, something more significant. Both are gifted coaches. I believe both could be successful NFL coaches. They had some seasons that proved it.

But Butch Davis the coach was sabotaged by Butch Davis the general manager.

And Eric Mangini the coach was sabotaged by Eric Mangini the general manager.

And those are two examples of why I don't like the "Coach As King" setup, where the coach has so much power.

I know, Bill Belichick makes it work. Part of the reason Belichick became a winner in New England is he trusted Scott Pioli with many of the duties of a general manager. After Pioli, Thomas Dimitroff held the position. It was never called "general manager." It always has been "Vice President of Player Personnel."

Pioli left the Patriots to become general manager of the Kansas City Chiefs.

Dimitroff left the Patriots to become general manager of the Atlanta Falcons. After Pioli was fired in Kansas City, he was hired by Dimitroff to be an assistant general manager in Atlanta.

Now, it's Nick Caserio who has a significant say in the Patriots' drafting and other player matters.

In the end, it comes down to Belichick. He makes the final decisions.

Other interesting and winning combinations had a CEO-type combined with a strong coach.

In San Francisco, it was Carmen Policy with coach Bill Walsh. Policy also won with coach George Seifert.

In Philadelphia, Joe Banner combined with coach Andy Reid.

Banner and Policy were NFL lifers. While their original expertise was salary cap and business matters, they picked up a lot of football over the years. They also had the respect of the coaches, even though the coaches had a major influence in how the roster was shaped and who was drafted.

The CEO/Coach format was supposed to be the formula when the Browns first started. Policy was the CEO in 1999, coming in with owner Al Lerner. Policy had the track record in San Francisco, and the Super Bowl rings. He hired Dwight Clark as player personnel director, but Clark was never in a powerful position. When looking at his drafts, it was hard to know what players he actually chose—and what players were picked by the coaching staff.

When Policy took over the Browns front office, he wanted to work with a coach, as he did with Walsh in San Francisco.

It's why he originally wanted to hire Butch Davis in 1999. Davis told me that it was never serious, there was no offer in 1999. But Policy did have an eye on Davis.

*   *   *

Butch Davis believes the beginning of the end of his chance for long term success with the Browns came on October 23, 2002. That's when Al Lerner died of cancer.

"Mr. Lerner was spectacular," said Davis. "A great businessman. He was an ex-Marine. That man was tough. Carmen Policy had been a part of Super Bowl winners in San Francisco."

Davis said Lerner told him that "This was a 10-year job." He was taking over an expansion team that was two years old.

"Listening to Mr. Lerner, I said, 'OK, this is a guy who gets it,'" said Davis.

Davis really thought he would have 10 years, assuming the team continued to make progress. He felt comfortable with Lerner and Policy. They recruited him and they empowered him.

But they also had his respect. Keep that in mind. They could put the brakes on Davis, who could be emotional and would make quick decisions.

"Mr. Lerner dying changed everything," said Davis. "Next were some conflicts between Randy Lerner (Al's son) and Carmen Policy. That led to Carmen starting his exit out of there."

Davis wonders what could have happened in Cleveland had Al Lerner lived longer and Policy remained at the top of the front office.

* * *

But it was more than the death of Lerner and the exit of Policy. And it was more than the inexperience and impulsiveness of Randy Lerner, who took over for his father.

It also was the draft.

On the day Davis was hired, Policy said he had no intention of hiring a general manager to run the draft. Nor would Dwight Clark have much of a role.

"Butch had a reputation for having an eye for talent evaluation," Policy said. "He had sent a lot of guys from Miami to the NFL."

Sounds good on the surface, but later Policy admitted to me: "If we had tried to bring in a GM, Butch would not have come."

Or as Davis also said: "I knew I needed a significant voice in the football operations. I didn't care about the marketing and business parts. But I wanted a voice in football—much like Jimmy Johnson had in Dallas."

With the Cowboys, owner Jerry Jones and coach Jimmy Johnson built the team into a power. Davis was a defensive coach on that staff. He modeled his career after Johnson, even coaching at the University of Miami as Johnson did from 1984 to 1988.

So it was Davis making some horrible picks in the first round. He was making the big decisions about veterans on the roster. He had

Pete Garcia as his player personnel director. But Garcia was a college guy, a former assistant to Davis at Miami. He had zero experience in the NFL.

Davis and the Browns needed an experienced NFL executive to run the draft. The team needed someone to tell Davis, "I know you loved Big Money (Gerard Warren) dating back to when you tried to recruit him out of high school. But we're not taking him."

The Browns still had Palmer's glowing recommendation of LaDainian Tomlinson as the impact player to change the offense. Several veteran Browns scouts favored Richard Seymour, a defensive lineman.

Player personnel director Dwight Clark was still with the team, but he had lost influence after Davis was hired. His idea for the 2001 draft was Michigan receiver David Terrell. He was the No. 8 pick in that draft (by Chicago) and had a very mediocre 5-year career.

The only ones who had Warren rated above Tomlinson and Seymour were Davis and Garcia. At least, I assume Garcia did. But the decision belonged to Davis. Carmen Policy was still with the Browns and had influence during the 2001 draft. But Policy had granted full power for Davis in order to entice him to come from Miami to Cleveland.

Policy also trusted Davis' judgment about defense. As Policy once said: "Butch played defense. He coached defense. He eats and sleeps defense."

Tomlinson became a Hall of Fame running back with the Chargers. Seymour was drafted by New England, where he became a Pro Bowl defensive lineman.

Warren's nickname dating back to high school and continuing at the University of Florida was "Big Money." He had the physical ability to be a Seymour-type defensive lineman. But scouts questioned his desire and work ethic.

Davis just saw the talent. The scouts were right. Warren became a journeyman lineman. He often started for teams but rarely distinguished himself.

I've always thought there should be a rule against drafting anyone named "Big Money" in the first round.

*   *   *

In the 2002 draft, Davis picked William Green in the first round. He was a running back from Boston College. Why Green? Because the Browns needed a running back. Why did they need a running back? Because they passed up Tomlinson in 2001.

Green was a young man with many personal problems dating to high school. He grew up tough in Atlantic City. Both of his parents died of AIDS. His father contracted it from heroin use. He passed the disease to his mother. Both parents were dead by the time Green was 12.

At Boston College, Green was suspended twice for marijuana use. Davis didn't care. He often took chances on troubled players. Green was a quiet, nice young man to talk to at that stage of his life. But lots of red flags were next to his name as the draft approached.

Davis passed up several good players to take Green. Two were Miami products: safety Ed Reed and running back Clinton Portis. He knew those players well.

Reed had a Hall of Fame-level career with Baltimore. Portis played nine seasons, rushing for more than 1,000 yards six times.

They missed others in that draft, but skipping the two Miami products for Green was especially baffling.

Green had a good 2002 rookie season, rushing for 887 yards and six touchdowns. He stayed out of trouble. The Browns were 9-7 and made the playoffs.

But the next season, Green was arrested for drunken driving and drug possession. He was wearing only one shoe and sock when the police found him. The NFL suspended him. He played only seven games.

Green had a variety of personal problems. He played only four seasons. He went into drug treatment.

To Green's credit, he became an ordained minister in 2012. He married his long-term fiancée and the couple is raising eight children. He does a lot of motivational speaking.

But that choice by Davis hurt the Browns long term.

*   *   *

But the biggest miss by Davis was in the 2004 draft. The Browns had the No. 7 pick in the draft.

At this point, Tim Couch was physically worn down after all the sacks and injuries in his four years with the Browns. The Browns still had Kelly Holcomb, but he was strictly a backup.

Before the 2004 draft, Davis signed veteran free agent Jeff Garcia to be a starting quarterback. That allowed him to draft someone else.

The prime quarterback prospect under consideration by Davis was Ben Roethlisberger from Miami of Ohio. The top quarterback prospect in the draft was Eli Manning, but the Mississippi product was destined to be the No. 1 pick in the draft.

But as Davis said before the draft, the real need of the team "is to win."

Lerner had died. Policy was being forced out. After their 9-7 record in 2002, the Browns fell to 5-11 in 2013. They started the season at 3-3, then lost 8-of-10 games to finish the season. Davis feared Randy Lerner planned to fire him if he had another disappointing season.

So that led to short-term thinking—and desperation.

It began with the signing of Garcia, who was 33 years old. He was a scrambling quarterback who'd had some success in San Francisco. But a coaching change happened, and Garcia fell out of favor. He also was arrested for drunken driving and blew a .237 alcohol test, meaning he was very drunk.

Garcia was a win-now decision.

So was the first round of the draft.

Davis entered the draft targeting three players. He wanted one from this group: Iowa left tackle Robert Gallery, Miami defensive back Sean Taylor or Miami tight end Kellen Winslow. It was no secret that Davis was absolutely enamored with Winslow.

The draft went like this:

1. Quarterback: Eli Manning.
2. Tackle: Robert Gallery.
3. Receiver: Larry Fitzgerald.
4. Quarterback: Philip Rivers.
5. Defensive back: Sean Taylor.

The Detroit Lions had the No. 6 pick. Before the draft, word was

Detroit wanted Texas wide receiver Roy Williams. The Browns were at
No. 7, and they were scared Detroit would select Winslow. The Lions
did a good job making Davis think that would happen.

Right as it was time for the Lions to make the No. 6 pick, the Browns
traded up one slot and grabbed Winslow.

The price? The Browns second-rounder, No. 37 overall.

I've heard the Browns had Rivers rated over Roethlisberger. That
may be true. But I also know the climate around the team at the time.
It was as Davis said—win now.

A second round pick was traded. It was an outrageously high cost
to move up one slot—because Davis believed Winslow would help
him win now.

As often happens around the Browns, desperation and panic set
in—and obliterated planning.

Roethlisberger fell all the way to Pittsburgh at No. 11, and he has
had a Hall of Fame career.

In true Browns fashion, Winslow broke his leg in the second game
of his rookie season. He was on special teams as the Browns were
trying to recover an on-side kick.

Winslow also had a major motorcycle accident in 2005 and had
ACL knee surgery. He could have had a very good career, but battled
knee problems after that. He also suffered a staph infection.

Winslow was with the Browns for four years, catching 219 passes
in 44 games. He played nine seasons total, and was hardly a franchise
changer.

Meanwhile Roethlisberger has tormented the Browns ever since
they passed on him in the 2004 draft.

*   *   *

The 2002 media guide reveals Davis had three assistants who
became NFL head coaches: Bruce Arians, Chuck Pagano and Todd
Bowles. A fourth was Terry Robiskie, who became the Browns' interim
coach after Davis quit in the middle of the 2004 season.

Davis had assembled a good coaching staff. He had inspired the
team to over-achieve. In its fourth season of existence, the new
Browns were a playoff team.

"I look back at that season, and we really weren't that far from making the Super Bowl," Davis said in 2017.

Then so much happened.

After the 9-7 season, the Browns were in a salary cap mess. Part of the reason was the team had given huge contracts to Tim Couch, Courtney Brown and Gerard Warren. They were high draft choices, and this was before the implementation of a rookie salary scale.

This gets complicated. Mistakes were made during the two years before Davis, and Davis made some poor moves.

He also overpaid for some free agents, just as Policy did before Davis arrived.

"Randy Lerner came in and wanted us to cut $30 million from the payroll right now," said Davis. "He said we weren't going to push contracts out to the future. We're not going over the salary cap. Those were things his father and Carmen had done in previous years. We started letting guys go who were a significant part of that 9-win team."

With Policy losing influence, Davis was gaining more power in the front office. He also had to deliver news to the players about the salary cap situation.

Among the players cut by the Browns were Corey Fuller, Earl Holmes, Dwayne Rudd, Dave Wohlabaugh and others.

"Some of the veterans thought we were going back to 1999 and 2000 again," said Davis. "Guys leaving seemed to be the happiest."

The mistakes made by Davis in the draft compounded the problems. He missed chances to draft stars, and none of the players he picked made a major impact.

Here are the facts: Davis drafted 29 players in four years. Only one ever made a Pro Bowl. That was Winslow, and it happened in 2007.

I'm not going to sort through who did what. It was clear Davis had taken on too much, acting basically as general manager and coach. Randy Lerner was overwhelmed as the owner. He never expected to be replacing his father so soon.

After the playoff appearance, the Browns were 5-11 in 2003. It was a mess with injuries and a lack of veteran leadership. The poor drafting also haunted the franchise.

*   *   *

The 2004 season was more of 2003. Jeff Garcia opened as the starting quarterback. The team kept losing. After a 58-48 loss to Cincinnati, the Browns record was 3-8.

Davis was feeling "a lot of anxiety." He said he had a panic attack
during that loss to the Bengals. He resigned after the game.

Davis doesn't want to say much about his departure.

But I heard Randy Lerner had become very disenchanted with
Davis and was planning a coaching change. When I mentioned this
to Davis, he said he also had heard it.

In other words, he was certain he was through after the season. He
wasn't feeling well. He no longer had the confidence of ownership.
So he left.

And think about this: Davis walked out the door more than a
decade ago with a very humble .407 winning percentage and one
playoff appearance. But that's the best since of any Browns coach
since the team returned in 1999.

Fans Write In . . .

Browns Jerseys

Browns fans were asked: What jerseys from the new Browns era (since 1999) do you own? Why did you buy them? Have you thrown any away? Are there any that make you embarrassed? (Responses were edited for clarity and brevity.)

I have Ty Detmer, Tim Couch, Jamir Miller, Kevin Johnson, Courtney Brown, Braylon Edwards, Kellen Winslow Jr. and a personalized jersey.

I bought all these because they were my favorite players on the team and I expected all to be great Browns for a long time. Apparently I am a horrible, horrible judge of talent. The majority were from my high school to early college years, with the Tim Couch jerseys being my favorite.

I was so unsuccessful at buying jerseys that I finally just bought a personalized jersey.

The Ty Detmer isn't embarrassing—it's cool and ironic. It's the hipster of all my jerseys. All of these were bought by myself or my parents at full price and I feel like the Browns should send us some type of gift basket or apology card.

—*David Robertson, Columbus, Ohio*

I have owned Tim Couch, Kelly Holcomb, Charlie Frye, Derek Anderson, Brady Quinn, Colt McCoy, Brandon Weeden, Brian Hoyer and, sadly, two Johnny Manziel jerseys.

My parents bought all of the jerseys as gifts up to Charlie Frye, but the rest have been on my dime. I really only regret the two Manziel jerseys as I was upset when they drafted him, but allowed myself to get caught up in the hype.

I still have my signed Kelly Holcomb jersey and my signed Brandon Weeden jersey; the rest have been sold to residents of Eastern Washington through various garage sales. I did luck out and sell the two Manziel jerseys on eBay right after the Browns released him for almost $20 per jersey. I was really surprised anyone bid but I billed them as a potential Halloween costume.

Although I have never purchased a jersey for $1, I have sold several of them at the price, always with pitying comments from the people purchasing them at our garage sales.

—*Scott Dayton, Airway Heights, Washington*

Since 1999, I have had multiple jerseys, but I still wish I had bought a Phil Dawson. Joe Thomas is the only jersey I have owned since 1999 that I do not regret, but Dawson was a player to be proud of as well.

I have owned jerseys from Shaun Rogers, Braylon Edwards and Courtney Brown. Edwards is particularly embarrassing due to his attitude and being from that school up north.

I was never quite foolish enough to own any QB jersey.

Most jerseys I've owned were gifts for holidays or birthdays. I've never bought any garage sale dollar jerseys because these were all the players that held my hopes and dreams and let me down. Seeing them makes me sad. They are very hard to sell even at garage sale and thrift store prices. They seem to be mostly snatched up by grandmothers with no interest in sports attempting to bring joy to someone. Most fans wish they would go away.

—*Ronald Mick, Meadville, Pennsylvania*

The only Browns jersey that I have ever owned is a No. 17, Braylon Edwards, which was free when I bought a set of tires. I have since taped over the name so that it now reads "Sipe."

—*Brian Reilly, Mentor, Ohio*

I own (or have owned) the following:

Lee Suggs—first jersey, bought at TJ Maxx just to have one.

Braylon Edwards—this was not an "official" adidas jersey, but I wanted to have a "good" Browns player.

Jamal Lewis—bought on sale, of course.

Joe Thomas—birthday present from my now-wife, and the only one bought full-price.

Joe Haden—sale at TJ Maxx in New York City.

Barkevious Mingo—TJ Maxx in Cleveland.

Paul Kruger—TJ Maxx in Cleveland. Bought it because it was the white away game jersey and I only had the brown home game jerseys up to then.

I have a weakness for jerseys on sale. I regularly find overstocked Browns jerseys at TJ Maxx, but I refuse to buy the jersey if the player has already left the Browns (never mind that each one becomes obsolete at most two years later), and I refuse to buy a QB jersey on principle.

I lost the Suggs jersey and threw away the Edwards jersey. I still have all the rest!

—*Shmuel Goldman, Beachwood, Ohio*

The jerseys I have are not just for me, but my kids. We have Kellen Winslow, Braylon Edwards, Colt McCoy, Trent Richardson, Brandon Weeden, Joe Haden, Corey Coleman, Josh Cribbs.

We haven't thrown any away. We're keeping them for grandkids.

Trent Richardson and Brandon Weeden jerseys are embarrassing. I bought a Richardson for me and won't wear it. At that point, I bought a Kosar throwback.

—*Paul Miller, Geneva, Ohio*

Wali Rainer and Joe Haden. I bought Rainer because I wanted one that most Browns fans wouldn't own. Haden was my favorite player at the time and he seemed to do a lot for the city.

—*Paul Moss, Apex, North Carolina*

I am down to six Browns jerseys. I have a bit of a jersey problem.

I started with a Chris Gardocki jersey bought at Value City off the clearance rack. When he signed with the Steelers, I could no longer wear it, so I took it to Ritchies Sporting Goods in Tallmadge and had the name plate changed to Sipe. And so it began.

As the new Browns continually overhauled their roster, I plucked jerseys from clearance racks and eBay at pennies on the dollar. I bought the

Browns media guide so we could look up the numbers of old players to have the name plates changed to someone from the "glory days" of my youth in the Sipe/Kosar era.

The only current jersey that still has the original name on it is a No. 73 Joe Thomas that I hope to get signed and framed. Scratch that, I just found a Courtney Brown and Willie McGinest in my closet while I was counting for this letter.

I have a 7-year-old son who has six jerseys. I did mention I have a jersey problem, right?

—*Jerry Lee Boatner, Akron, Ohio*

I have Colt McCoy and Joe Thomas jerseys. It's my name on the back for McCoy. I got Joe Thomas's jersey for the person he is, the standard he set and being a career Hall of Fame Browns player.

—*Martin McCoy, El Dorado Hills, California*

I have Brady Quinn and Johnny Manziel. I thought they would be "the answer" at quarterback. I loved Quinn's childhood photos of himself wearing a Kosar jersey. I loved that he was (mainly) a local boy who flourished at a big time college program. I loved the excitement Manziel brought. I drank the pre-draft Kool-Aid. I haven't thrown them away, but I don't wear those. My kids felt sorry for my choices and bought me a Kosar jersey I wear on draft days and game days.

—*Gregg Bollinger, Columbia City, Indiana*

I own a Willie McGinest jersey. At the time, the really expensive jerseys were Braylon Edwards, Kellen Winslow and Brady Quinn. I wanted to save some money. McGinest probably cost about a third of the most expensive ones. I could never throw that jersey away. It would feel like getting rid of a part of my childhood.

I am strangely proud when I wear my McGinest jersey. And I will continue to wear it to every game I go to, even after the fortune of this franchise finally turns. A random Browns jersey from years ago shows that I stuck with the team through the bad times and I never jumped on the bandwagon of any other team. It's like a badge of honor that shows your loyalty.

—*Tyler Lance, Chagrin Falls, Ohio*

I purchased a really nice ($100) shirt with Jordan Cameron's name. I've never done that before.

My daughter got to meet him at a Browns promotional event and he was so very kind when he heard about me. At the time I was going through chemo for breast cancer and Jordan was my favorite player. My daughter brought a get-well card and asked him to sign it for me, which he did.

Later, when she and her children were leaving, he made a point of stopping them and again extending good wishes for my recovery. It meant a lot to me and I carried that card with me for moral support to all of my chemo treatments. When he left the Browns, it was a sad day for me.

—*Terrie Ruic, Strongsville, Ohio*

I own two jerseys, Courtney Brown and Johnny Manziel. I'm 29, so my father passed down the Brown a few years after he was drafted. It was my go-to for home games until . . . I fell hook, line and sinker for Johnny. I was making the "money sign" with my fingers on draft night. I wore it for one home game and will never wear it again (Goodwill soon).

My friends and I (under 30) have no good memories of the Browns, not even sadness—nothing. We openly talk and laugh about not buying a jersey until the second contract.

As always, the group chat is very excited at draft time. Hope.

—*Joe Hoffman, Columbus, Ohio*

I have a Phil Dawson jersey. He was without a doubt the best player on the Browns at that point. Sadly, it was a statement that our best player was our kicker.

—*Jim Fulton, New York, New York*

I own a white Nike Trent Richardson jersey that my good friend bought brand new and later threw on the ground at a tailgate and never picked up

after Richardson got traded. I picked up the jersey to prevent littering. I didn't buy, but I do own it.
—*Chris Brenner, Cleveland, Ohio*

My family and friends continuously crack jokes about the jerseys I buy that usually end up in a trash can or the back of the closet. I have owned Willie McGinest, Brady Quinn, Trent Richardson, Johnny Manziel and Joe Haden (both the old design and the new uniforms). McGinest was supposed to be LeCharles Bentley, but he was injured the day after I went to the team shop to have it made.
—*Sean Ferguson, Boardman, Ohio*

I have every quarterback jersey except Cody Kessler, Robert Griffin and whoever starts this season. I got all of them at various Goodwill stores.
—*Wayne Stripe, Wadsworth, Ohio*

The only jersey I still own is a brown Braylon Edwards. I bought it because he was having a good year (2007) and I thought that was going to be just the beginning of a long, storied career. Seriously, that's what I thought. Besides, everybody was getting Joe Thomas jerseys.
I did not get it cheap; however, I firmly suspect two jerseys I once owned (received as gifts) were, in fact, purchased from clearance racks. Both were for players no longer even with the team when I received them—Courtney Brown and Reuben Droughns.
Whether I am embarrassed depends on the audience. Among Browns fans, yes. Among other people who don't know the difference, no.
—*Geoffrey Funkhouser, Washington Court House, Ohio*

I was superstitious that everyone's jersey I bought instantly became worse and left the team. So I avoided buying a Joe Thomas or Joe Haden jersey because I loved them on the Browns.
—*John Bebbington, Broomfield, Colorado*

I bought five Jeff Garcia jerseys from the clearance rack about an hour after Frye was drafted. Garcia was No. 5 and I figured Frye would be No. 5 as well, since that was his college number. I had a friend who worked in a local sports store make new name plates that could be put over Garcia's name, and I was going to give them to my buddies and my father, who took us to University of Akron games. Little did I know that Frye would pick No. 9, which ultimately caused my Garcia jerseys to become the jerseys for our annual Turkey Bowl game on Thanksgiving.

—*Jason Light, Twinsburg, Ohio*

I have Orlando Bobo and Andra Davis. I bought Bobo about five years ago because I never saw anyone else wear one. I bought Davis because I liked him and it was greatly discounted, around $10. I still have them both and wear them occasionally on game day. I'm not embarrassed by either of them, but I'm very thankful I never purchased a QB jersey.

—*Joel Hassinger, Huron, Ohio*

I own two of them, both Chris Spielman. When I was growing up, my parents were huge fans. My grandpa coached his little league team in Massillon. I saved up all my money to buy one when he signed, and was a devastated 17-year-old when he got injured and retired. I still wear it to the Twin Cities Browns Backers every Sunday.

—*Dan Wise, Maple Grove, Minnesota*

I bought the Trent Richardson orange jersey at a gas station that was bootlegging them for $50, I think. Wore it once or twice and he was gone.

Later, I went to the Mike Adams charity Halloween event at Champs in Westlake and bought his game-used brown one at auction for $200 since it was for charity and he was a class act. I never wore it to games—I didn't want to ruin it with a chili cheese dog or something. The real jerseys are pretty nice compared to the knock-offs.

—*Greg Gierszal, Westlake, Ohio*

I have No. 82. Gary Barnidge. I met Gary through his Twitter movie contests. I'm a movie nerd and won often. On a whim I asked him if he would come to my house in Wooster and help me surprise my wife for her birthday. Well, he drove down in his giant green truck! Spent over three hours hanging out and eating pizza and just talking to everyone. Everyone still talks about it. Gary reinvigorated our Browns fandom just by being a good guy. That's the jersey I wear proudly no matter what the record is or where he plays.

—*Charles "Matthew" Teach, Wooster, Ohio*

I have a brown Nike Josh Cribbs jersey for myself, and purchased a brown Joe Haden and brown Joe Thomas for my young children. These jerseys were specifically selected because these three players truly embody the spirit of Cleveland, supported the city, and played for something greater than themselves. All three are class acts that we as a family were proud to support.

—*Mary Clare Lane, Shaker Heights, Ohio*

I have owned only a single Browns jersey in my adult life. I am extremely embarrassed to admit that it was a Johnny Manziel jersey. I bought the jersey because I was stupidly optimistic about him, ignoring all the pre-draft warning signs.

I threw the jersey away the moment he went to rehab.

As punishment for wasting $100+ on this jersey, my wife will not let me purchase a Browns jersey again unless the player plays two straight seasons as the Browns' QB. As a Notre Dame alum, I found it difficult to not buy the DeShone Kizer jersey . . . but my wife's rule ended up being a blessing in disguise!

—*Kyle Chormanski, Universal City, Texas*

Here Comes Phil Savage!

"A perpetual expansion team."

By 2005, we were starting to see a pattern with the Randy Lerner ownership.

In 2001, Butch Davis was hired as head coach. Carmen Policy was still around as team president, but Policy was eventually pushed out by Randy Lerner. That never would have happened if Al Lerner had remained alive and in control of the team. The senior Lerner was paired up with Policy in 1999, helping him secure the Browns expansion franchise. They were very close.

But on October 23, 2002, Al Lerner died of brain cancer at the age of 69. His son, Randy, took over. He was 40 years old.

Policy left the Browns on May 1, 2004. But he had lost influence with Randy Lerner at least a year before that. That was a mistake on the part of the young Lerner. Policy was a savvy NFL operative. He knew the salary cap. He knew all the owners and the key people in the NFL front offices. He came into the league in 1983 with the San Francisco 49ers.

Policy was connected and he could have helped Randy Lerner, but Randy had other ideas.

Randy thought he and Butch Davis could run the team. It was a "Coach as King" setup. There was no general manager or team president with any clout.

When that fell apart during the 2004 season and Davis resigned, Randy went looking for a front office model. He had gotten to know some people in the NFL, and they told him to hire a strong general manager.

In other words, change the business model.

1. Hire the general manager first.
2. Allow the general manager to hire the coach.
3. The coach would report to the general manager.
4. The general manager would report to the owner.

Randy called Ozzie Newsome, the former Hall of Fame tight end with the Browns. Newsome was the highly successful general manager of the Baltimore Ravens. He was under a long-term contract with the Ravens, who had no interest in allowing him to take over their rival Cleveland Browns. I also doubt Newsome wanted to leave Baltimore, where he put together the team that won a Super Bowl in 2001. He'd win another Super Bowl later in 2013.

The man who was running the college drafts for Newsome was Phil Savage. That was the same Phil Savage who was with the Browns from 1991 to 1995 under Bill Belichick.

Savage was a "hot name" when it came to general manager candidates.

He had interviewed with Philadelphia and Chicago in 2001. He talked to Jacksonville in 2002 and Miami in 2003.

"I pulled out of some of those because they weren't real GM jobs," said Savage. "I wanted a legitimate GM job where you'd be in control of football operations."

Late in the 2004 season, Newsome walked into Savage's office.

"Cleveland called and they want to talk to you," he said.

"Is it going to be a true GM job?" asked Savage.

"I think so," said Newsome. "They'll be in touch with you."

*   *   *

John Collins was team president in charge of the business side of the Browns. Randy Lerner and Collins met with Savage at the Baltimore-Washington Airport.

"That was a get-to-know-you thing," said Savage. "That night, I got a call from Collins inviting me to meet with him and Randy in Long Island, where Randy lived. That happened the next day."

After that meeting, Collins flew back to Baltimore with Savage.

"John said they were offering me the job," said Savage. "I said I wanted to talk to my wife and sleep on it."

It didn't take long after Davis left for the Savage-to-the-Browns rumors to start.

I don't recall if I was the first to write it, but I know I campaigned for Savage a lot in print. I liked the strong general manager model. I have a lot of friends with the Baltimore Ravens and they all spoke highly of Savage. He was 39 years old and had been scouting players since 1993. By 2003, he was Newsome's top assistant.

He seemed ready for the job.

There were some problems between Collins and Savage's agent. Or at least, that was the version Collins told Savage.

A few days after their meetings, Collins called. They had a deal. I think it was just Collins trying to drive a hard bargain. Savage was being represented by Neil Cornrich, who is based in Cleveland. He wanted his client to run the Browns. Savage was excited about the job because he was the only candidate being pursued by the Browns.

"I also had a special place in my heart for the Browns," he said. "It was where I started my NFL career. I like the city. I know the fans love the team. I was there when the team moved. I knew winning was not easy, and it wasn't going to be easy there. But I also knew if you could turn that franchise around, it sets you up for life."

Savage said something I'd later hear from many other coaches and general managers—they all dreamed of being the guy who turned the Browns into winners.

"It is a special place," said Savage. "I'll always believe that."

Savage understandably didn't want to discuss money.

But my sources say he was making about $600,000 with the Ravens in 2004.

He signed this contract with the Browns:

2005: $1 million.

2006: $1.1 million.

2007: $1.2 million.

2008: $1.3 million.

2009: $1.4 million.

* * *

Savage's first job after taking over the Browns was to find a coach. He talked to everyone from scouts to assistant coaches to trainers to video people. He talked to some people on the business side of the team. Savage discovered what many of the media close to the team knew—there were trust issues with Davis, at least in his last two seasons.

"Some of it came from Butch being both coach and GM," said Savage. "It's hard when a coach has some say over a player's contract. That creates a disconnect."

Just as Randy Lerner looked for a different model to run his team— the strong general manager—Savage was seeking to change the personality of the head coach.

"We needed a believable figure who could connect with the players and myself," said Savage.

* * *

Before Savage was hired, Lerner and Collins talked to Brad Childress about being the coach. He was 48 years old and the offensive coordinator for the Philadelphia Eagles. He later would become the head coach of the Minnesota Vikings from 2006 to 2010.

But why interview a coach when you knew you were going to hire a general manager . . . and the general manager was supposed to hire a coach?

Well, they did. It meant little once Savage was hired.

Savage interviewed Terry Robiskie, who finished the 2004 season with a 1-4 record as the Browns interim coach. It was mostly a courtesy to a good man who was thrown into an impossible situation when Butch Davis resigned with five games left.

Savage had an interest in Kirk Ferentz. They worked together with the Browns in the 1990s under Belichick. But Ferentz was the head coach at Iowa and really liked his situation.

Savage interviewed Russ Grimm, a Pittsburgh Steelers assistant. He also talked to NFL veteran assistants Mike Nolan and Jim Bates.

But from the start of the search, one name emerged as the leader and it never changed—Romeo Crennel.

"I had an out-of-the-box candidate," said Savage. "That was John Harbaugh, who was the special teams coach with the Eagles. Back then, you usually didn't hire a special teams coach to be a head coach. But I had always liked John from a distance."

Savage said the Browns had already interviewed Crennel and liked him. He was the defensive coordinator with New England when they won three Super Bowls – 2001, 2003 and 2004.

For several years, word in the NFL was Crennel was ready to be a head coach. He came from the coaching tree of Bill Parcells and Belichick.

Crennel had been with the Browns in 2000, the defensive coordinator under Chris Palmer. That was before he joined Belichick in New England.

"John Collins didn't think there was any reason to talk to Harbaugh," said Savage. "We were close to settling on Romeo, so we just went forward with him."

Harbaugh later won a Super Bowl as head coach of the Baltimore Ravens.

Savage admitted he wanted someone different from the mercurial Davis.

"Romeo was a fatherly figure," said Savage. "One of the reasons we picked him was that he was the opposite of Butch. I didn't know Romeo well, but we had some of the same roots from Belichick. He was just a solid choice."

And Crennel was widely praised.

He was 57 years old when hired. He had never been a head coach at any level. All of his coaching experience was with special teams or on the defensive side of the ball.

Crennel had been consistently passed over by younger (and mostly white) assistant coaches for other head coaching opportunities. He never complained. He just worked harder. Crennel became the first black head coach of the Browns. Or at least the first full-time coach. He replaced Robiskie, the interim who also is an African-American.

"In many cases I've been the only African-American on the coaching staff or in the neighborhood," Crennel told the media on the day he was hired. "The way I carry and conduct myself . . . carries an impact on the rest of America, and on African-Americans in particular. The best thing I can do for other minority candidates is to be successful."

Crennel is a huge man, weighing about 280 pounds. He was a former defensive lineman at Western Kentucky. Coaching the defensive line was his specialty. He had an immediate connection with most of the big men on the defensive line.

He also said this: "My skin color is black, but I'm a head coach. I hope I possess the qualities needed in a head coach . . . taking the reins of a team and trying to run a whole program is going to be a big challenge. But I think I'm ready."

*   *   *

Savage nearly was fired after his first season. Team president John Collins and Savage had a clash late in the 2005 season, Savage's first with the Browns. I was never sure exactly what was the problem, other than Collins thought Savage was on the road too much scouting.

"The plan was for me to be on the road the first few years," said Savage. "We had to find players. We had to draft well. Randy and I agreed on this when I was hired."

Near the end of the season, ESPN even reported Savage would be fired.

It was very, very close to happening.

The Browns were finishing up a 6-10 season. Nothing special, but better than the previous two years of 4-12 and 5-11. Savage and Crennel did bring some stability to the shaky ship left behind by Butch Davis.

After Randy Lerner broke up with Carmen Policy, he hired Collins as CEO on May 1, 2004. Collins helped Lerner conduct the search for the general manager. That led to Savage being hired. He also had a hand in the hiring of Crennel.

At that point, the best move would have been for Collins to back off and let football people do their jobs. Collins came from the NFL's New York headquarters where he worked in marketing and sponsorship deals. He also helped start the NFL Network channel.

But he had zero experience in actual football operations. Nonetheless, Lerner allowed Collins to have some control over Savage. Soon, the general manager and Collins were at odds over more than Savage's scouting trips.

Collins also thought control of the salary cap should be in his department.

Savage said Collins wanted to replace salary cap expert Trip Mac-Cracken.

"We had worked out our cap and approach to free agency," said Savage. "It was all in writing. Then Randy informed me everything was to run through John Collins."

Most general managers believe they should be in charge of the salary cap, relying on a lawyer/salary cap expert. Naturally, the owner is part of this. He writes the checks.

MacCracken had been with the Browns since 1999, working his way up in the team's legal department. Collins thought the team didn't handle some contracts well. At the very least, he wanted to replace MacCracken.

Savage said the Browns were about $30 million under the salary cap, so what was the problem?

Meanwhile, Lerner sat back and watched his two most important front office people duel it out behind the scenes. When ESPN reported Savage would be fired after the season, most fans and media members were outraged. How could they fire Savage after one season? It seemed the team was heading in the right direction.

Lerner was stunned by fan and media criticism of the move—much of it aimed at him. After all, he was the owner. This was happening on his watch. Finally, Collins "resigned."

Collins is a talented man. He later became chief operating officer of the National Hockey League and did a very good job.

Because Lerner was so murky when it came to who was in charge of what, Collins thought he could have a major say on contracts. After all, it was business.

Savage thought he needed to control the cap because that was part of picking players, without having to clear it through Collins and the new salary cap person.

* * *

A few weeks after Collins resigned and Savage survived, I had a 90-minute sit down meeting with Lerner. This was on January 20, 2006. I found the story that I wrote for the Akron Beacon Journal.

"I can't let anyone get between Phil Savage and myself," Lerner told me. "I handled this clumsily."

Lerner admitted "the salary cap is in great shape." He called the problems between Savage and Collins "like a marriage gone bad."

This was the start of Randy Lerner's fourth year as owner. He had already made it clear to Policy that he should leave. He had given Davis a 4-year extension, then watched Davis quit before he finished his first year.

Lerner then paid Davis about $12 million remaining on the contract.

He hired and fired John Collins in a span of 18 months.

He went from the "Coach As King System" to the "General Manager in Charge" model—sort of—but allowed Collins to be in the middle.

Then Collins departed.

In the meeting, Lerner told me: "If we don't keep our football operation in order, we'll be a perpetual expansion team. That's beyond unacceptable to me. That will lead to nightly vomiting, divorce and personal ruin."

Yes, the man said "nightly vomiting, divorce and personal ruin." I'm not making that up.

Of course, many fans probably felt the same way.

Lerner was living in Long Island, but commuting to Cleveland by private jet a few days each week during the season.

He told me, "When they ask who is in leadership, it's me. I'm digging in to do this job. I can have various people report to me."

I remember sitting in Lerner's office, wondering if the 43-year-old owner would ever figure it out. He loves modern art. In the few personal conversations I had with Lerner, he was the creative man whose mind seemed to jump from topic to topic. He was almost the opposite of his father. Al Lerner was a former Marine, a hard-driving banker and a bottom-line business man.

I was hearing, "Randy can be very influenced by the last few people who talk to him."

For a while, Collins had convinced Lerner that there were major problems with Savage.

Then the fans and media screamed to keep the general manager.

Lerner went from having Butch Davis running everything, to Collins/Savage/Crennel—then to Savage/Crennel.

"I wanted Phil Savage," Lerner said. "I recruited Phil Savage . . . Phil and Romeo should be the public faces of the franchise . . . Phil and Romeo have given me reason to hope."

For a little while, Lerner was right.

Could It Have Been Different for Brady Quinn?

"He could have been a good NFL quarterback."

A few years ago, Phil Savage was talking to Brady Quinn.

Savage was the Browns general manager in 2007. He put together a bold trade with Dallas in order to draft Quinn, the star quarterback from Notre Dame, in the first round.

He was with Quinn and Bruce Feldman, an author of several books including the New York Times bestseller *The Making of a Quarterback*.

Savage put his hand on Quinn's shoulder and said, "For the life of me, I can't figure out how this young man isn't an established quarterback in the NFL, the face of a franchise and the guy who got the Browns to the playoffs."

At that point, Quinn was out of the NFL and building a broadcasting career.

"I know Brady had some weaknesses," said Savage. "But I still believe he could have been a good NFL quarterback."

And Savage believes it could have happened in Cleveland. He also thinks the ever-changing general managers and coaches led to some of Quinn's problems.

"A young quarterback needs a sponsor, an advocate," said Savage. "When I was fired, Brady lost that. The same is true when Romeo (Crennel) and Chud (offensive coordinator Rob Chudzinski) were fired (after the 2008 season). Brady was ready to take over the team then, but the sponsors who believed in him were gone."

That's Savage's version, and there might be some truth to it.

But there are other factors.

*   *   *

First, let's consider Quinn.

"I grew up a Browns fan," he said. "Growing up, I wanted to play for the Browns. That was my dream."

Quinn was born in Columbus and attended Dublin Coffman High School. He was an All-Ohio quarterback and then went to Notre Dame, where he set 29 different passing records. Heading into the 2007 draft, the Browns were looking for a quarterback. They had Charlie Frye and Derek Anderson on the roster.

Savage really liked Quinn.

"They brought me to Berea," said Quinn. "I had a great meeting with RAC (coach Romeo Crennel), Chud and Phil Savage."

He was hoping the Browns would take him with the No. 3 pick in the 2007 draft. Savage told Quinn's agent that was not likely to happen. He had his heart set on Joe Thomas, the future Hall of Fame tackle.

*   *   *

Heading into the draft, I knew Savage liked Quinn.

But I also knew the general manager loved Joe Thomas, the left tackle from Wisconsin.

In 2006, the Browns had a 4-12 record with Charlie Frye and Derek Anderson as their quarterbacks. The Browns offensive line allowed 54 sacks, third most in the NFL. The quarterbacks had thrown 15 touchdown passes compared to 25 interceptions. As usual for the Browns, quarterback was a problem. But the offensive line was part of the reason the quarterbacks were being assaulted when they dropped back to pass.

Savage made his reputation in his first draft with the Baltimore Ravens. He picked future Hall of Famer Jonathan Ogden in the first round. Ogden was a left tackle. Savage was the Ravens' scouting director. It was Baltimore vice president Ozzie Newsome who had to green-light the selection. But there was no doubt that Savage was a strong advocate for Ogden.

And Savage saw a lot of Jonathan Ogden in Joe Thomas.

"If Joe was there at No. 3, we were taking him," said Savage. "About two weeks before the draft, I was at home looking at tape of Thomas. I finally clicked it off and knew we were taking Joe. We had to take Joe."

In fact, Savage called Quinn's agent before the draft to say he had no plans to pick the quarterback at No. 3.

As the draft dawns it seems nearly everyone in the NFL is lying (or at least not telling the whole truth), so the Quinn camp wasn't sure what to think of Savage's call.

Savage liked Quinn and knew Quinn was dreaming of wearing an orange helmet. He wanted Quinn to know that was not about to happen at the top of the draft.

The first pick in 2007 draft was quarterback JaMarcus Russell. He had a disastrous career with Oakland, playing only 31 games.

The second pick was Calvin Johnson, who became a Hall of Fame caliber receiver with Detroit.

Then the Browns picked Thomas.

"We had Adrian Peterson and Marshawn Lynch rated high in that draft," said Savage. "Peterson had some knee injury issues at Oklahoma. We really liked Lynch, too. But I had decided to put our problems on the offensive line to bed."

Before the 2007 draft, Savage signed guard Eric Steinbach as a free agent from the Cincinnati Bengals.

Once he added Thomas and Steinbach, Savage began to think about Quinn.

*   *   *

Meanwhile, Quinn was in the green room on draft day in New York, waiting for a team to call his name.

It seemed the cameras were on him for hours. Every time a team drafted someone other than Quinn, the bright, unforgiving TV lights focused on Quinn . . . being rejected.

"A lot of people make a big deal about that," he said. "I knew what I signed up for. If I wasn't sitting in the green room in New York, I'd have been in a room somewhere else waiting for the draft."

Quinn expected to be selected by Miami at No. 9.

The Dolphins took receiver Ted Ginn Jr. from Ohio State.

"At that point, I wondered where I'd end up," he said.

His face looked as if someone had just stolen his favorite dog. Cleveland and Miami were the two teams showing the most interest in him. He was convinced Miami was the most likely destination.

After Miami passed on Quinn, Savage began calling other teams— trying to trade back into the first round. His next pick was number 36. He knew Quinn would be gone by then.

"Right before the 22nd pick, I got a call from Baltimore," said Quinn. "They had a trade all set up with Kansas City. They were going to trade for the 23rd pick and take me."

Quinn was warming to the idea of being a Raven "and beating the Browns. During the draft, I kept thinking about all the teams who passed on me . . . and how I wanted to beat them."

Quinn had expected to be drafted in the top 10. That was also what most draft experts projected.

After the top 10 picks, Savage had a list of players that he'd consider trading back into the first round to acquire: Darrelle Revis, Marshawn Lynch and Quinn.

Lynch went No. 12 to Buffalo. Revis was selected by the New York Jets at No. 14.

And Quinn just kept sitting in the room. At times, he appeared to be sweating.

Savage was working the phones. He knew Quinn was dropping. He and his front office people were making calls, trying to see who'd make a trade. Savage later admitted he wasn't even sure who other teams were drafting after the 12th pick. He was laser-focused on finding a trading partner so he could draft Quinn.

"The night before the draft, we had targeted Dallas as a possible trade partner," said Savage.

The Cowboys' owner Jerry Jones also served as general manager. He loved to make trades. He had the No. 22 pick. He had Tony Romo as his quarterback, so he didn't need Quinn.

Savage became even more determined to acquire Quinn when he heard Baltimore wanted the Notre Dame quarterback. From his Raven background, Savage knew the strengths of Newsome and his scouting staff. He didn't want Quinn to end up in Baltimore, which also was looking for a quarterback.

Savage suddenly swung a deal with Dallas. He shipped the No. 36 pick and the Browns' 2008 first round pick to the Cowboys for the 22nd pick . . . and a chance to draft Quinn.

"I went from thinking, 'I can't wait to beat the Browns' to being with the Browns," said Quinn. "It was a whirlwind."

In the Browns draft room, people were cheering, laughing, slapping palms.

Perhaps the happiest man was Rob Chudzinski. The offensive coordinator absolutely loved Quinn and was pushing for Savage to take Quinn at No. 3.

When Savage talked to the media after the first round, he was still on an adrenaline high. He had been able to draft two of the players he prized the most.

"I could not have imagined Brady would end up falling back in our lap at No. 22," Savage said that draft day. "I don't think Brady or his people could have anticipated this type of situation . . . this will probably be the day that defines the Browns turnaround, if that indeed happens."

As for Quinn, he now considers draft night one of his favorite memories.

"I was with my family in New York City waiting to be picked in the NFL draft," he said. "Some of them had never been to New York. It was a neat experience. Then my favorite team traded up to get me. How great is that?"

*　　*　　*

Browns fans were overjoyed with the 2007 draft.

The "Build-the-line-first" types were thrilled with Thomas.

"One of our scouts told me something before the draft that resonated," Savage said that day. "They said since 1999, this team has tried to serve apple pie for dinner. We needed to do something different with our interior line. So we took Joe Thomas, and we could serve steak and potatoes for dinner."

But Quinn became the surprise dessert.

ESPN's Mel Kiper gave the Browns a "B+" on their draft. On the air, Kiper said, "Quinn will be a good, solid quarterback in the NFL."

At one point, Kiper had Quinn as the top pick on his Big Board. As the draft neared, his top five in order were Calvin Johnson, Joe Thomas, Adrian Peterson, JaMarcus Russell and Brady Quinn.

We hear a lot about analytics now as if they are new. Now, there are more stats and facts to consider than years ago. But there was something in 2007 called the Lewin Theory of Quarterbacks. I wrote about this right after Quinn was picked.

It began with former Dallas scout Gil Brandt, who did some research. He believed first-round quarterbacks who had at least 40 starts at major college programs had a higher success rate than those with fewer starts—especially less than 25.

David Lewin wrote for Football Outsiders. He took Brandt's 40-start baseline, and dropped it to 35. He also believed the more a quarterback completed at least 60 percent of his passes, the higher the success rate in the NFL.

So his goal was to find a quarterback in the first round with at least 35 starts and 60 percent completions. This was before the spread offenses took over the college game and inflated stats.

Quinn started 46 games at Notre Dame, completing 58 percent of his passes. In his last two seasons, he completed 63 percent with 69 touchdowns compared to 14 interceptions.

Savage paid a heavy price for Quinn. He traded the Browns' 2008 first-round pick and the 36th pick in the 2007 draft to Dallas for the quarterback. But in terms of the data available back then, the trade appeared to have real merit.

Here's a list of quarterbacks from 1999 drafted in the first two rounds who started at least 35 games and completed 57 percent of their passes: Peyton Manning, Donovan McNabb, Daunte Culpepper, Ben Roethlisberger, Eli Manning, Philip Rivers, Drew Brees, Byron Leftwich, Chad Pennington, Jason Campbell, Carson Palmer, Matt Leinart and Jay Cutler.

So Quinn was in very good company in terms of the early analytics.

*   *   *

Looking back, Savage can see some flaws in Quinn's game.

"He wasn't a pinpoint accurate passer," said Savage. "He was a muscle-bound thrower in some ways. But I also kept thinking about all the quarterbacks who went low in the first round and later. But hindsight is 20/20. If there are reasons you're not taking a quarterback at No. 3, then you shouldn't take him at No. 22. But I still think Brady could have been a solid quarterback with the right team."

The Browns were not the right team.

When it comes to quarterbacks—any quarterback since 1999, the Browns never seem to be the right team.

In 2007, the Browns already had Charlie Frye and Derek Anderson. Quinn missed part of training camp due to a contract dispute. This was before the NFL rookie salary scale was put in place. But the Browns had no plans to open the season with Quinn at quarterback. Savage wanted Frye or Anderson to start. In his mind, it made no sense to start a rookie in the opener.

Coach Romeo Crennel went with Frye, who was benched in the second quarter of what became a 34-7 loss to Pittsburgh. Anderson took over. Two days later, Frye was traded to Seattle. Anderson became the starter, Quinn the backup.

Then an amazing thing happened.

For one glorious season, Anderson got hot. He threw 29 touchdown passes compared to 19 interceptions. The Browns were the surprise of the NFL, finishing with a 10-6 record. Anderson also stayed healthy all year, a rarity for Browns quarterbacks.

In 2007, Quinn threw only eight passes.

In 2008, the Browns had injuries. Derek Anderson returned to the form that made him a backup quarterback. After a 3-5 start to the season, Anderson was benched. Quinn was given a chance to start.

In Quinn's first start, the Browns lost 34-30 to Denver. Quinn looked good, completing 23-of-35 passes for 239 yards, two touchdowns and no interceptions.

In his next start, the Browns beat the Bills, 29-27. It was a near blizzard in Buffalo, a Monday night game. Phil Dawson kicked an incredible 56-yard field goal through the wind to win it.

Quinn was 14-of-36 passing for 185 yards, no touchdowns or interceptions. It was a very tough night to throw the ball with 22-degree wind chills and gusts of 30 mph.

After two games, it was clear Quinn had poise. His arm was not super-charged. There were times when he poorly missed open receivers. But he had the makings of a decent quarterback.

But something happened in that Buffalo game. He broke his right index finger. He also suffered some tendon damage. He tried to play the next week against Houston, "but I could barely grip the ball. I had no accuracy."

He was replaced by Anderson during the game. Quinn then had season-ending surgery on the finger.

What if Quinn had not been hurt?

Would he have been the Browns quarterback for the next few years? Would the Browns have won a few more games, and perhaps that would have been enough for Savage to keep his job?

Then Quinn would have had his "sponsor," as Savage called the general manager or coach who backs the quarterback.

But he did get hurt.

So did Anderson.

And the Browns ended the season on a 6-game losing streak, their record being 4-12.

"I was so comfortable playing that season," said Quinn. "It was my second year in the league, and my second year in that offense. I really felt ready . . . then I got hurt . . ."

His voice trailed off.

After all, there was not much more for Quinn to say.

*   *   *

In 2009, Eric Mangini was the new coach. He also served as his own general manager, although George Kokinis had the job for a few months.

Mangini did open the season with Quinn as the quarterback. He also had Anderson.

"They dismantled the team," said Savage.

Top receiver Braylon Edwards was traded. Talented but troubled tight end Kellen Winslow was traded.

The Browns were playing rookie receivers Mohamed Massaquoi and Brian Robiskie. A college quarterback and NFL return man, Joshua Cribbs played some receiver.

"It was a completely new offense," said Quinn. "Brian Daboll was the offensive coordinator, and it was the first time he'd called plays. We were so young, there were lots of growing pains."

The Browns lost 11 of their first 12 games.

Late in the season, Mangini installed a no-huddle quarterback system. He wanted to run the ball a lot, throw few passes. He put Quinn in charge because Quinn was smart enough to set up his teammates without a huddle. He also could recognize defenses and switch plays at the line of scrimmage.

The Browns beat Pittsburgh, 13-6, in the first game with the new system. The wind chill was minus-6. Quinn did what Mangini asked, he stayed away from turnovers and kept the offense organized.

In the next game, the Browns beat Kansas City, 41-34. Quinn was 10-of-17 passing, two interceptions and no touchdowns. It was not a good performance. The Browns won because Jerome Harrison ran for 286 yards and three touchdowns. Joshua Cribbs returned two kickoffs for touchdowns.

Quinn suffered a major foot injury in that victory in Kansas City. His season was over.

Quinn started nine games and had a 2-7 record. He completed 53 percent of his passes, eight touchdowns compared to seven interceptions.

Anderson had a 3-4 record as a starter, completing only 44 percent of his passes. He had three touchdowns compared to 10 interceptions.

Both quarterbacks watched their careers sink.

*   *   *

I wondered what I wrote about Quinn after he was injured.

Here is part of my Plain Dealer column from December 22, 2009.

"There is so much we still don't know about the third year player from Notre Dame, partly because he has played so little . . . His arm strength is average at best. He has days when it seems he's wearing a blindfold because his passes are so far off target. Yet, he runs the no-huddle offense masterfully, not easy with so many receivers and running backs who are rookies or in their first seasons as starters. Nor is he blessed with a strong line or an established tight end.

"Quinn is the 26th-rated quarterback (67.2) with eight touchdowns and seven interceptions this season. Behind him are some big names: Mark Sanchez (29), Matt Stafford (30), JaMarcus Russell (33). All were first-round draft picks. Russell has been such a disappointment, he first lost his job to Bruce Gradkowski. After the former Browns backup was injured, Oakland started another former Brown (Charlie Frye) over Russell.

"Some quarterbacks are simply victims of being young on a bad team, and Quinn certainly fits into that category. They need to play a lot for the team to find out if these young guys can handle the position. But for the second year in a row, Quinn is hurt. He had started the last six games, his longest streak of starts. In his career, he has a dozen starts and a 3-9 record. His career quarterback rating is a humble 66.8, completing only 52 percent of his passes, 10 touchdowns compared to nine interceptions.

"What can be said about Quinn's future with the Browns? New team president Mike Holmgren will have the final word, but Quinn has played so little and with such mediocre talent, about all that can definitely be said is that there is still so much we don't know about Quinn."

*   *   *

Only now after digging up this column did I remember Holmgren was hired as president before the end of the 2009 season.

His response?

The Browns traded Quinn to Denver for Peyton Hillis on March 14, 2010.

"I didn't want to be traded," said Quinn. "I loved being with the Browns. I wanted to get out there, stay healthy and see what I could do."

In his last game with the Browns, Quinn suffered a season-ending Lisfranc foot injury. He had to decide about surgery. Instead, he took a more conservative approach of rest and rehabilitation. It took at least six months.

It's hard to understand why Denver traded for Quinn. The Broncos had Kyle Orton, a so-so starter who had an 8-7 record in 2009.

Maybe Quinn was supposed to be the backup. But coach Josh McDaniels drafted Tim Tebow in the first round of 2010—after acquiring Quinn.

Then McDaniels was fired after a 3-9 start. Quinn never played in a game for the Broncos.

"Brady had no real chance in Denver," said Savage. "They had Orton. Every time Tebow stepped on the practice field, the fans were screaming for him. Then McDaniels got fired."

Quinn then signed with Kansas City. He started eight games in 2012 and had a 1-7 record. That team finished 2-14.

*   *   *

In 2014, Quinn supplied the analysis for several NFL games on Fox television with veteran play-by-play man Dick Stockton.

After one of the games, Stockton looked hard at Quinn and asked, "What's wrong?" Stockton thought they had done a good job on the broadcast. Quinn was learning the television game.

"I miss it," said Quinn. "I miss the game. I miss competing. I miss the guys. I miss playing. I miss all of it."

At the time, Quinn was 29 years old.

"I was watching my one true love," said Quinn. "It hurt so much to watch someone else do it. I wanted to be a part of it."

Early in the 2014 season, Quinn had worked out with New England. He went to training camp with Miami.

"Turned out, I was just a camp arm," he said.

That's the extra quarterback brought to training camp simply to throw passes in practice. He has virtually no chance of making the team.

Even when he was doing some television games in 2014 and 2015, he still wished he could play. He spent seven seasons in the NFL.

"It just went by so fast," he said.

Injuries were a major factor.

He believes he never fully recovered from his Lisfranc foot injury late in the 2009 season. He skipped surgery and tried to have it heal on its own.

In 2012 with Kansas City, he suffered two major concussions.

He also had a back that required surgery to repair two herniated disks. By the end of his career, he knew he wasn't throwing the ball as well as he once did.

He said he also tried out with Seattle, New England, the Jets, and Miami. He spent two months with the Rams in 2013.

Quinn has been considered a draft bust by some experts. For some fans, the most vivid memory of Quinn's pro career is him sitting in the draft room in 2007, waiting hours for someone to finally call his name.

Quinn was 3-9 in parts of three seasons with the Browns. Overall, he had a 4-16 record as an NFL starter. He threw 12 TD passes compared to 17 interceptions.

"I kept getting hurt," he said. "It didn't end the way I wanted. But most football careers don't end the way you want."

I asked him if he had any hard feelings against the Browns.

"There's no reason to carry a grudge," he said. "There is no grudge. How many kids have an opportunity to play in the NFL? How many kids have their favorite team trade up to get them?"

Quinn has become a rising star in the media with Fox Sports. He is often on talk shows. He talks about the game very well.

He still deals with football injuries. He said his back will eventually require surgery. So will his foot.

"I never felt the same in the last few years of my career," he said. "I have some nerve issues in my leg stemming from the back problems. The only regret I have is I wish it had worked out better for me in Cleveland. I wanted to make it work for the fans and for Cleveland. But the Browns will always be my favorite team."

The Halley's Comet Season

"We were so close."

Maybe it wasn't a team built to last, but the 2007 Cleveland Browns were built to win.

This was the third season for Phil Savage as general manager. When you know you're still searching for a quarterback, a way to help the situation is to build the offensive line.

Savage began doing that in 2006.

He signed LeCharles Bentley, who had been a Pro Bowl center with the New Orleans Saints. Bentley is a Cleveland native who played at Ohio State. Bentley was 26 years old, right in his prime as he was entering his fifth pro season. It was a 6-year, $36 million contract with $13 million guaranteed.

Bentley was delighted to play for his home team. Savage was convinced he had an anchor for the center of his offensive line.

In late July, the Browns had their first 11-on-11 drill in training camp. The players were not in full pads, just shoulder pads. This was not heavy-duty blocking and tackling.

On the first play . . .

In the first practice . . .

After Bentley made his first snap . . .

He fell to the turf, suffering a massive knee injury.

"It was unbelievable," said Savage.

Bentley would never play another NFL game. He was supposed to be the "face of our free agent class." Instead, Bentley's hometown fans never saw him play a game in a Cleveland orange helmet.

But Savage would keep trying to help the line. He brought in veterans Hank Fraley, Kevin Shaffer, Seth McKinney and Eric Steinbach to join rookie left tackle Joe Thomas.

I mention this because Savage took a unique road trying to revive the Browns compared with everyone else running the team since 1999. Only Thomas was a draft pick. The others were acquired as free agents or through trades.

"Once we got a line, I went looking for a running back," said Savage.

In 2007, he found Jamal Lewis, who had tormented the Browns for years as a member of the Baltimore Ravens. Lewis was only 28 years old. He was coming off a season where he rushed for 1,132 yards.

But the Ravens thought Lewis was losing some of his speed. Even in the early 2000s, an analytics warning sign was when a good running back suddenly stopped averaging 4.0 yards per carry.

In 2005, Lewis was at 3.4 yards.

In 2006, Lewis was at 3.6 yards.

Savage was with Baltimore when Lewis was at his best (2000–03).

"I always liked Jamal," said Savage. "I knew he'd bring us toughness. We knew we'd get his best because he had something to prove— that he could still play."

Savage also added veteran receiver Joe Jurevicius in 2006. He was from the Cleveland suburb of Mentor, and a big target at 6-foot-5.

He had drafted Braylon Edwards, an athletic, 6-foot-3 receiver in the first round of the 2005 draft.

I'm detailing some of the moves because Savage took a realistic approach of what to do on offense when you didn't have a good quarterback. Add talent and experience at other positions.

1. He brought in five new offensive linemen: Thomas, Fraley, Shaffer, McKinney and Steinbach.

2. He brought in a veteran running back who had rushed for 1,000 yards in five of his six pro seasons.

3. He brought in two big receivers: Jurevicius and Edwards.

4. He kept Kellen Winslow, a gifted tight end drafted by Butch Davis. Winslow had a sometimes difficult personality and battled

injuries. But when healthy and focused, Winslow was an excellent pass catcher. Often, there is a tendency for a new front office to trade the draft picks of the previous front office. Winslow was drafted in 2004. He played only two games and broke his leg. In 2005, he missed the entire season after suffering a major knee injury in a motorcycle accident. Would this guy ever be healthy? That was the question. In 2006, Winslow caught 89 passes and played all 16 games.

5. Savage kept shopping for quarterbacks. He drafted two of them: Charlie Frye (third round, 2005) and Brady Quinn (first round, 2007). He picked up Derek Anderson off the Baltimore Ravens practice squad.

*   *   *

I had a close relationship with Savage when he was with the Browns.

For two years, he talked about his plan—the veteran line, the strong runner, the talented receivers.

The result was a 10-6 season in 2007, but no one saw that coming.

Not after the Browns were 6-10 (2005) and 4-12 (2006) in Savage's first two seasons as general manager.

Savage worked with head coach Romeo Crennel to reshape the coaching staff instead. Hiring Rob Chudzinski as offensive coordinator was the major change.

While Savage is an Alabama native, he understood the culture and mentality of the Browns fans. He had been with the Browns from 1991 to 1995 as a member of Bill Belichick's coaching staff. He knew the fan base was traumatized by the franchise move to Baltimore. He was part of the front office that relocated.

Savage's idea was to assemble a high-powered offense. He compared it to a jet-fighter. The quarterback would be the pilot. But he'd have a swift, well-tuned plane to fly.

"It should be an attractive cockpit for any quarterback," Savage told me.

*   *   *

Then the Browns opened the 2007 season with a 34-7 loss to Pittsburgh in Cleveland. Frye started the opener and was pulled in the second quarter. He was 4-of-10 passing for 34 yards and was sacked five times. He also threw an interception.

Frye looked shell-shocked. Anderson took over and was mediocre, completing 13 of 28 passes for 184 yards and a touchdown.

At this point, the Browns were 10-23 under Savage and Crennel.

The jet-fighter could barely get off the ground. The revamped offensive line looked like five guys who arrived on five different buses and had never seen each other before.

Newcomer Jamal Lewis? He looked old and slow, 35 yards rushing in 11 carries.

Anderson had been a sixth-round pick by Baltimore in 2005. That was Savage's first season in Cleveland, but he always paid close attention to what his old team was doing.

"In the AFC North, you play in a lot of bad weather and a lot of wind," said Savage. "I've always thought you needed a big guy who could throw the ball through that wind."

Anderson is 6-foot-6, 230 pounds. He has always looked the physical part of an NFL quarterback.

Two days after the Steelers game, Frye was traded to Seattle for a sixth-round pick.

In the back of Savage's mind, he thought Quinn could possibly start at some point in 2007. But he didn't want it to happen early in the season. He wanted to give the rookie from Notre Dame time to acclimate to the NFL.

Anderson started the second game of the season and something incredible happened: The Browns beat Cincinnati, 51-45.

That's right, the Browns scored 51 points!

That jet-fighter soared. Anderson threw five touchdown passes. That's right, five touchdown passes!

Jamal Lewis? He rushed for 216 yards.

Braylon Edwards and Kellen Winslow? They combined to catch 14 passes for 246 yards.

Joe Jurevicius? The 6-foot-5 receiver played what Savage called "tall ball." Near the goal line, the 6-foot-6 Anderson lofted passes above the defense—and they were hauled in by a leaping Jurevicius. He caught two in the end zone.

Anderson wasn't sacked at all as the offensive line was a wall protecting the quarterback and opening holes for Lewis.

* * *

Suddenly, the Browns jet-fighter was flying high.

The Browns beat the Ravens—TWICE!

They beat Miami, 41-31. Anderson threw three touchdown passes, all to Braylon Edwards.

They beat Seattle, 33-30, in overtime.

They beat Buffalo, 8-0, in a Cleveland blizzard.

OK, they lost twice to the Steelers. But this was a remarkable season.

They went to Cincinnati with a 9-5 record, A victory over the Bengals would have put the Browns in position to clinch a playoff spot. It was wild, windy afternoon in Cincinnati.

"Our bus was rocking in the wind on the way over to the game," recalled Savage.

For some mystifying reason, the Browns came out throwing. Anderson had trouble with the wind. It also seemed for the first time, his confidence was shaky. He threw two interceptions in a span of 40 seconds right at the end of the first half that were turned into 13 quick points for the Bengals.

In 2016, ESPN's Tony Grossi interviewed Anderson, who said: "I had the opportunity to take my team to the playoffs, and it was one of the worst games I ever played."

Chudzinski had been an aggressive play caller all season. It usually worked. But not on that Sunday.

Anderson threw the ball 48 times—and four of them became interceptions.

The 19-14 loss is a game that still haunts Anderson, Chudzinski and Savage.

At different times over the years, all three men have mentioned that game with true regret. Chudzinski wishes he had run the ball more often. Anderson wishes he hadn't felt the pressure and forced so many poor passes that led to interceptions.

As for Savage, he knew how hard it was for a Browns team to make the playoffs—and this was a team good enough to do just that. The Browns led the AFC North in scoring, and had the No. 8 offense in the NFL.

They all know what it would have meant for the Browns to make the playoffs. They finished with a 10-6 record. But Pittsburgh went into the post-season because of two victories over the Browns. Tennessee was also 10-6 and earned the second wild card playoff spot.

"We were so close," said Savage.

It turns out this was a Halley's Comet season for Anderson and the Browns. It seemed to come out of nowhere. It was a beautiful sight . . . and then it was gone.

Why Josh Cribbs
Was Special

"He plays the game with the right attitude."

I won't take credit for the Browns signing Josh Cribbs.

But I will say that right after the 2005 NFL draft—when Cribbs wasn't picked—the Plain Dealer's Elton Alexander and I spotted Phil Savage. We had been talking about how the Browns should bring in Cribbs, who was a star quarterback at Kent State.

Savage had just taken over as the Browns general manager. This was his first draft with the team.

I remember telling Savage, "Cribbs is an elite athlete. He can do something on a football field."

Alexander covered Cribbs for all four of his seasons at Kent. He knew Cribbs well. Savage and Alexander had an in-depth conversation about the character of Cribbs, who pleaded guilty the year before for possession of marijuana.

It was the only time Cribbs was in any trouble at Kent State.

"They found marijuana in his apartment or something," recalled Savage. "That probably was why no one drafted him. I liked Josh in college. We had talked to him before the draft about trying to be a receiver."

Savage doesn't remember much of our conversation about Cribbs—other than Alexander and I thought the Browns should give him a shot.

Not long after that, Savage called Cribbs.

"I came in the hard way as a free agent," said Cribbs. "I was signed for five grand. I was eaten up by bills. This opportunity was all I had to change my life."

Cribbs had an incredible career at Kent State.

Golden Flashes coach Dean Pees recruited Cribbs in 2001 out of Dunbar High in Washington, D.C. Several larger programs were interested in Cribbs, but not as a quarterback. Most wanted him to try defensive back.

Pees had a 3-30 record in his first three seasons as KSU's coach. He knew Cribbs could immediately energize his offense because he was a tremendous runner and a decent passer.

The Flashes were 6-5 in his first season at quarterback. He started all four years, throwing for 45 touchdowns and running for 38 more. He also caught three touchdown passes. Cribbs rushed for 3,670 career yards—a 5.8 per carry average.

Twice, he ran for more than 1,000 yards in a season. He ran the ball 632 times. Why mention this? Because the 6-foot-1, 210-pound Cribbs took a physical beating before he even stepped on the field in the NFL.

"I always thought he could have been an NFL running back," said Lee Owens, the former University of Akron coach who faced Cribbs in Mid-American Conference games.

Kent State had a 14-18 record in the MAC during the tenure of Cribbs, pretty good for a team that has struggled for decades in football.

"If nothing else, I figured Cribbs could help us on special teams," recalled Savage. "I also thought he had some ability to become a receiver."

*   *   *

"There were 30 of us."

That's how Cribbs begins to tell the story of joining the Browns.

He meant 30 players who were not drafted. Thirty players who were easy to cut—because the team had so little invested in them. Of the 30 players, the $5,000 Cribbs received was the biggest bonus.

But that's barely a penny in the economy of the National Football League.

The 30 undrafted free agents were not in Berea at the same time. Some were at the team complex for spring mini-camps. Others arrived during veterans camp late in the summer.

But they kept coming . . . body after body.

I say "body," because that's how most undrafted free agents are viewed in the NFL.

They also are called "a JAG." That means they are Just Another Guy.

Romeo Crennel was the head coach. One day he told Cribbs, "If you can run down the field and tackle a punt returner in a double vise, you have a spot on this team."

Cribbs said, "I'll do it."

He walked away from the conversation wondering, "What is a double vise?"

Cribbs laughs now as he tells the story.

"I'd never played special teams in high school or college," he said. "Quarterbacks didn't play special teams. But I had to make the Browns. I had to make the team. So I asked people, 'What's a double vise?'"

Not long after Cribbs arrived in Berea, Savage spotted him in the team cafeteria.

"Josh," said the general manager. "Right now, don't even worry about making the team as a wide receiver. Just concentrate on special teams. Cover kicks and punts. Run back kicks and punts."

"Yes sir," said Cribbs.

"That's the way you'll punch your ticket in this league," said Savage. "Take it and run with it."

*   *   *

Desperation.

That's what Cribbs felt in that first year.

And fear.

Desperation and fear bubbling up inside.

He was married with a daughter. He was certain a team would draft him after his sensational career at Kent State. But nothing happened.

Nothing but the $5,000 bonus . . . the invitation to Berea . . . the chance to impress the coaches.

"I was willing to do anything to make the team," he said. "I'd play anywhere . . . offense . . . defense . . . special teams. If they told me to play on the defensive line, I'd have tried to play on the defensive line."

Instead, it was all-special teams, all-the-time.

Cribbs was unique because most guys who are excellent tacklers on special teams do not return punts and kicks. Running and tackling are their specialties.

Most guys who return punts and kicks are not good tacklers. Their specialty is running the ball.

"I could do both," said Cribbs.

He learned to do both.

"He was such a fierce competitor," said Savage. "He'd run back a kick for a touchdown, then he'd run down the field on the next kickoff and make the tackle. You just don't see that. After some practices, he'd be out on the field, catching passes from the Jugs Gun . . . wanting to learn to be a receiver."

He was a fearless player driven by fear.

"I had to make the team," he said. "I just had to make it. This was my life."

If that meant learning how to cover punts and kickoffs, he learned.

If it meant learning how to tackle, he became consumed with tackling.

If it meant catching punts and kickoffs and running into defenders at ridiculously high speeds—and risking concussions and other injuries, he did it.

"I didn't want to have a 'What if?' moment," said Cribbs. "I didn't want to say, 'I would have made the team if I did this . . .' No 'What Ifs' for me . . . I did everything I could to make it."

Cribbs paused, then said, "You have to find a way to make them keep you."

*　　*　　*

As time passed, his heart beat a little faster each day he walked into the training facility.

"I'd go to practice each day hoping not to get tapped on the shoulder and told to go see the coach," said Cribbs. "I kept seeing guys getting the tap on the shoulder, every day. They had to turn in their playbooks."

Bodies. JAGs. One guy passing through. Some only survived a few days, others a few weeks.

"I knew I made the team on the last day (before the opening game)," he said. "I noticed there was no one getting tapped on the shoulder. It was cut down day. No one tapped me on the shoulder. I still had the playbook in my hand."

Cribbs said Romeo Crennel called a team meeting. The guys stared at the coach, who said, "This is our team."

Cribbs looked around the room to see if any other undrafted free agents had survived.

"There was one guy," said Cribbs. "But he was assigned to the practice squad. I was the only one of 30 undrafted free agents who made the active roster."

Cribbs said he went into the bathroom, looked in the mirror and said, "I made it."

The face staring back at him was an NFL player—at least for now.

"NFL . . . Not For Long," said Cribbs. "I never forgot that."

*   *   *

As a rookie, Cribbs was second on the team in special teams tackles. The Browns only used him on kickoff returns in that 2005 season, and he returned one 90 yards for a touchdown.

Cribbs soon became one of the NFL's premier special teams players. He remained driven and dedicated.

"Every year you have better players coming after your job," he said. "They are faster . . . stronger . . . cheaper. You have to out-play all these young guys."

In his mind, he kept telling himself, "Do things to make them keep you."

So he worked on becoming a receiver and caught a few passes. He played some wildcat as quarterback, taking long snaps from center and running the ball.

He is tied with Leon Washington for the NFL record of returning eight career kickoffs for touchdowns. When it comes to all-around special teams players, Cribbs was Hall of Fame caliber.

"Playing consumed my life," said Cribbs. "The next contract consumed my life because I came in making the minimum. Winning consumed my life. I knew the more I could do for the Browns, the longer they'd keep me."

And he played hurt. By 2009, his knee was bone-on-bone.

"I'd go to the doctors because my knee was all messed up," said Cribbs.

Then he'd ask one question, "Is it functional?"

"Yes," the doctor would say. "But it's going to be painful."

Cribbs would ask, "Is it just pain or injury?"

The doctor would explain about how most of the knee cartilage was gone, bones were rubbing against each other.

"It was pain," said Cribbs. "I could play through pain. I pushed through it. I'd take the injections, the medicine, whatever I needed to get through the pain."

He knew they were coming . . .

The younger guys . . .

The faster guys . . .

The guys on cheaper, rookie contracts . . .

In his eight seasons with the Browns, Cribbs missed only four games.

Two were in his rookie season, when his right knee was first injured.

He played with battered toes. Former Browns coach Eric Mangini once told me that he couldn't believe how bad some toes on Cribbs' feet looked. His fingers sometimes were mashed. His knees often ached.

Know what happened in 2009—the year it was determined Cribbs had the knee with "bone-on-bone"?

He ran back three kickoffs for touchdowns. He ran back a punt for a touchdown. He caught 20 passes as a receiver. He ran the ball 55 times from the wildcat formation, averaging 6.9 yards per carry.

"That was Coach Mangini," said Cribbs. "He often said 'Players make plays.' So he wanted to find ways to get the ball in the hands of playmakers."

Mangini loved Cribbs, praising his passion and toughness.

*   *   *

Cribbs said there was a day in 2008 when "we just kept losing . . . and I was losing that fire."

The Browns had lost a home game.

"I was really down," he said. "My wife and I were driving and we saw a Pop Warner game going on at St. Ignatius Field."

Cribbs pulled over and watched it for a while.

"That day, I didn't give my all on the field," he said. "I lost my heart a bit. I looked at those little kids playing football. I thought about how I was once one of those little kids, dreaming of the NFL. At that moment, I re-dedicated myself to playing like I should."

*   *   *

One of the more remarkable stories was when Cribbs wanted his contract re-worked—and how the fans wanted it to happen.

Cribbs played for the rookie minimum (about $350,000) in 2005 and 2006.

Heading into the 2007 season, he signed a 6-year, $6.8 million contract—but only the $2 million signing bonus was guaranteed.

Savage was preparing to rework Cribbs' contract starting in 2009— but the general manager was fired after the 2008 season.

Mangini took over as coach and had a lot to say about contracts. He also wanted to give Cribbs a new deal—but it was stalled.

Finally, after the 2009 season, Cribbs signed a 3-year, $20 million deal. Only $7 million was guaranteed, but suddenly he was set up for life.

"I'll never forget how the fans supported me," said Cribbs.

A public internet campaign called PAY THE MAN! was created.

I remember talking to Jim Brown about Cribbs. This was in 2009.

"He is a spiritual force," Brown said. "What he does is so pure. He runs the ball. Then he runs down the field and makes a tackle. He plays the game with the right attitude."

That's what the fans sensed.

They knew his story of being an undrafted free agent from nearby Kent State. They saw the physical price he paid on the field.

In 2005, he had a helmet-to-helmet hit. After the game, he didn't remember what happened in the game.

In 2010, he had a significant concussion when he was hit in the helmet by Pittsburgh linebacker James Harrison.

In 2012, he returned a punt against Baltimore. Linebacker Dannell Ellerbe hit Cribbs under the chin. His helmet went flying. He dropped to the turf and was down for quite a while. The action stopped. Players from both teams went on their knees to pray. Cribbs lay flat and stared at the heavens—not sure what had happened. He eventually left the field with yet another concussion.

"I don't know how many concussions I had," he said. "It was a lot."

Cribbs said he has "no regrets" about his career or the injuries he suffered.

*   *   *

After the 2012 season, the Browns didn't renew his contract.

As Cribbs knew, they'd finally found a player who was "younger . . . faster . . . cheaper" to replace him.

That was Travis Benjamin.

The injuries were wearing him down. He played six games with the Jets in 2013, and six more with the Colts in 2014.

At the age of 31, he was finished as an NFL player.

"My main motivation was to make it to the NFL for my family, " said Cribbs. "But I also was motivated to play well for the fans. They work so hard for us, spending their hard-earned money to watch us play—and we wouldn't win. The least we could do was give them all we've got."

I remember after one frustrating loss, Cribbs told several of us, "We almost always almost win."

There was a lot of truth in those ALMOSTS.

Cribbs remembered going to the 2012 Pro Bowl with teammates Joe Thomas and Phil Dawson.

"We were in Hawaii," said Cribbs. "We were smoking cigars. I was thinking, 'Here we are . . . one of football's greatest kickers . . . one of the greatest tackles . . . and me, a great return man . . .' We accomplished something with the Browns."

Cribbs said one of the best compliments he ever received was from Dawson.

"Phil once told me, 'I can tell my kids I played with Josh Cribbs,'" said Cribbs.

Then Cribbs said: "I tell people, 'I played with Joe Thomas. I scored on a play where he blocked for me.' That means something."

I talked to Cribbs before the 2018 season. He was an intern special teams coach with the Browns.

He had graduated from Kent State in 2010, picking up his communications degree while he was an NFL player. He played 10 seasons in the NFL and is one of the best all-around special teams players ever.

"There wasn't just a 1 percent chance that I'd make the team," said Cribbs. "It was .01 percent . . . or maybe lower. But I did make it. To me, playing in the NFL is an honor. It hurts me when people talk bad about the Browns. This team will always be dear to my heart."

Fans Write In . . .

Browns Quarterbacks

Readers were asked about Browns quarterbacks since 1999: Who was the best? Who deserves the most sympathy? Have you met any of them? (Responses were edited for clarity and brevity.)

Derek Anderson came out of nowhere to lead us to a surprise 10-win season and so painfully close to the playoffs (in 2007). He didn't have any huge expectations or hype, he just played with grit and gave it his all when he was given the opportunity to start.
—*Christopher Schlosser, Cuyahoga Falls*

I was always impressed with Derek Anderson's big arm, and his deep ball was a thing of beauty. He could be fooled by complex defensive schemes and his inaccuracy was his undoing here, but he was by far our best quarterback. Tim Couch deserves the most sympathy. He was thrown into an impossible situation, so it's hard to know what might have been under different circumstances. He never had a chance to succeed.
—*Aaron Trella, Youngstown*

Tim Couch was the only QB who got better each season and the last to bring us to a playoff game. He beat the Steelers multiple times, and I'll never forget the Sunday night game where he ran in for a touchdown and flexed to the Steelers crowd (a 33-13 Browns win on Oct. 5, 2003). I met him at the Smokey Bones in Mentor about 10 or 12 years ago. I believe he bought everyone who was at the bar a round. I don't think he got a fair chance in Cleveland, and I believe we ruined his career.
—*Umberto Barbera, Mentor*

I still bristle when I see NFL Network's Top 10 Biggest Busts episode and see Tim Couch listed. He doesn't deserve it. He wasn't a bust–he got busted by a historically inept organization. He was a tough SOB who took all the hits and always got up and was a pretty damn good 2-minute QB as well. His teammates liked and respected him. He also led his team to the playoffs in his fourth year. He would've gone about 11-5 with a roster approximating the one that Hoyer/Manziel went 7-9 with.

—Sean Beck, Burbank, California

Spergon Wynn deserves the most sympathy. He will always be the guy we took instead of Tom Brady.

—Drew Harnett, Lexington, South Carolina

Tim Couch is the best, hands down. The kid was shoved into duty early, in an offense that did not maximize his strengths, and on a team void of playmakers.

Couch was mauled behind a weak offensive line as he learned how to play in the NFL and actually improved enough to take a team that still lacked talent to the playoffs in 2002. I would have loved to have had Couch in 2007 and beyond with some of the offensive weapons we had, but, alas, it is the reality of a Browns fan.

Couch deserves the most sympathy. The guy was sacked 117 times in his first 38 games. His one steady playmaker was Kevin Johnson, who everyone loves in Cleveland, but sadly, nobody else remembers. On top of this, we treated the guy like crap, booing him when he was lying hurt on the ground. His career was shortened because of the abuse he took and he still loves us all. Sympathy is more than due.

I met [center] Hank Fraley's father in the hours leading up to the Browns-Giants' Monday night game in 2008. He assured me that the team was behind Derek Anderson, but that Brady Quinn was the future from the locker room's perspective. UGH! LOL

—Patrick Eugene Martin, Middleport, Ohio

Best QB since 1999? Tough question. Derek Anderson made a Pro Bowl. Hard to argue against that. I liked Jeff Garcia's game. Tim Couch deserves the most sympathy. Brian Hoyer never had a real shot, and I hated the

Johnny Manziel pick (I knew he would not only bust, but would tear the Browns apart).
—*Brian Oldaker, Decatur, Indiana*

The most successful was Kelly Holcomb since he's the only QB to get us into the playoffs. Tim Couch deserves the most sympathy. We'll always wonder what he could've done behind a strong line.
—*Christopher Ard, Virginia Beach, Virginia*

The statistics back up my memory of the glimmer of contention from 2002, the only glimmer since 1999. I strongly believe the best QB is Kelly Holcomb. He got the Browns closest to being a contender since 1999, which is how I define best QB. In the 2002 season, Holcomb had magic whenever he filled in for Couch. Holcomb had a 92.9 rating and almost beat the Steelers in the only Browns playoff game since 1999. The Browns lost 36-33 and Holcomb threw for 429 yards with a 107.6 rating.

I wonder how Tim Couch's career would've gone on a good Eagles team under QB guru and maybe Hall of Fame coach Andy Reid? Derek Anderson was a poor man's Vinny Testaverde.
—*Matt Lazar, Tulsa, Oklahoma*

I have to go with Tim Couch. He had no one to throw to and had no line but he was by far the best. We should have had a lot more winning seasons with him. I think a close second is Brian Hoyer.

Hoyer is about 20 days younger than I am. He went to high school at St. Ignatius and I went to St. Edward. He beat my Eagles in the two years that he started. He played baseball with my next-door neighbor. I did wait on his dad once when I was bartending. His dad was really nice. We graduated the same year. His mom and my mom worked together while they were pregnant with Brian and me. Clearly, Hoyer got the better genes (lol).
—*Andrew Tima, Cleveland*

Judging by record and success, the best is Brian Hoyer. People forget what impact that knee injury against the Bills in 2013 caused Hoyer. Add to that the uninformed fans clamoring for Johnny 8-Ball a few months later, as well as the belligerence between coach Mike Pettine and general manager Ray Farmer, and it is easy to see how Hoyer never received a fair shot.

I met Bruce Gradkowski when he was an underclassman at a party at Toledo. He promptly destroyed me in a game of Madden on PlayStation 2. I didn't even know who he was until my friend told me later that night.
—*Nikolaos Hazinakis, Seven Hills, Ohio*

Kelly Holcomb was the best quarterback for throwing for 429 yards in a playoff game. Josh McCown and Tim Couch are second and third. Couch deserves the most sympathy . . . he would have been an above-average quarterback in the right situation.
—*Mike Ehrman, Sagamore Hills, Ohio*

Brian Hoyer deserves the most sympathy. He beat the Pittsburgh Steelers at home, and you could not buy his jersey or a T-shirt in the team store. Fans had to make their own Hoyer jerseys and T-shirts. ESPN and ESPN Cleveland wanted the overrated Johnny Manziel.
—*Mark Thut, Wooster, Ohio*

The expectations placed on Tim Couch were completely unrealistic. Fans have forgotten, it seems, that he was the last quarterback to start all 16 games in a season. It would have been interesting to see what a healthy Couch could have done playing on a normal "Browns bad" team instead of the expansion "Browns bad" teams.

The sympathy question is a toss-up between Couch and Brian Hoyer. How can we not be sympathetic to the story of the local kid that dreamed of playing in Cleveland and bounced around the league before getting his shot? After blowing out his knee, he works his tail off to rehab and be ready for the next season only to become collateral damage in the Manziel fiasco.
—*Chris Lally, Chester, Virginia*

I am from Mansfield and have lived in Berlin, Germany, the last 12 years. Seeing the Browns in 2017 at Twickenham [in London] was the first time since 2004. DeShone Kizer deserves the most sympathy. The guy has

a huge upside and can make it in the league. He was not ready and was entrusted to lead a team of rookies while learning the ropes himself.
—*Steve Squires, Berlin, Germany*

Brian Hoyer was a winner and did the best job overall of any on the long list. He also dealt with more pressure than any of them, with the Johnny Manziel arrival. Had JM not come along, I think you would've seen an entirely different Browns career from Hoyer. The most sympathy definitely belongs to Tim Couch! I didn't agree with the pick, but he has earned my respect over the years by the way he has handled himself!
—*Tom Goodsite, Sanford, Florida*

Derek Anderson is the best quarterback. He had one shining season where he led an offense that looked like it belonged in the NFL. All other QBs have had a series or two where they looked mediocre or OK but then halftime arrives and the defense makes an adjustment and the magic disappears.
—*Deb and Pat Hogan, Louisville*

The QB who I felt the sorriest for was Tim Couch. The NFL did the Browns no favors when it came to acquiring talent. The team ended up with nothing but castoffs and a coach who was in over his head. Couch had the physical tools and an attitude to be successful. What he lacked was good coaching and NFL-caliber starting teammates.
—*Terry L. Reed, Lake Worth, Florida*

The best is Brian Hoyer. He had a winning record and for at least a half season gave us hope. I wanted to like Derek Anderson, but with the playoffs on the line he had a terrible game against the hapless Bengals, so it's Hoyer.

I haven't met a post-1999 Cleveland quarterback. That's odd, because there are so many of them running around. You'd think I'd meet one by pure chance. Seriously, the 27th most recent starting QB for the Browns is Tim Couch. The 26th most recent starting QB for the New York Giants is Y.A. Tittle.
—*Phil Barth, Batavia, Ohio*

As a Notre Dame and Browns fan, I think Brady Quinn is the quarterback who I feel the most sympathy for. How could you not feel for him when you think about his draft, just sitting there and the cameras keep turning to the poor guy? How could you not feel for him when you see a picture of him as a kid in a Kosar jersey? The first time he came back with Kansas City, my brother and I were tailgating, both wearing our No. 10 Quinn jerseys. A woman comes up to us, wearing a KC Quinn jersey and says, "I'm Brady's aunt, and that's his mother. I want to tell you it means so much to us that you still support Brady." My brother and I said how much we've liked him since Notre Dame. We might have made their day, but she also made ours.

—*Rick Fawcett, Youngstown, Ohio*

Randy Lerner's Desperate Decision

"Everyone will remember what you did there."

Nothing was working.

That's how it seemed to Randy Lerner after he fired general manager Phil Savage and coach Romeo Crennel after the 2008 season.

Lerner thought he could hire Bill Cowher as coach and give him power to run the entire football operation. It was much the same setup Butch Davis had with the Browns from 2001 to 2004.

A Super Bowl-winning coach with Pittsburgh, Cowher had little interest in running the Browns. He was making more than $1 million a year as a football analyst for CBS Sports.

He retired as head coach of the Pittsburgh Steelers after the 2006 season. He'd spent 15 years with that organization.

After Cowher left coaching, every few years there were rumors of Cowher buying a house in Strongsville or another West Side Cleveland suburb. It was supposed to signal a move to the Browns. But a house in the Cleveland area was never sold to Cowher.

Cowher discovered television work was profitable and far less stressful than being an NFL head coach.

Lerner also had conversations with Scott Pioli, who was general manager of the New England Patriots and a Bill Belichick disciple. This happened a few times during Lerner's tenure.

But Pioli simply couldn't see the Browns as the right situation for him.

* * *

Lerner was meeting with the Cleveland media about the firing of his front office when he heard Eric Mangini was fired as head coach of the New York Jets. He learned of it in the middle of a discussion with about a dozen of us.

Several media members wrote something like, "Lerner's eyes lit up," when told Mangini was suddenly available.

I was not alone on that day thinking, "If Mangini wants the Browns job, it's his."

There was desperation in Lerner's voice along with confusion when discussing what he planned to do next. He didn't seem to have a good idea after Cowher and Pioli.

And they weren't coming.

But Mangini?

Lerner had a house in New York. He knew Mangini had some success with the Jets. In 2006, he was 10-6 as a rookie head coach. He was only 35 years old, a former New England defensive coordinator. The New York tabloids dubbed him "Mangenius!"

In his next season, he was 4-12. Suddenly, Mangini was being called other names. But that 10-6 record as a rookie coach bought him a third year.

Mangini had a 9-7 record in 2008. He was fired after losing 4-of-5 games to end the season. The Jets had imported veteran quarterback Brett Favre. He was 39 years old. Mangini was 37. They did not get along.

To Lerner, Mangini suddenly was a reason for hope. Here was a young head coach with two winning seasons in three years. Mangini longed to coach again, to wipe out the bitter taste of what he considered to be an unfair firing in New York.

Furthermore, Mangini had started his pro football career as a ballboy and public relations intern with the Cleveland Browns in 1994. Bill Belichick had hired him.

So part of Mangini connected with Cleveland.

"It always has been a special place for football," Mangini once told me. "I knew how the city would respond if they ever started to win."

It's the same thing every new general manager and coach has said when coming to the Browns.

If they could win in Cleveland . . .

"Everyone will remember what you did there," said Mangini.

It was an easy sell.

Mangini wanted the job.

Lerner wanted Mangini.

And best of all for Mangini, Lerner was willing to hire him first as coach—and then let Mangini hire his own general manager.

That set up Mangini to run the team, much like his mentor Bill Belichick.

* * *

The press conference where Eric Mangini was introduced as the new Browns head coach revealed some of the problems that were to come.

It began with Mike Keenan.

He was the team president, although few people knew it. He rarely appeared in public. Before introducing Mangini, Keenan first introduced himself to the media.

This should have been Lerner's job, but the owner refused to do it.

Mangini talked for about 10 minutes, clearly excited by the job. There were references to his time as a Browns ballboy and intern.

"I know Cleveland fans," Mangini said. "They don't just love football. They live football."

When Mangini finished his opening remarks, he started to walk away from the podium.

The media began screaming questions.

He returned to the podium. He wasn't sure if he was supposed to take questions. The Browns had no strong presence running the front office or the public relations department.

The disorganization was embarrassing, and did little to help Mangini create a good first impression.

The main finger of blame should be pointed at the Browns organization. No strong leader over the business department. No leadership in public relations. No owner who appeared to have even thought about how best to present a new coach to the public.

Furthermore, it was hard to remember a Browns coach arriving in Cleveland with as much animosity awaiting him as Mangini. He was vilified by the New York media. When Browns writers talked to those who covered the Jets, they were told Mangini was a lousy, insecure, nit-picking, dictator of a coach. Listening to them, you'd have sworn Mangini had been lucky to win three games in three seasons with the Jets.

Mangini knew how he was portrayed in New York—and in many parts of the national media.

He had to be aware that media members talk to each other.

But Mangini did very little to plan his own press conference. Perhaps he thought he should just follow the plan of the front office, but not much was left of the front office with the departure of Savage.

No matter, it came off poorly.

*   *   *

I was one of the few positive voices about the Mangini hiring.

Part of the reason was Mark Shapiro, who was the general manager of the Cleveland Indians in 2009. Mangini was married to Shapiro's sister, making them brothers-in-law. I knew Shapiro well and he spoke highly of Mangini.

I also looked at the Jets record. Mangini was 10-6, 4-12 and 9-7 in his three years with the Jets.

Two winning seasons in three years? Two winning seasons in three years for the Jets?

How bad could he be?

I began my Plain Dealer column: "If I had to pick a coach for the Browns, it would be Eric Mangini. He's the best coach available with two winning records in three seasons. At the age of 37, he's in the prime of his coaching career. He should be smart enough to learn from some of his mistakes in New York, especially early in his tenure when he was hard on some players and sometimes did a poor imitation of Bill Belichick."

I wrote of the Browns needing discipline after four years of the grandfatherly approach of Romeo Crennel.

I worried about the Browns hiring a coach first, then a general manager.

There were rumors of Mangini wanting to hire George Kokinis as general manager.

Right there is a problem.

The coach should not be picking the general manager, unless the general manager would be general manager in name only. And that was the system Mangini wanted. It was the setup a desperate Lerner was willing to give him.

Lerner didn't speak at the press conference when Mangini was hired.

But he did tell Cleveland radio station WKNR: "When you are going out to hire a head coach and a general manager, it seemed to me that the head coach hire is the more urgent one. The longer you wait, the less people are available."

Lerner also said, "If you have a long-standing head coach that has been a part of the continuity of an organization . . . that guy would take a leadership role in the hiring."

But the Browns didn't have a "long-standing head coach."

They haven't had a "long-standing head coach" survive more than five seasons since Sam Rutigliano in 1978 to 1984.

So it was hard to understand what Lerner was talking about, other than it made no sense.

And he was hiring Mangini, and hoping Mangini would not only coach the team—but build the entire football front office.

At that point, I should have known Mangini was set up to fail.

* * *

When Mangini came to the Browns, he fell into the same trap as a young Bill Belichick had done in Cleveland.

In 1991, former Browns Owner Art Modell turned over the entire football operation to a 39-year-old Belichick.

Lerner gave the same power to a 38-year-old Mangini. The difference was Mangini had three years as a head coach with the Jets. But the Jets had Mike Tannenbaum in place as assistant general manager. He pushed for the hiring of Mangini. He was promoted to general manager not long after Mangini was hired.

So Mangini had an experienced football man above him. They had known each other for years. But Mangini was not in charge of the entire football operation.

Mangini came to Cleveland and hired Baltimore Ravens pro player personnel director George Kokinis as general manager. I was told Kokinis was reluctant to take the job. He knew Mangini well. They both were with the Browns under Belichick in 1994–95, although in very low level roles. Kokinis feared he would not have the true power of a general manager—only the title.

But Kokinis also realized if he didn't take this job, it could be his last chance at being a general manager.

I was told within a month of taking the job, Kokinis knew it was a mistake. Mangini was preparing the draft and doing all the work on possible trades. Kokinis also is a shy man who came off poorly in press conferences.

Kokinis had a long relationship with Mangini and promises in writing from Randy Lerner that he'd be in charge of picking the 53-man roster. He also believed he'd run the draft and have other duties associated with being a general manager. But that was simply a way for the Browns to hire him.

Mangini ran the 2009 draft, where he made a good move by passing up a chance to take quarterback Mark Sanchez with the No. 5 pick.

Instead, he kept trading down. He took Alex Mack with the 21st pick, and he became a Pro Bowl center.

But Mangini also picked up three former New York Jets players in those trades—veterans Kenyon Coleman, Abram Elam and Brett Ratliff.

In the second round, the Browns drafted not one but two receivers: Brian Robiskie and Mohamed Massaquoi.

They had a third pick in the second round and grabbed David Veikune, a defensive end from Hawaii. The selection had the folks in the media room scrambling to figure out, "Who is David Veikune and why are the Browns taking him the second round?"

It turned out he was a 4-3 defensive end in college. The Browns wanted to turn him into a 3-4 outside linebacker. It never worked. He had five NFL tackles for his career.

Other than Mack, the draft was a disaster.

I remember having a long background conversation with Kokinis not long after the draft. He had a very hard time explaining why the Browns did what they did—because it was Mangini's idea. He never said that, but it was obvious with all the Jets players being added.

At that point, I knew Kokinis would not be with the Browns for long.

He was fired at mid-season. The team was 1-7. There were a lot of rumors of him supposedly having some personal problems. Those were never established.

Here was the statement the Browns released when Kokinis was fired: "Cleveland Browns General Manager George Kokinis is no longer actively involved with the organization. In response to rumors and reports that Kokinis was escorted out of the building today, the Browns deny those reports. In the interest of protecting the parties involved, we will withhold further comment."

The entire episode was embarrassing to the Browns, Mangini and Kokinis. The Browns tried to avoid paying the $4 million left on his contract. That ended up with a settlement in 2010 with terms not disclosed. Kokinis returned to the Baltimore Ravens as a special assistant to general manager Ozzie Newsome.

If Kokinis had personal issues (as some reports hinted), Newsome would not have brought him back to the Ravens.

Kokinis had huge doubts about the job, and they quickly became reality when Mangini was making the big decisions. Kokinis quickly went into a shell. He never should have left Baltimore.

* * *

In pure football terms, I thought Mangini was the best coach the Browns have had since they returned in 1999.

Butch Davis had a better record. Romeo Crennel had a 10-6 season in 2007. But I thought Mangini did more with less than any Browns coach. Of course, part of the reason Mangini had "less" was the moves he made in terms of trades and draft picks in 2009.

Meanwhile, Mangini was vilified by many in the Cleveland media based on his problem with the New York media.

After Mangini was fired, Gary Myers of the New York Daily News wrote: "His secretive, paranoid ways were suffocating the organization from top to bottom. The Jets had turned an 8-3 season into a 9-7 nightmare. The players didn't have Mangini's back. They quit on the coach. He had to go."

General manager Mike Tannenbaum and Mangini were very close

friends. So the parting was heart-breaking for both men. Tannenbaum knew under the right circumstance, Mangini could be a successful coach.

One of Mangini's regrets in New York was not fighting harder
against the Jets acquiring Brett Favre. The aging star quarterback was
brought in by ownership to help sell tickets as the Jets were moving
into a new stadium in 2010.

That's why Mangini wanted as much control as possible when
Lerner contacted him. As usual, Lerner could not decide what type
of front office/coach situation would work best. So he simply let
Mangini do everything.

"I always thought if Eric had better players, he'd still be the coach,"
said Josh Cribbs. "I learned more football from him than anyone in
the NFL."

Mangini demanded players take detailed notes. He'd stop them in
the hallways and ask questions about game plans and strategy. He
wasn't afraid to quickly cut or trade players he considered malcon-
tents.

He hated penalties. He loathed penalties. He saw them as a lack of
preparation and mental toughness.

If a player jumped offside or made another mental mistake in practice, he had to run a lap around the field. Film sessions were ugly for
those who made mental blunders.

"But he took us from being one of the most penalized teams in the
league to one of the fewest," said Cribbs.

In 2008, the Browns had the ninth most penalties in the NFL.

In Mangini's first year, they had the third fewest.

Mangini had four tenets he called Four Core Values: Communica-
tion, Focus, Finish and Trust.

Those words were on the walls in the locker rooms and team
meeting rooms.

He'd stop players in the hallway and ask them to name the four
values.

This annoyed some players. They thought Mangini was treating
them like high school or college players, rather than pros. Mangini
was desperate to build a winning team and have it based on those
values.

Legendary Browns left tackle Joe Thomas called Mangini his "least favorite" Browns coach. He thought Mangini nit-picked players and "did so many things to make your life miserable."

Thomas liked Mangini the person. He called Mangini "a smart football coach." But Thomas and others didn't like Mangini's coaching style.

The Browns started the 2009 season with a 1-11 record.

Then they finished with four consecutive victories. They were only the second team in NFL history to open at 1-11 and end up with a 5-11 record. The other was the 1993 New England Patriots.

As the 2009 season went along, the Browns did improve. They became a tougher, more disciplined team. They may not have liked Mangini the coach, but they played hard for him when most teams quit at the end of the year.

With two games left in the 2009 season, Lerner shifted gears again, hiring Mike Holmgren as team president. Holmgren was a former Super Bowl coach with Green Bay and Seattle.

On the surface, this move had potential.

Holmgren even kept Mangini for another season—although most people close to the Browns knew that football marriage would not last long.

What Could Go Wrong?

"I should never have sent it."

So much went right for the Browns to win 10 games in 2007.

And everything went wrong in 2008.

That's right, everything—or at least almost everything.

It began with the approach to the season.

For the first time since the Browns returned in 1999, there were real expectations for the Browns to win.

And win big.

The 2008 Browns were given five national TV games at night. That's right—*five!*

The theme for the season was supposed to be, "The Browns are back." Or at least, that's how the national media was selling it.

Owner Randy Lerner was extremely excited. He had given coach Romeo Crennel, general manager Phil Savage and offensive coordinator Rob Chudzinski contract extensions. Lerner wanted the Browns to make a serious run for the Super Bowl. That put pressure on Savage to bring in more veterans to win right now—and trade away draft picks for what he hoped would be quick fixes.

"Our biggest problem was stopping the run," said Savage. "We were coming off a 10-win season. We felt like we had a chance of winning big, so we had to go for it."

Savage is a man who loves the draft. The Browns were without a first-round pick because of the 2007 draft-day deal with Dallas for Brady Quinn.

"We had a chance to trade for Shaun Rogers," said Savage. "We weren't going to find anyone in the second or third round who could stop the run like Rogers."

Rogers was a 6-foot-4, 350-pound bulldozer of a man. He was 29 years old and had played seven years with the Detroit. He had been named to two Pro Bowls (2004, 2005) and had seven sacks in 2007.

It was *Win now. Think Super Bowl!*

Savage shipped a third-round pick and defensive back Leigh Bodden to the Lions for Rogers. Bodden led the Browns with six interceptions in 2007.

In 2007, the Browns ranked No. 27 vs. the run. They gave up an average of 4.5 yards per carry, fourth-worst in the NFL. Savage decided one defensive lineman wasn't enough.

He made another draft-day deal, shipping his second-round pick to Green Bay for defensive lineman Corey Williams. He had seven sacks in each of the previous two seasons.

Win now. Think Super Bowl.

And Savage also put this in capital letters: STOP THE RUN.

If it meant trading out of the second and third rounds in 2008 to do so, go for it.

The Browns never even made a pick until the fourth round.

Disaster hit during the off-season and minicamps.

1. Receiver Joe Jurevicius was the team's best clutch receiver in 2007. He had some knee problems, came down with a staph infection and didn't play in 2008. He never played another game in the NFL.

2. High-priced cornerback Gary Baxter tore patellar tendons in each knee in a 2006 game against Denver. He missed all of 2007. He appeared to be making a comeback in 2008 when he suffered another knee injury in minicamp. He never played another game in the NFL.

3. Newly acquired Corey Williams suffered a significant shoulder injury in June during a minicamp. He played rather than have surgery, but "really could only use one arm," recalled Savage.

4. Starting right tackle Ryan Tucker suffered a hip injury and needed surgery. He only played one more NFL game in his career.

5. "In the preseason, Derek Anderson and Jamal Lewis both suffered concussions," said Savage. "We signed Donte Stallworth and he pulled a hamstring in WARM UPS before our opener with Dallas. It was one thing after another."

It became a nightmare, especially because the quarterbacks kept getting hurt.

Anderson often played when he wasn't close to being healthy. He was 3-6 in nine starts. This came after his 10-5 record in 2007. It seemed that awful game he had in 2007 in Cincinnati robbed him of his confidence in 2008.

Brady Quinn played respectably in three starts, but suffered a season-ending injury to his right index finger that required surgery.

By the end of the season, the Browns were starting Ken Dorsey, Bruce Gradkowski and a mentally and physically beaten down Anderson.

At one point, they had a 3-4 record. They finished the season by losing 8-of-9.

"Braylon Edwards caught 16 touchdown passes in 2007," said Savage. "Lots of us got contract extensions. In 2008, he dropped 14 passes and we all got fired."

Actually, Edwards dropped an NFL most 16 passes!

Savage knows that's not the entire story, but it illustrates the sad story of the Browns in 2008.

In addition to injury and bad luck, some players drastically under-performed.

Edwards went from 16 TD catches to three—along with those league-leading 16 drops.

Kellen Winslow went from a Pro Bowl tight end to a player angry about his contract and having a staph infection in his knee.

It was a year of staph infections and player discontent. Crennel seemed helpless when it came to keeping order. Savage struggled at times because so much went so wrong.

It was so bad, the Browns' offense didn't score a touchdown in the final six games!

* * *

"Then there was the email," said Savage with a sad sigh.

Somehow, a fan found Savage's email address and sent the following to the general manager:

"You are easily the worst GM in the NFL. Chud, Crennel and Tucker should NOT have jobs. How the hell do you play prevent defense the entire game? How do you NOT use Jerome Harrison more? . . . This is official a regime that is worse the Butch Davis. By the way, just like last week—this email was written last week when the Browns had the lead."

Savage read it on the bus after the Browns beat Buffalo, 29-27. That was Game 10 of the season, making the Browns record 4-6.

Savage replied, "Go root for Buffalo, f---- you"

"This guy had been beating me up for about a month," recalled Savage. "It was after the game. I don't eat much of anything during games, some cheese and crackers. I was angry about how the season was going. I was exhausted after that game."

Savage was finally feeling good after the Buffalo game. Quinn had taken over at quarterback and led the team to a victory. Savage's wife, Dorothy, is a singer. At that point, she was living in New York. He was supposed to connect with her, but she had a knee injury! Even his wife couldn't stay healthy!

"She couldn't travel to see me," he said. "Everything just got to me."

The email exchange became public. Savage is a Christian and takes his faith seriously. He rarely swears.

"I just lost it," he said. "Now, people would sort of laugh about it. But it was a big deal back then."

But with all the Browns' problems and terrible performances on national television, it seemed the general manager also had problems.

"I should never have sent it," he said. "A million times, I'd wished I never sent it."

To this day, Savage has real remorse about it.

"In the next game, Brady broke his finger," said Savage. "DA (Anderson) took over, and he ripped up his knee in the following game. It was unbelievable."

Remember, this team started with *Win now. Think Super Bowl.*

*   *   *

When the Browns lost Quinn and Anderson for the season in a two-game span, Savage had an honest conversation with Randy Lerner.

The team was 4-8. They were looking at Ken Dorsey as the starter for the rest of the season. Dorsey had a 2-8 record throwing eight touchdown passes compared to 11 interceptions. That was with the San Francisco 49ers in 2004–05.

The Browns added him as a reserve quarterback. He didn't start a game in 2006 or 2007. He was the No. 3 quarterback when the 2008 season opened. He was never intended to be a starter.

But with four games left, Dorsey was the only healthy player in the quarterback room that opened the season.

With that in mind, Savage told Lerner, "It's hard to fathom, but we have to get our heads around the fact we could finish 4-12."

Savage said Lerner wanted to fire Romeo Crennel at that point. The same coach who was 10-6 in 2007 was 4-8 in 2008. He was having some trouble keeping discipline with some of his young, headstrong players.

But fire him at that point? With four games left? And no legitimate NFL starting quarterback?

"Randy, that's foolish," said Savage. "First of all, we don't have anyone on the staff who can be an interim coach. Even if we did, it won't go well anyway. We all have respect for Romeo. The players respect him. Firing him would not be right."

Savage remembered the Browns' 34-7 opening day loss in 2007.

He said Lerner wanted to fire Crennel after that game. That's right, after the first game of the 2007 season!

"Randy, if you want to fire Romeo, I'm not going to do it," said Savage. "You can go downstairs and tell the team that you want to fire the coach after the first game of the season. If you do that, you'll have a mutiny on your hands. I'm not having anything to do with this."

Lerner agreed to wait.

Then the Browns won 10 of their last 15 games.

Move forward to the 2008 season when Lerner wanted to fire Crennel again—this time with four games left.

"Randy, I understand the frustration," said Savage. "But you can't do that now. Romeo has a sterling reputation in the NFL. He is a dignified man. He is not going to quit and he shouldn't quit. And I'm not going to fire him. You have to let us finish it out. We know it's not going well."

Savage did agree to begin looking for a new coach to start the 2009 season. At that point, he had no idea he would be fired.

"Randy was telling me to look for a new coach, someone I could work with," said Savage.

*　　*　　*

Bill Cowher.

That's who Lerner wanted to hire as coach.

The former Pittsburgh coach had retired after the 2006 season. He wasn't interested in the Browns or any other team in 2008. Savage told Lerner as much.

"I told Randy to deal with Cowher," said Savage. "I'll deal with everyone else."

The Browns kept losing.

During the last week of the season, Savage met with Lerner.

"Who's on your list?" asked Lerner.

"The two names who interest me the most are Rex Ryan and Marty Schottenheimer," said Savage.

"I don't like those names," said Lerner.

A few days later, Savage was scouting a bowl game. On the sidelines was Butch Davis, coaching the North Carolina Tar Heels.

Savage looked at Davis and realized, "He's off the clock."

By that, Savage meant Davis was not going to be paid in 2009 by the Browns. He had been paid by the Browns and Lerner from 2005 to 2008 after quitting the team in the middle of the 2004 season. Lerner had honored a recent contract extension he'd given Davis.

The next day, Savage received a call from Lerner while he was waiting for a plane back to Pittsburgh to join the team for the final game of the season. He was at the Charlotte Airport.

"I've got bad news for you," said Lerner. "We're going to make a change and start fresh with everybody."

THE BROWNS BLUES

"Really?" asked Savage.

"Yes," said Lerner. "I just feel we need to start fresh with a new set of people."

"Randy, I've got four years left on the deal you just gave me (at the start of the 2008 season)," said Savage.

"That's all right," said Lerner. "We can sort through all that."

The Browns were playing in Pittsburgh the next day. It was the final game of the season.

"Do you want me to go to the game tomorrow?" asked Savage.

"You can do what you want," said Lerner.

"I would never quit in a million years," said Savage.

He went to Pittsburgh the night before the final game. He met with Crennel, and told him the news. Crennel figured he'd be fired, too. But the coach had not heard anything.

Savage went to the game.

At halftime, he pulled me aside in the press room.

"There's going to be some news after the game," Savage said. "I'll update you later."

I assumed Crennel was being fired. Many of us in the media were reporting that for weeks. I didn't know Savage also was gone until he called me about an hour after the game, just as the Browns released the news of Savage and Crennel being fired.

Savage wanted to meet with Lerner in person. He wanted to make his case to stay, or at least have a discussion of why he was being fired. He went to the office Monday after the game. He hung around, talked to people—said goodbye.

He never got a chance to meet with Lerner, who hated confrontation.

Lerner had a press conference where he told the media he had talked with Cowher.

"He said he was very focused on his kids and his life in North Carolina," Lerner said "(and) the way he's living in a non-coaching, or if you will, a civilian existence. He wasn't finished with that."

That was a classic, meandering Lerner explanation.

Lerner said he had been granted permission to interview Scott Pioli, who was New England's vice president of player personnel.

In the middle of the press conference, he learned Eric Mangini had been fired as coach of the New York Jets. Lerner's eyes lit up.

As for Savage, he went on to spend six years running the Senior Bowl for the NFL.

"I travel a lot through the Charlotte Airport," he said. "I was sitting in those white rocking chairs they have when I got fired on the phone. Every time I'm in that airport and see those chairs, I think of that."

When The Big Show Came to Cleveland

"I'll always be a coach."

* * *

Mike Holmgren arrived wearing a Super Bowl ring that glittered in the lights of his introductory press conference.

The hulking 6-foot-5 Holmgren dominated the room without saying a word. He had presence. He had a face known to most football fans. When he did speak, his voice boomed and oozed confidence.

Mike Holmgren, the new president of the Cleveland Browns.

In many ways, it was hard to believe it was Holmgren standing in front of the media on December 22, 2009. Holmgren was 61 years old with leathery skin around his eyes that came from squinting through the sun during decades of afternoon football practices.

Mike Holmgren wasn't just a good NFL football coach, he was a great one. His resume sparkled with 14 winning records in 17 seasons. He went to playoffs 12 times in those 17 years.

Mike Holmgren went to the Super Bowl three times with two different teams.

Mike Holmgren was known as The Big Show for his huge personality that made everyone assume, "Here's the man in charge."

He talked about growing up in San Francisco: "There was a time when you could walk into Candlestick Park or Kezar Stadium, buy a ticket and sit down anywhere (to watch the 49ers play). That was quite different from the time when I was coaching and we were expected to go to the Super Bowl every year."

Holmgren began his pro career as an assistant coach with the San Francisco 49ers. In six seasons under head coaches George Seifert and Bill Walsh, the 49ers won two Super Bowls.

His next stop was Green Bay in 1992, where he became an NFL head coach for the first time.

"They had been in one playoff game in 24 years after Vince Lombardi retired," explained Holmgren.

Actually, Holmgren's facts were a bit off. There were 23 years between Lombardi leaving the Packers and Holmgren being hired. The team went to the playoffs twice, had a 1-2 record.

Holmgren missed the playoffs in his first Green Bay season (1992), then went to the playoffs the next six years. There were two trips to the Super Bowl—one victory.

Next stop was Seattle in 1999.

"In Seattle, we hadn't been to the playoffs in 12 years (actually 10 years) and we became a consistent playoff team," said Holmgren.

He took the Seahawks to the playoffs six times in 10 years, including a Super Bowl appearance.

I mention what Holmgren said and his history to remind fans of the excitement that greeted him in Cleveland.

The Big Show had arrived. Maybe Mike Holmgren could fix the Browns.

Certainly, he had the experience not to be overwhelmed with the Browns' history of losing.

Right?

Why not try Mike Holmgren?

The bigger question is why Holmgren would take the Browns job. He is a West Coast guy and loved his home in Seattle.

"I found out something during my year off," said Holmgren. "I didn't want to get away from the game."

What was his job?

"I get the final say on everything, which is fun," Holmgren said. "Randy Lerner is my boss. I answer to Randy."

At that press conference, I asked Holmgren if he planned to coach the Browns.

"My coaching . . . as far as in the near future, I'm not going to do that," Holmgren said. "Things can change down the road, but this year I accepted this new challenge."

Lerner was handing the Browns to Holmgren, and The Big Show could write any script he wanted for himself—and then hire others to fill the roles.

Seattle also had offered Holmgren a front office position, but nothing close to the power granted him by Browns owner Lerner.

But there was another factor.

At the press conference, Holmgren said he had a 5-year contract.

Later, it would be learned it was a 5-year, $40 million totally guaranteed contract, giving him the freedom to define his own job.

It was the largest deal of its kind ever given to an NFL executive.

And that was a big reason Holmgren decided to come to Cleveland.

*   *   *

By the middle of the 2009 season, Randy Lerner knew he had made yet another blunder by putting the entire football operation in the hands of coach Eric Mangini. So he went on a hunt for what he called "a credible football man."

The search led him to Holmgren, who was out of a job. Holmgren had coached the Seattle Seahawks for 10 years (1999–2008). He had a 4-12 record in his final season, ending a streak of five consecutive trips to the playoffs.

Holmgren thought he needed a break from coaching. So he sat out for a year.

That's when Lerner found him.

Holmgren was represented by Bob LaMonte, a powerful agent.

LaMonte's clients included many top NFL and college coaches along with NFL front office people. The moment Lerner began looking at possible football executives, it didn't take long for him to be in contact with LaMonte. Holmgren was LaMonte's first significant client. They knew each other dating back to the late 1970s when both were high school coaches and teachers.

By late in 2009 when Lerner was on the prowl for someone to save the Browns—again—LaMonte was a man with lots of clients and plenty of ideas.

But he had one huge one—Mike Holmgren.

The Browns needed The Big Show. Lerner needed The Big Show because the Browns had become a horror movie to Browns fans.

Lerner also was burned out in his role as owner of the Browns. It had been seven years of frustration since his father died in 2002. Lerner didn't want to deal with the media, the coaches, or most people in the front office.

As Jimmy Haslam said when he bought the Browns in 2012, Holmgren had become the "de facto owner" of the team.

It became clear at Holmgren's introductory press conference that Lerner was stepping out of the Browns' public picture. New team senior advisor Fred Nance introduced Holmgren. Nance led the City of Cleveland's legal battle to bring a franchise back to town after the old Browns moved to Baltimore after the 1995 season.

I don't know if Lerner was even at that press conference. I don't recall seeing him there. I can't find any story online mentioning Lerner attending. His last time before the media was when he fired general manager Phil Savage and coach Romeo Crennel following the 2008 season—the same time he learned Eric Mangini had become available.

The hiring of Holmgren for a staggering $40 million was Lerner's attempt to revive the Browns and save himself the grief that comes with having the responsibility of running the franchise.

The plan was for Holmgren to handle it.

*   *   *

It didn't take long for Holmgren to make his first mistake. But I also must confess, I thought he did the right thing.

Check that.

I thought it was a good idea for Holmgren to keep Eric Mangini as the head coach for the 2010 season because I had developed a relationship with Mangini. I liked him as a person, respected him as a coach.

I thought with a strong front office, Mangini could do what he does best—coach football.

Furthermore, the Browns finished the 2009 season with four consecutive victories.

Holmgren had several meetings with Mangini. He seemed to like the coach, who was only 38 when the 2009 season ended. Maybe Holmgren could coach the coach. Maybe having some continuity would work.

Maybe I was just trying to talk myself into believing yet another Browns football shotgun marriage could defy the odds and succeed.

I should have known better.

I should have known that Mangini and Holmgren come from two very distinct and sometimes conflicting schools of coaching.

Mangini favored a 3-4 defense.

I thought Holmgren didn't care much about defense. He served as his own play-caller when he was a head coach.

I thought wrong. Holmgren was a strong believer in a 4-3 defense— something Mangini considered to be antiquated.

Holmgren believes in the West Coast offense. I'm not going to dwell on all the nuances, but it's very different from the offense used by Mangini.

Why was this a big deal?

Because Mangini was not going to change his core beliefs.

And because Holmgren was not going to have a lot of patience if Mangini's style of coaching failed to show significant improvement.

*   *   *

Armed with Lerner's checkbook, Holmgren hired experienced people to run the front office.

Tom Heckert was brought in as general manager. Heckert had a 20-year career with the Miami Dolphins and Philadelphia Eagles, including three years as the Eagles general manager.

Bryan Wiedmeier was hired as executive vice president to run the business side of the franchise. Wiedmeier had a terrific reputation among NFL executives. He spent 29 years with the Miami Dolphins.

Gil Haskell was hired as "Senior Advisor to the President." He had been an assistant for years when Holmgren coached.

All were represented by Bob LaMonte.

Holmgren interviewed four candidates before picking Heckert as general manager. All of those were LaMonte clients.

To be fair, LaMonte represented so many coaches and executives, you could build a strong front office/coaching staff with his clients. Nonetheless, Holmgren seemed to be focused solely on LaMonte's clients when filling key jobs.

I was aware of the LaMonte connection.

But I also thought Heckert and Wiedmeier were good selections. They had been successful. Heckert had worked for Joe Banner and Andy Reid in Philadelphia to revive that franchise.

One key person not represented by LaMonte was Mangini. The fact that Holmgren retained him spoke to the fact that not everyone had to have a LaMonte connection.

The new front office and Mangini started off well.

Mangini told me how Holmgren and especially Heckert were very interested in the kind of players he needed to be successful.

And the 2010 draft came off very well, given the new front office was in place for only four months.

Heckert had fallen in love with Joe Haden, the defensive back from Florida. There were rumors of Haden not being as quick as scouts believed.

As Daniel Wolf wrote in the Bleacher Report:

"Haden is the top cornerback (in the draft) and he ran a very disappointing 40-yard dash time with an official 4.57. Even though 4.57 is still considered pretty fast, a cornerback needs to run as close to 4.4 as possible because they need speed at their position to run with wide receivers . . . Haden disappointed in his vertical leaping ability, too, jumping only 35 inches."

In his pro day at Florida, Haden was a little faster.

"I didn't worry much about his performance at the combine," said Heckert. "I just looked at the tape and our scouting reports. Haden was all we wanted in a cornerback."

Heckert told me that a few weeks after taking Haden with the No. 7 pick in the 2010 draft.

Mangini favored trading down. But he also wanted a defensive back, and the Haden selection was OK with the coach.

Heckert picked safety T.J. Ward and running back Montario Hardesty in the second round. Hardesty's career was hampered by injuries. Ward and Haden would both make Pro Bowls during their careers.

When the third round came up, Holmgren inserted himself into the proceedings.

The Browns had already signed veteran quarterback Jake Delhomme and traded for Seneca Wallace.

That signaled the end of Brady Quinn and Derek Anderson battling to start at quarterback. Both were gone. Holmgren had Wallace as backup in Seattle. Holmgren admired Delhomme, who had some good years with Carolina but now was 35 years old.

In the third round, Holmgren wanted to make his own pick—a quarterback.

It was Colt McCoy from Texas.

Heckert wasn't sure. Neither was Mangini.

McCoy was listed at 6-foot-1, 215 pounds. He looked smaller, played smaller and had sustained a significant shoulder injury in his final college game. He owned 47 Texas school records.

According to what Holmgren would later tell Sports Illustrated's Peter King, Holmgren said, "Let's do this."

I don't know who the Browns had on top of their draft board at that point, but it wasn't McCoy.

"Let's pull the trigger," Holmgren told Heckert.

They pulled the trigger and—boom—McCoy was a member of the Browns with the 85th pick in the 2010 draft.

Later, Holmgren admitted to the media, "I kind of pulled rank a little bit."

At the 2010 pre-draft press conference, I asked Holmgren how things would work if there was a division of opinion.

"I'm the chief tie-breaker . . . the big boss," he explained.

*　　*　　*

McCoy would have a respectable career as a backup in the NFL. And he wasn't supposed to play at all for the Browns in 2010. He was No. 3 on the depth chart.

But in usual Browns fashion, the quarterback plans didn't work.

Delhomme was injured in the opener. Wallace took over and by the fifth game of the season, he was hurt. That left McCoy to start in Pittsburgh.

I'm not going the dredge up all the gory details.

The Browns finished that season at 5-11. Quarterbacks could not stay healthy. McCoy ended up starting eight games. He was 2-6. Delhomme was horrible, throwing only two TD passes compared to seven interceptions in his four starts. Wallace was a competent backup, but he started only four games.

But the Browns found a star . . . at least for a year.

On March 14, 2010, Heckert traded Brady Quinn to Denver for a running back named Peyton Hillis. Mangini absolutely loved Hillis. The day of the trade, we had a private conversation where Mangini praised Heckert for making the deal—and taking the input from the coach.

Mangini outlined how he planned to use the 6-foot-1, 240-pound Hillis.

"He can run over people," said the coach. "But he's really skilled. This guy can catch passes. Denver never used him for that. He was mostly special teams. I'm telling you, he can be special."

And in 2010, Hillis was indeed special. He was everything Mangini predicted and more.

Hillis rushed for 1,177 yards, averaging 4.4 yards per carry. He ran for 11 TDs. He caught 61 passes. He was a force.

Browns fans loved him. The coaches liked him. He was only 24 years old and looked as if he would have a long and wonderful career in Cleveland—regardless of who became his coach.

The Browns finished the 2010 season with four consecutive losses. Mangini was fired.

*   *   *

Like many Holmgren press conferences, the one announcing Mangini's departure was a bit off.

Holmgren was immediately asked if he would name himself to replace Mangini.

"I was hired to be President of the Cleveland Browns and I think I have grown into the job," he said. "Having said that, I'm also a coach. I'll always be a coach. Heck, people in the building call me 'Coach.' To tell you I'll probably never coach again be it here or any place, that probably wouldn't be honest. You know that, I know that."

I remember listening to those words and wondering, "What is he talking about? If he wants to coach the team, coach the team. Fans and the media will love it."

Then Holmgren talked more about being the president and explained, "My job is to find the best coach available. That's what I'm trying to do and it doesn't include me right now."

OK, fine.

But then he said, "To say I'll never coach again . . . I probably won't coach again, but I don't want to lie to you ever."

Most of the press conference revolved around why he would not just coach the team in 2011. At that point, Holmgren was 62.

As one media reporter asked, "When would you coach again, if not now?"

Holmgren asked, "How old is Joe Paterno?"

At that point, Paterno was 84 years old. The Jerry Sandusky scandal had not become public at Penn State.

The Paterno comment led to questions about Holmgren changing his mind.

It was as if Holmgren enjoyed teasing the media about the possibility of returning to coaching. Or perhaps, he was thinking about it.

Looking back, it was handled poorly.

*   *   *

So was the coaching search that led to the hiring of Pat Shurmur.

The only other candidates interviewed by Holmgren and Heckert were Perry Fewell and Mike Mularkey. Fewell was a defensive coordinator with the Giants. He also fulfilled the NFL's requirement that a minority be interviewed for a head coaching position.

Mularkey was a veteran NFL assistant and head coach of the Buffalo Bills for two years.

Neither had much chance of landing the job.

Shurmur had more going for him than being the only candidate represented by Bob LaMonte. His uncle was Fritz Shurmur, a former Green Bay defensive coordinator when Holmgren was the head coach. Pat Shurmur had been an assistant in Philadelphia for several years when Heckert worked for the Eagles.

He entered the interview process as the favorite and was hired. His last stop before that was a 2-year stint with the Rams as offensive coordinator.

Furthermore, Shurmur planned to run the same West Coast offense used by Holmgren for years. He planned to hire Dick Jauron as defensive coordinator. He ran a 4-3 defense.

In other words, Holmgren was hiring a coach who would use the offense and defense that he favored—and it was the opposite of what was used by Mangini.

Which means he should have simply fired Mangini after the 2009 season in order to bring in a guy to build the team the way Holmgren wanted it constructed.

So the 45-year-old Shurmur came to town and Holmgren did him no favors. He allowed Shurmur to be his own offensive coordinator. It also was clear Shurmur would learn some painful lessons as a rookie head coach.

*   *   *

Looking back, so many mistakes were made starting with how Holmgren was hired.

Lerner gave him zero guidelines. Holmgren's only NFL experience other than coaching was also serving as Seattle's general manager from 1999 to 2002. That was in his first four years with the Seahawks, where he was coach and general manager. Ownership determined Holmgren didn't do both jobs well. He then became the full-time coach.

Three Holmgren drafts were enough for Seattle Seahawks president Bob Whitsitt in 2002, who asked Holmgren to remain as coach.

When Holmgren left Green Bay for Seattle, he insisted on also being his own general manager. The Seahawks complied. But after records of 9-7, 6-10, 9-7 and 7-9 . . . one playoff appearance . . . Holmgren lost front office power.

He also became a better coach, taking Seattle to the playoffs in each of the next five seasons.

As Browns president, Holmgren tended to hire people and then stay out of their way—except when the mood struck him to intervene. But usually, he sat back and watched.

In 2011, it quickly became obvious Shurmur was making the mistake of many coordinators who are suddenly promoted to head coach. He was doing everything he did on his old job—plus all the added duties of his new head coaching job.

Holmgren should have insisted Shurmur hire an offensive coordinator. That would happen before the 2012 season when former Minnesota head coach Brad Childress (also a LaMonte client) was added to the staff to help Shurmur.

But how could Holmgren not see the need in 2011? The excuse that Holmgren called his own plays wasn't good enough. The head coach can still call plays, but he needs someone to run the team meetings for the offense.

The head coach can't do everything.

Even worse was how he handled— or didn't handle—the Peyton Hillis situation.

After his breakout 2010 season and even being put on the cover of the Madden NFL 12 video game, Hillis was one of the NFL's most popular players.

Hillis went into the 2011 season with $550,000 remaining on his contract. He wanted a long, lucrative extension.

The Browns were concerned because Hillis had hamstring problems in college. He tore a hamstring in 2008 with Denver. In 2009, he had a major concussion. He had some minor hamstring issues the previous few years.

And punishing, physical running backs tend to wear down quickly.

The Browns didn't offer a long-term deal to Hillis with a lot of guaranteed money. The running back also went through four agents in 14 months. It was chaotic.

Then Hillis became angry. Very, very angry.

He went from a determined blue-collar running back to a guy who was convinced the Browns didn't appreciate him.

"At one point, the situation with him was toxic," said star left tackle Joe Thomas to several Cleveland media members in 2012. "He didn't want to be here. The players didn't want him here."

Hillis didn't seem to be working as hard and wasn't as engaged in training as he was the year before. Shurmur didn't see the same Hillis who played for Mangini in 2010. In the third game of the season, Hillis showed up at the stadium and then refused to play. It was announced he had strep throat.

"You think strep throat and I don't know what else should keep you out of an NFL game?" Thomas asked. "All I know is Alex Mack (Browns center) had appendicitis. His appendix blew up, and he played."

Shurmur seemed overwhelmed trying to answer the media's questions about Hillis. He also didn't seem to know how to handle the troubled running back.

"To have Peyton going through a contract dispute and basically refusing to play, it was a big distraction," said Thomas. "He decided his contract was more important than coming out and playing and helping his team win."

Thomas said this in 2012, the year after Hillis left the Browns. But it was what the Browns players were saying during the Hillis mess.

The situation begged for Holmgren to help Shurmur behind the scenes with Hillis. Holmgren said he talked every week with the coach and Hillis, but it was obvious Hillis was drifting further from the team.

A stronger leader would have at least suspended Hillis, or perhaps traded him.

Hillis missed six games that season. He rushed for only 587 yards, a 3.6 average. The hamstring problems were back.

At the end of season, the Browns allowed Hillis to leave via free agency. He played in the NFL only three more years, never gaining more than 309 yards in a season.

The Browns were right about not offering Hillis an extension with a lot of guaranteed money. But how they handled Hillis made a tough job for Shurmur even more difficult.

After two years of the Holmgren Era, the Browns had records of 5-11 (Mangini) and 4-12 (Shurmur).

Holmgren hated it whenever anyone in the media wrote or said, "Same old Browns."

But that was how it looked heading into the 2012 season.

The 2012 Draft: How It Went Wrong

"He can do all the things we ask a quarterback to do."

The 2012 draft was supposed to be a franchise changer for the Browns. They had the No. 4 and No. 22 picks. They would pick 11 total players.

Here's what didn't happen.

1. Browns president Mike Holmgren offered his entire 2012 draft—that's right, every pick—to Indianapolis for the top pick and the right to take Stanford quarterback Andrew Luck. Holmgren said he made the offer to Colts general manager Ryan Grigson. They were sitting by a swimming pool having "umbrella drinks," according to Holmgren. The Colts turned him down.

2. Holmgren had done this before. In the 2010 draft, he offered his entire draft to the St. Louis Rams for the top pick—and the right to draft Sam Bradford. The Rams turned him down.

3. After Luck, the No. 2 rated player in the 2012 draft was Baylor quarterback Robert Griffin III. Holmgren didn't offer his entire draft, but he offered a lot. He never said exactly what. The Rams (with Bradford at quarterback) didn't needed Griffin III. They were determined to trade the second pick. Washington made the deal, parting with first round picks in 2012, 2013, 2014 and a second round pick in 2012. Holmgren insisted his offer was just as good as Washington's.

So the 2012 draft opened with the Browns knowing they would not be able to pick the top two quarterbacks in the draft. In 2011, the Browns had gone through Jake Delhomme, Seneca Wallace and Colt McCoy at quarterback. They didn't like any of them.

The most exciting non-quarterback available was Trent Richardson, who had rushed for a school-record 1,679 yards for national champion Alabama. He was third in the Heisman Trophy voting— behind Luck and Griffin.

ESPN's Mel Kiper wrote: "(Richardson) has everything you look for in a top flight feature back at the pro level . . . He's going to do a lot of great things in the NFL."

Former Colts president Bill Polian is a respected evaluator of talent. For years, he appeared on ESPN and other media outlets giving opinions on the draft. In an interview with Sirius XM Radio, he labeled three "sure thing" players in the draft: Luck, Griffin III and Richardson.

In 2011, Peyton Hillis led the Browns with 587 yards rushing. He pouted most of the season because he didn't like the contract extension offered by the Browns. He missed one game because of a sore throat. He went from a determined, physically-punishing back who rushed for 1,177 yards in 2010 to a guy who seemed like he didn't want to play in 2011.

Or at least, Hillis didn't want to play for the Browns.

He left after the season as a free agent, signing with Kansas City. Hillis would never come close to that 2010 season again—a year that landed him on the cover of the Madden football game.

So the Browns needed a running back.

Browns fans love running backs, dating to the great Jim Brown in the 1950s-1960s.

Trent Richardson was the best running back in the draft, according to most experts.

ESPN's Todd McShay called Richardson: "The most complete back to enter the draft since Adrian Peterson in 2007."

Just about everyone loved Richardson.

After the Colts selected Luck and Washington drafted Griffin, the No. 3 pick belonged to Minnesota.

Minnesota's running back was Adrian Peterson, who was five years into what looked like a Hall of Fame career. The Vikings didn't need Richardson.

The Browns were at No. 4. They had set their hearts on Richardson.

Somehow, Minnesota convinced the Browns that another team was willing to trade up for the Vikings' No. 3 pick—and select Richardson. If the Browns really wanted the Alabama back, they better make a deal.

So that's what the Browns did.

They traded their No. 4 pick.

Their No. 118 pick.

Their No. 139 pick.

Their No. 211 pick.

All to move up one spot for Richardson.

You can say those are lower picks—fourth, fifth and seventh rounders along with the No. 4 pick. But that's still a lot to move up one spot.

Browns general manager Tom Heckert was a friend of Rick Spielman, who was Minnesota's general manager in 2012.

At the draft night press conference, Heckert said Minnesota had another offer, "and we beat it. We're pretty fired up. Trent was the guy we really wanted and I'm glad it worked out. He can run. He can catch. He's a tough, tough kid."

Just about everyone was raving about the selection of Richardson.

"He's passionate," said coach Pat Shurmur. "He's productive and durable. He's the kind of runner we feel is going to help us put an offense together to win games . . . He's going to be one of those players that our fans and community will be able to watch run the ball for a lot of years."

Here's what ESPN's Kiper wrote right after the draft: "The Browns traded up to No. 3 to get Richardson. I think they'll get him 250 or more carries in 2012, if he stays healthy. This is a guy as physically ready as we've ever seen for the NFL at the running back position."

Holmgren defended the Browns moving up to trade for Richardson: "Some said it was too expensive . . . I think it will be a bargain."

*   *   *

When I look back at what I wrote about Richardson, I should have been drug tested.

It's embarrassing.

I was campaigning for the Browns to draft him.

"I'm enamored by Richardson," I wrote. "He's a bullish back who can be stealth as he changes directions. Yes, running backs wear out. But if Richardson gives the Browns 7,000 yards over the next five years, will anyone complain?"

Yes, I actually wrote, "7,000 yards in five years."

That breaks down to 1,400 yards a season. No one in modern football does that, at least in terms of rushing. I can try to explain I actually meant a combination of rushing and receiving yards—but that's still a ridiculous statement. I should have been drug-tested after those words.

Richardson had a sensational college career.

In his last season at Alabama, he rushed for 181 yards against Florida . . . 203 against rival Auburn . . . and 96 yards in 20 carries in the national title game against LSU.

"There has to be a player whose jersey the fans can not only wear proudly on Sunday, but who brings them to edge of their seats (if not on their feet) every time he touches the ball," I wrote. "Richardson has a chance to be that player. If you can't have a powerhouse passing attack (and the Browns won't), then why not run the ball with authority?"

Before the draft, I wrote a long story under the headline "Making the Case for Trent Richardson."

I went through the drafts from 2006 to 2011. I checked all the backs drafted in the first round. There were 15. Only five even had one season where they rushed for at least 1,000 yards.

By 2012, research was emerging warning teams to stay away from running backs in the first round, especially in the top five. Before the 2012 draft, the Plain Dealer ran a story by Bill Lubinger and Rich Exner pointing out how only two of the previous 10 Super Bowl winners had a 1,000-yard rusher.

The running back was being devalued.

But in my story, I mentioned how in 2001 the Browns passed up a chance to draft future Hall of Fame running back LaDainian Tomlinson and instead picked Gerard Warren at No. 3.

I tossed in the stat that Richardson fumbled only once in his final season at Alabama. Skipping Richardson "is a choice that can be regretted for years," I wrote.

*　　*　　*

There were some warning signs.

He had his knee scoped after the season and didn't run the 40-yard dash at the NFL Combine. But he did run at the Alabama pro day, where his times were 4.46 and 4.52. That's quick for a 227-pounder.

Richardson had surgery on both ankles in high school. He had surgical screws installed in each ankle. Some doctors wondered if he could run again.

By his senior year in high school, Richardson was an elite college prospect—recruited by Nick Saban at Alabama.

He did have some knee issues at Alabama, but played through them.

Pro Football Weekly's Nolan Nawrocki wrote: "Long-term durability could be a concern given his physical running style and history of knee injuries."

As far as I can tell, he had only the one knee "scope" at Alabama.

Browns head coach Pat Shurmur discussed his conversation with Nick Saban. Once upon a time, Shurmur and Saban were on the same Michigan State coaching staff. Saban was the head coach. Shurmur was sure Richardson had been well-trained for the NFL because of his experience under Saban.

It's a reasonable assumption. Saban had been the Browns defensive coordinator under Bill Belichick in Cleveland from 1991 to 1994. Saban later was head coach of the Miami Dolphins. He had an NFL background.

More revealing was Jim Brown telling Pro Football Talk: "The problem is he's just ordinary . . . the size, the speed, the moves."

At the time, Brown was feuding with Holmgren. I thought some of his comments about Richardson were flavored by the sour relationship. But Brown always insisted that was not the case. He was simply stating his opinion.

Brown offered the theory that Richardson was unable to beat out Mark Ingram at Alabama. Ingram became a very average NFL running back.

Most Browns fans know what happened.

Richardson had a promising rookie year—running for 950 yards and 11 touchdowns. He also caught 51 passes.

But two games into the 2013 season, he was traded by CEO Joe Banner to the Colts for a 2014 first-round pick. Richardson couldn't stay healthy. His last NFL season was 2014.

* * *

After taking Trent Richardson, the Browns were in a quarterback frenzy. They had the No. 22 pick. Andrew Luck and Robert Griffin III were gone.

The next quarterback on their draft board was Ryan Tannehill. He was picked at No. 8 by Miami. I was not a big fan of Tannehill. He spent his first two seasons at Texas A&M as a wide receiver. He was a starter, catching 101 passes in 24 games—nine for touchdowns.

He moved to quarterback his last two seasons, throwing 42 touchdown passes in 26 games—compared to 21 interceptions. He completed 62 percent of his passes. The stats looked good, but it appeared he still had a lot to learn about being a quarterback.

In retrospect, the Browns would have been better off taking Tannehill at No. 4 rather than Richardson. In his first five seasons, Tannehill proved to be a respectable NFL quarterback with a 37-40 record. He completed 63 percent of his passes, 106 touchdowns compared to 66 interceptions.

OK, I digress.

Tannehill was never a real possibility for the Browns. Most NFL experts thought Tannehill was drafted "too high."

Meanwhile, Mike Holmgren did not want to go through another season with his 2011 quarterbacks—Colt McCoy and Seneca Wallace.

The Browns had fallen into what was primarily a romance of convenience with Brandon Weeden.

While Tannehill was a former wide receiver, Weeden was a former minor league pitcher.

In 2002, Weeden was a second-round pick by the New York Yankees. He received a $565,000 bonus. He pitched five years in the minors, never rising above Class A. His minor league record was 19-26 with a 5.06 ERA.

At the age of 23, he enrolled at Oklahoma State hoping to become a college quarterback. He was an all-state football player at Edmond Santa Fe High School in Oklahoma. So why not give it a shot?

He was a red-shirt in 2007 and played only one game in 2008. He didn't emerge as a starter until 2010 and then set several school passing records.

By the time of the 2012 draft, Weeden had spent five years in the minors. He spent five more at Oklahoma State. He was 28 years old. Other than Roger Staubach coming out of the Navy at the age of 27 to join the Dallas Cowboys (in 1969), it was hard to find another successful NFL quarterback who started his pro career so late.

Holmgren was enamored with Weeden. When the draft rolled around, Weeden was 6-foot-3, 220 pounds and fully physically developed. After all, he was 28. He had an extremely strong arm. It's why the New York Yankees drafted him in 2002.

Other quarterbacks bloomed in their late 20s—Kurt Warner and Rich Gannon were two examples. But they had been wandering around the world of pro football for years before that happened.

At Oklahoma State, Weeden played in the rather simplistic "Air Raid" system. The quarterback is always in the shotgun position. He never huddles up. He doesn't vary the snap count. He usually has four or five receivers going out for passes. He usually looks to only one side of the field.

It's nothing like most NFL systems.

The Browns brought Weeden to Berea for a visit. They thought his time in baseball's minor leagues was a plus. So was his age. They believed it made him far more mature than most rookie quarterbacks. He also had to deal with the failure of his baseball career, followed by rebuilding himself as an athlete in football. He patiently waited two years to start at Oklahoma State.

All of that was true. Weeden had some very positive personal characteristics—and was no trouble off the field.

ESPN's Kiper wrote: "It might feel odd to call a guy who is 28 and likely to be drafted in Round 2 underrated. But evaluators agree that if Weeden were younger, he'd be (drafted) far higher . . . I think Weeden projects as a start-early QB who can help a franchise for 7-8 years, easy. And who in this league has a 9-year plan?"

Sounds like what the Browns were thinking.

The one draft expert who turned out to be prophetic about Weeden was Nolan Nawrocki of Pro Football Weekly. He called Weeden's stats "inflated" because Oklahoma State had a "simple" offense. He said Weeden had "limited mobility" and struggled under pressure.

Most NFL experts had concerns about Weeden's age, but thought he'd have a respectable pro career. Few had a first round grade on him.

*   *   *

When the No. 22 pick arrived, I heard Browns general manager Tom Heckert was not ready to draft Weeden. He had another player in mind.

The Browns had the No. 37 pick. Many in their draft room thought Weeden would still be available there. Not Holmgren. He mentioned how Miami surprised most teams by taking Tannehill at No. 8. Most teams had Tannehill being available late in the first round—perhaps even at No. 22 for the Browns.

Holmgren was team president. He hired Heckert and the others in the personnel department.

As Holmgren told radio station 92.3 FM The Fan in Cleveland: "I said if we're going to take Weeden, let's just take him. Some other team could pop up there and get him with Tannehill already gone . . . we loved the quarterback, so we just went ahead and did it . . . We drafted a quarterback we think can come in and play right away. He has that kind of maturity."

The Browns had talked themselves into Weeden. That happens when a team not only wants a quarterback in the draft, but wants that quarterback to *start right now*.

Pat Shurmur said Weeden "can do all the things we ask a quarterback to do."

Shurmur also said of the 6-foot-3, bulky Weeden: "You like guys who have a little bit of size so they can take a pounding."

Shurmur then added: "When we don't hand it to Trent, we'll have Brandon throw it in there. He displayed the ability to get his team in the end zone and win games . . . We think he's going to project into being an outstanding NFL quarterback. We were able to see that in the way he competed in college. We felt all along he was going to make us better."

Weeden had a 23-3 record at Oklahoma State. He threw 71 touchdown passes in two years.

*   *   *

The Browns opened the 2012 season with Weeden as the starting quarterback.

That was a bad idea for a few reasons. The first is rookie quarterbacks tend to struggle, especially on bad teams—and especially when that bad team is the Browns.

Furthermore, Shurmur was using a form of the West Coast offense. It was the offense preferred by Holmgren. It was absolutely the wrong offense for Weeden. The West Coast offense often required a quarterback to take snaps directly under center, take three steps back, and then throw a pinpoint short pass.

At Oklahoma State, Weeden played almost always in the shotgun—meaning he received the snap about five yards behind the line of scrimmage. He often threw longer passes. He never started the offense from a huddle.

In his rookie season with the Browns, the following happened:

1. Virtually every play began with a huddle.

2. He threw 298 passes under center compared to 219 in the shotgun.

3. He opened the season by throwing four interceptions and was 12-of-35 passing for 118 yards in a 17-16 loss to Philadelphia.

4. He lost his first five starts. He threw five touchdown passes compared to nine interceptions. It was a miserable way to begin a pro career.

5. Weeden ended up with a 5-10 record as a rookie. He threw 14

touchdowns compared to 17 interceptions, completing 57 percent of his passes.

6. Weeden started five games in 2013 and lost them all. He was waived after the 2013 season. His career with the Browns lasted two seasons, a 5-15 record.

7. Weeden bounced to Dallas and Houston after that as a backup.

* * *

Looking at the top quarterbacks drafted in 2012, there are some surprising facts.

1. Four quarterbacks were picked in the first round. Only one, Andrew Luck, went on to have a career winning record. The others were Robert Griffin III (15-25), Ryan Tannehill (37-40) and Weeden (6-19).

2. Only one quarterback was picked in the second round. That was Brock Osweiler (Denver). He briefly was with the Browns in 2017 but never appeared in a regular season game.

3. Two quarterbacks won Super Bowls . . . and both were picked in the third round: Russell Wilson (Seattle) and Nick Foles (Philadelphia).

4. The first quarterback to receive a fully guaranteed three-year deal was picked in the fourth round. That was Kirk Cousins, selected by Washington. He signed a 3-year, $84 million deal with Minnesota after the 2017 season.

5. If you had to re-rank the quarterbacks, Wilson would be No. 1 in the draft thanks to his two appearances in the Super Bowl. Luck would probably be No. 2, but injuries have haunted him. Third would be Cousins.

6. In this draft, the Browns missed on a quarterback. But it's also fair to wonder what would have happened if they had picked Wilson or Cousins or Tannehill—all available to them at one point. Holmgren, Heckert and Shurmur were all fired after 2012 as the team was sold to Jimmy Haslam. There would have been another coaching change, another front office not heavily invested in the quarterback picked by the previous regime. It's life with the Browns.

Fans Write In . . .

Browns Coaches

Readers were asked: Who is the best Browns coach since 1999? Which coach got the rawest deal? Did you ever meet one of them? What memories do you have of watching a Browns coach at training camp? (Responses were edited for clarity and brevity.)

Butch Davis was the best coach. It's not even close. But Butch Davis the head coach was completely undermined by Butch Davis the personnel guy. He had a sense of his players and his schemes really worked to maximize them, as much as could be done. But the building pressure of everything just ate him alive.

The easy answer is Rob Chudzinski on which coach got a raw deal. He got one year, an awful roster and surrounding chaos. But the actual answer is Chris Palmer. After the success of the Carolina Panthers and Jacksonville Jaguars as expansion teams, the NFL stacked the cards against the Browns, so early on, that Palmer stood no chance to succeed even remotely. The only thing he had going for him was that he knew it was never going to work, so the pressure likely wasn't as bad.

—*Logan Andress, Lyndhurst, Ohio*

The best coach is Romeo Crennel. He had the best results and the fans and players loved him. The main argument against him was that he was too soft. I think the Browns could have solved that by adding a tough assistant coach or front office person to support him. Rob Chudzinski got the rawest deal. I still cannot believe how he was fired after one year.

—*Sami Khorbotly, Valparaiso, Indiana*

Butch Davis probably got the most out of his players. He was also my favorite coach to watch during training camp as well as the regular season. Always animated. Was surprised that the pressure got to him, given his successful college background. Would've liked to see what he could've done in another year or two.

As far as getting a raw deal, it was Eric Mangini. I felt that he was as close to a Bill Belichick as we've seen. They gave up on him way too soon.

—*Christopher Ard, Virginia Beach, Virginia*

Butch Davis had the highest winning percentage, still below .500, but one playoff appearance.

The rawest deal goes to Rob Chudzinski. One season?

I delivered Papa John's to Eric Mangini in '95 when he and five other guys shared an apartment in Berea.

—*Jake Pease, Lakewood, Ohio*

Eric Mangini was the best coach and worst GM. Had he been able to coach the team and let someone else pick the roster, he'd have stuck around much longer.

Mangini got the rawest deal. Mike Holmgren coming in cemented his fate right when the Browns were starting something. It tainted Mangini's career forever.

I had a fleeting moment of watching Romeo Crennel's engagement with the team. He was quiet and giving direction. Nothing about him screamed "leader." It was his first season, and that just left a bad taste and more worry about the future.

—*Dan Clay, Joliet, Illinois*

The best coach is a tough question. Bruce Arians would be the best coach but he was a coordinator. I am embarrassed to tell you I long for the Butch Davis era lately. You never knew what you were going to get with good old Butchie.

The rawest deal? I liked Eric Mangini. Maybe because he was the first coach to sense how much we loved the Browns locally or the fact he tried to at least bring discipline and professionalism to the organization.

I sat next to [general manager] Dwight Clark on a flight from San

Francisco to Cleveland months after he was fired. Mr. Clark answered every football question I ever wanted answered (how many plays does the QB have at the line of scrimmage in the West Coast offense). I asked him about every draft pick he selected and he had a solid reason for every player. He never ducked a question and even drew out the "catch" on a legal pad. A real class guy. Mr. Clark told me a story about coaching his son's pee wee football team and he scripted out the first dozen plays to ease his nerves.

—*Ming Chang, Copley, Ohio*

The best coach was Butch Davis, who got them to the playoffs. Romeo Crennel got the rawest deal.

We provided software to the Browns, and sent our most football illiterate installer to do the job so that we wouldn't have someone onsite that was star struck. Our installer was cute, in her 30s, and called Coach Crennel "Coach Romeo." He had her sit next to him at the coaches' table during team meals and the coaches laughed at everything she said. I still credit her with the 10-6 season in 2007.

—*Jay Volk, Richfield, Ohio*

The best coach is Butch Davis. Unfortunately, he had a hard time dealing with pressure. It didn't help not having a true GM.

Probably Mangini got the rawest deal. He came in to build his own football program. He did not receive his full opportunity before they brought in Mike Holmgren.

—*Anthony Cardenas, Toledo, Ohio*

I worked for a security company that "secured" the training camp motel for the players. I was 19 or 20 years old, and at 5'10", 160 lbs, with nothing but a walkie-talkie, I did not provide any "security." I started about 8 or 9 p.m. on my assigned floor. Players had bed check shortly thereafter. No one allowed in, no one out. One night I heard players talking about going out for the night. I sat at my desk pretending to read my magazine, but I was listening to what they were saying. I heard one player say, "What about him?" Full knowing they were talking about me, I played dumb, looking at my magazine. A couple of minutes later, I was approached by a player and asked "if it would be cool if a few guys left for the night." I told him no problem. (These are adults, it's their career, let them do what they want, is how I felt.) Not to mention, most players had legs bigger than me. So I got a handshake with incentives ($$$) included. Once bed check was done by the coaching staff and they left the floor, I knocked on the players' door to give them the OK. Four players left that night. It was the 2001 training camp. That is how I remember the Butch Davis era. This was his first camp and players were already sneaking out.

—*Daniel McGinnis, Cleveland, Ohio*

The best coach is Butch Davis. Too bad he was not a very good GM.

Mike Pettine got the rawest deal. Pettine didn't get a fair shake because of his GM, Ray Farmer. Farmer drafted Justin Gilbert as the 8th overall pick, which he followed with Johnny Manziel at #22. Both picks are now out of the NFL. The following year he drafted Danny Shelton (#12) and Cameron Erving (#19). Four first-round picks without ANY first-round impact. Epic drafting failure!

I remember watching Pettine react to a training camp fight between Mitchell Schwartz and Justin Staples ending in Joe Thomas at the bottom of a pile. This practice was open to season ticket holders. The team had to line up on the sidelines and run sprints across the field. Of course Joe Thomas ran with the offensive unit even though he was a bit dinged up from playing peacemaker.

I sat on the offensive side of the practice fields and watched Johnny Manziel in passing drills hesitate on his reads, check down, and otherwise demonstrate that he clearly did not grasp the pro game. It was evident that he didn't have "it." It's a shame Brian Hoyer wasn't given more organizational support. It was clear he knew what he was doing. All of this was clear in August of 2014 and yet the Manziel train wreck was unfurled for all to see.

—*Rob Richman, Pittsburgh, Pennsylvania*

Best coach is a tough call. Butch Davis had a good run but he flaked out and was bad when he tried to be GM as well. I had high hopes for Hue Jackson. The jury is still out on him. I guess I would say Rob Chudzinski, because I thought he had potential.

Chris Palmer got the biggest hose job, even more so than Chud. Why fire a coach on a new expansion team after only two years?

I met Eric Mangini, sort of. I was one of the managers at Barnes & Noble in Woodmere and had to go up and help run the register and Mangini came up and purchased a computer book. I was surprised to see him since it was a few months after he had been fired. He was very pleasant.

—*Jason DiDonato, Fairlawn*

Butch Davis is the best coach the Browns have had since 1999 as the only coach to lead us to the playoffs. A close second would be Romeo Crennel with the 2007 squad.

Which coach didn't get a raw deal? I'll go with Chris Palmer since he had practically no talent from the start.

I went to a training camp in the Eric Mangini years. I did like the discipline he brought to camp where events were very structured. I guess the military man that I am liked that.

—*Christopher W. Urban*

I went back and looked at all the records of the former coaches. It's hard to believe that with the exception of Marty Schottenheimer, there hasn't been a coach with an overall winning record since Nick Skorich!

—*John Bednarowski*

The best coach is Butch Davis, the only coach to get us to the playoffs since 1999. I think history could have been different if Alfred Lerner didn't pass away during his coaching regime.

A few coaches got a raw deal, but Rob Chudzinski may have received the rawest. Sixteen games with that roster?

—*Jonathan Joch, Neenah, Wisconsin*

The best coach is Romeo Crennel. They won 10 games (in 2007). It was fun going to the games that year.

The coach who got the rawest deal was Mike Pettine. He was forced to use Johnny Manziel.

I had [former special teams coordinator] Chris Tabor speak at an event and he was great. Had some great stories and was very funny. Too bad he is not around still to see the team turn around. I know his numbers were down a bit the last couple years.

Gregg Williams is the most memorable coach as you can hear him talking loudly to his defense. I still have it on a short video.

—*Len Gold, Aurora, Ohio*

The best coach is Butch Davis without a doubt. He turned that team into a playoff team. Unfortunately, Butch Davis the GM seemed to do him in. Too much on his plate and he imploded.

The rawest deal went to Chris Palmer. Being the first coach of an expansion team is a thankless job. He seemed like a decent person in a tough spot.

—*James Lovelace, Ravenna, Ohio*

The Curtain Drops
on The Big Show

*"Don't come to me for extra tickets to
a playoff game or something."*

About two years after leaving the Browns, former team president Mike Holmgren gave the kind of interview that drives Browns fans crazy.

"I really just should have coached the team, but (Randy Lerner) wouldn't let me," Holmgren told Sports Illustrated's Peter King on April 21, 2014.

Oh, boy!

Lerner would have allowed Holmgren to coach, especially after the 5-11 record in 2009 with Eric Mangini. Lerner just wanted someone—anyone—to stop the pain.

He was paying Holmgren $40 million for five years. The one thing Holmgren could do was coach.

So we are to believe a beleaguered Randy Lerner would have stopped Holmgren? And Lerner would have said, "You're right Mike. The team is better off with a rookie head coach (Pat Shurmur) than you."

It's outrageous.

But it's classic Holmgren, who was always called "Coach" by everyone associated with the Browns.

In several press conferences, Holmgren admitted he was not ready to coach again. He also seemed to enjoy working the structured hours of a top executive who has others doing the heavy-lifting, time-consuming duties that come with coaching or running the office.

Holmgren was often criticized for not working hard in Cleveland. I don't know how much of that is true.

But I do know Holmgren sounded like a guy who liked the idea of coaching in the abstract. Being in his early 60s when he was in Cleveland, Holmgren did not seem to want to take on the emotional and physical challenges that come with trying to turn around a destitute franchise such as the Browns as their head coach.

And Holmgren contradicted himself on this subject at his final Browns press conference in 2012.

He was asked if he thought about taking over as coach for Mangini.

"We were compiling a list of coaching candidates," said Holmgren. "I asked (general manager Tom Heckert) and the selection people . . . 'You don't have to say yes, but tell me tomorrow if I should be on the list.'"

So what happened?

"I don't know if they were afraid to come to me and say, 'Are you kidding, an old guy like you, you shouldn't be on that list,'" said Holmgren. "But they didn't. It gave me a chance to think about it a bit more, and I did what I did."

So in 2012, Holmgren admitted he was free to put himself on the list of coaching candidates.

In 2014, he said Lerner would not allow him to coach.

Go figure.

Back to 2012. Why didn't he coach?

"At that particular time, I wasn't ready to do it again," he said. "I thought I'd be short-changing the organization."

Know what needed to happen? Lerner had to go to Holmgren and say, "Mike, either coach or shut up about coaching. Make up your mind."

But Lerner never did.

It seems like everyone else who was around "Coach Holmgren" during his tenure in Cleveland, Lerner was afraid to confront the man who was brought in to save the franchise—but had little idea how to do it.

*   *   *

Holmgren periodically surfaced to give some of the most colorful press conferences in the history of the new Browns.

They weren't always accurate, and they often said more about Holmgren's state of mind than the state of the franchise.

Near the end of the 2011 season, Colt McCoy was flattened in what became a 14-3 loss to Pittsburgh.

You didn't need to be a doctor to guess McCoy probably sustained a concussion, or at least should immediately be tested for a concussion. He took a helmet-to-helmet hit from Steelers linebacker James Harrison.

It was possible the medical staff was working on other players when McCoy went down. That's what the Browns said. But as I wrote at the time, "There were coaches on the sidelines. There were coaches in the press box (who did see the replay of the horrendous Harrison hit). But no one said, 'Hey, someone better check McCoy.'"

Someone should have said something because enough people with the Browns saw it.

The press conference became ugly, including Holmgren still trying to explain his job nearly two years into it.

"My definition of my role is hire good people and support them the best I can," he said. "That's why I don't do press conferences. That's why I don't have a radio show. I have done that for 25 years. I support my people behind the scenes. We have a very competent young coach who will be here a long time."

But Holmgren sometimes gave interviews to a radio station—in Seattle!—while he was still running the Browns. He had connections with the host. When that happened, the Cleveland media naturally went apoplectic. Why was the president of the Cleveland Browns talking to a station in Seattle while turning down requests from the Cleveland media at the same time?

And when he did address the Cleveland media, he didn't like some of their questions.

At one point in that 2012 press conference, Holmgren lost focus. Anger boiled over.

"When winning does happen, don't come to me for extra tickets to a playoff game or something," he said. "Don't do that. You're either with us or you're not."

This sounded like Coach Holmgren chastising his team.

Unfortunately for Holmgren, that became his signature line with the Browns.

*   *   *

At the start of the 2012 season, the Browns were sold to Jimmy Haslam.

Holmgren never saw that coming. Haslam hired Joe Banner as CEO. That was basically Holmgren's job under Lerner. When the sale was finalized by the end of the season, Holmgren knew he was finished.

"Mike was very accepting of the reality of the team being sold and the new owner was bringing in his own people," said Banner. "Mike was very helpful in terms of explaining what they did and why they did it. He talked about how he felt about certain people in the building and what he would have done if he had stayed."

Banner had no reason to praise Holmgren when I interviewed the former Browns CEO in 2018. But Banner did just that, especially in terms of how Holmgren tried to get the new ownership group off to a good start.

"He wasn't resentful," said Banner. "Anything I asked, he tried to help. He handled it all extremely well."

In Holmgren's three seasons, the Browns had a 14-34 record. They started five quarterbacks. They went through two coaches. Holmgren insisted he worked hard to change the franchise, but it was more of the same.

On October 23, 2012, Holmgren had his final press conference.

Here are some highlights:

1. He said he went to owners meetings and league meetings representing Lerner. "As you all know, he was uncomfortable being out front and that's why he asked me to come."

2. He went through quarterbacks Jake Delhomme, Seneca Wallace, Colt McCoy and Brandon Weeden. As he was departing, he said Weeden "is an excellent passer. I like how he leads . . . I think his future is bright. I think the organization has found their quarterback."

3. "I know this: I've learned a lot of things in the last three years. One of the things I thought I knew, but now I'm sure, I do miss the coaching part of it, I really do."

Sigh.

When Holmgren was sitting at that press conference in 2012, I had a sense he thought someone would contact him to coach again. Why else would he keep bringing it up?

In the short term, Holmgren said: "I'm going to ride my motorcycle a lot. Perhaps go to the beach a little bit, go to Hawaii."

After the 2012 season, Holmgren would have two years left and $16 million on his contract.

His final words at that 2012 press conference?

"Kathy (his wife) and I are going to go someplace where it's warm with those little drinks with the umbrellas in them," he said. "Then kind of think about what the future is all about . . ."

And with that, The Big Show came to a close in Cleveland.

Josh Gordon:
Talent, Suspensions,
Frustration

"I don't plan to ever go back there."

As I was writing this book, I wondered what to do about Josh Gordon.

Doing research, I realized far more had been written about Gordon than Phil Dawson and Josh Cribbs.

And probably more than about Joe Thomas, at least until Thomas said he was retiring in the spring of 2018.

That says something about the Browns since 1999, how Gordon dominated the news while contributing so little compared to so many other dedicated players such as Cribbs, Thomas and Dawson.

That's why I'm not going to dwell on Gordon, a troubled soul who says he has battled addiction problems most of his life.

But the basics of his story show how the Browns ignored many warning signs about Gordon.

Former Browns general manager Tom Heckert decided to pick Gordon in what is called the "Supplemental Draft." That was in 2012. The Browns committed their 2013 second-round pick to select Gordon a year earlier.

Heckert knew Gordon's story. He knew Gordon had played only 22 college games. That was for Baylor in 2009–10. His college career featured five starts, 43 receptions and seven touchdown catches.

He also was suspended several times for breaking team rules.

In 2011, Gordon left Baylor and went to Utah. He was basically kicked out of Baylor. He had to sit out the 2011 season in Utah before he could be eligible. He never played for Utah. Instead, he entered the 2012 supplemental draft, where he was selected by the Browns.

Not long after the Browns picked Gordon, I had a background conversation with Heckert. The general manager admitted Gordon had a problem with marijuana. Like so many others who dealt with Gordon, Heckert thought the young man "was a pretty good kid." He believed Gordon wanted to put his life on the right track. Heckert also said Gordon had gone to accountability groups while in Utah and was "doing the right things."

But a few weeks later, a report surfaced that Gordon also had flunked a drug test at Utah. There was some question of him being eligible to play for Utah in 2012, so he decided to turn pro.

I still don't know if Heckert was aware of the failed drug test at Utah, or simply ignored it. But it was yet another warning sign with Gordon.

At first, Gordon denied he failed the test at Utah. But later he admitted he did indeed flunk it.

"It was against school policy," Gordon told the Cleveland media. "I was suspended in the summer. I've definitely put that part of my life behind me. I don't plan to ever go back there. It was a difficult time, but I've learned from it and moved on."

When Heckert drafted Gordon, he had a conference call with the Cleveland media:

"We expect him to come in and play right away," said Heckert. "Anytime you pick somebody that early, you're hoping he's a good football player and we think Josh is. Most years, there's not a player of Josh's caliber in the supplemental draft. We're getting a really good football player and getting him early."

When I wrote a story about Gordon being drafted, here's what Heckert told me:

"I talked to a zillion guys at both Baylor and Utah. To be honest with you, I couldn't find anybody to say one thing bad about the kid. I enjoyed meeting with him . . . We think we've done our homework. But to say we're 100 percent, we're not 100 percent on anybody in the draft. But we felt good enough that we think he's going to be a positive influence on our team."

I do know several teams were not willing to risk a second-round pick on Gordon. A few wanted no part of him.

* * *

For the Browns, there was a major problem with using that second-round pick on Gordon. It also led to Gordon receiving a second-round contract.

Gordon's deal was $5.4 million over four years.

He also was given a $2.3 million signing bonus.

Let's consider the message being sent to the 21-year-old Gordon. He had acted irresponsibly in college, flunking drug tests at two different schools. He didn't play or even produce that much—43 total catches.

The season before he was drafted, he was out on a suspension.

But the Browns handed him a $2.3 million signing bonus.

In Gordon's mind, playing the game (and life) his way paid off.

* * *

As a rookie with the Browns, Gordon played all 16 games for the only time in his NFL career. He caught 50 passes, five for touchdowns. At 6-foot-3 and 225 pounds, Gordon made the game look easy. But there were times when he seemed a bit confused when it came to play calls and what was the proper pattern to run.

Overall, it appeared Heckert's gamble had paid off. It seemed the best was yet to come for Gordon.

But on June 9, 2013, the NFL announced Gordon had failed a drug test and was suspended for two games. Gordon released it was for codeine, and he had used it in cough medicine because he was sick.

By the summer of 2013, the Browns' new front office of Joe Banner and Mike Lombardi was in place. They were absolutely terrified Gordon would flunk more tests and face more suspensions.

When Banner was working in the Philadelphia front office, they wanted no part of Gordon.

To some people, Gordon's explanation seemed to have merit.

Many people have taken prescription cough syrup with codeine. But Gordon didn't get the prescription from the Browns' doctors. They would have used another type of cough syrup that would not have been a problem with the NFL's drug policy.

Furthermore, there is a party drug concoction known as "Purple Drank." It's a combination of codeine and a soft drink, usually Sprite.

Gordon served the two-game suspension. He also was fined four game checks.

Then he came back to have one of the best seasons of any Browns receiver—ever.

Gordon caught 87 passes, setting a franchise record with 1,646 yards receiving. He caught nine TD passes and had five carries for 88 yards. He was a Pro Bowl receiver.

He was everything Heckert imagined—and more.

*   *   *

But five weeks into that 2013 season, reports surfaced that the Browns were willing to trade Gordon.

"We're absolutely not shopping Josh," Banner told USA Today. "We're not going to shop him and we don't have any plan to trade him. When we did the Trent Richardson trade, the perception was we were throwing in the towel. So we got calls on players."

The Browns traded Richardson to the Colts after the second game of the 2013 season. They received a 2014 first-round pick in return.

"If you're in this long enough, you learn never to say anything absolute," continued Banner. "Then something comes up and you look like you lied. I personally would be completely shocked if we ended up trading him. Josh is playing great. He's working his butt off."

Accurate but not true.

That's how to view Banner's comment.

Banner had little faith Gordon could stay clean. He knew another failed drug test could trigger at least a 10-game suspension, or perhaps an entire season. He knew of Gordon's history of failed tests in college.

He was absolutely interested in trading Gordon when those reports surfaced.

But coach Rob Chudzinski was adamantly against it, already suffering from the loss of Richardson. More importantly, new Browns owner Jimmy Haslam wanted to keep Gordon. He was sure Gordon would be a star.

This also was Haslam's first exposure to Gordon, who can be very engaging and seemingly sincere when talking about his desire to change his life.

So Haslam would not allow Banner to trade Gordon. That's why Banner could say there were no plans to trade the receiver.

I know Banner had a couple of offers of at least a second-round pick for Gordon. He wanted to make the deal. The 2013 season already was going to be rocky. It made sense to load up for the 2014 draft.

By trading Richardson and Gordon, Banner would be adding extra first and second round picks in 2014.

When the season ended, it appeared Haslam was right. Gordon set records.

All was well . . .

Until it wasn't.

*   *   *

When the 2014 draft opened, Banner and Lombardi had been fired. Ray Farmer was the general manager.

And a report surfaced on draft night of another failed drug test by Gordon.

This led to a suspension for the first 10 games of the 2014 season. Gordon played five games, and looked disengaged. He didn't know the plays. He didn't practice hard. The team suspended him for the final game of the 2014 season. He was partying the night before with Johnny Manziel.

For a long time, Gordon and his camp insisted his only problem was marijuana. In November of 2017, he finally admitted using all different types of drugs in a GQ Magazine interview. He also insisted he was high on something before every game.

Who knows how much of that is true, other than Gordon's addiction problems were deep and very serious long before he ever joined the Browns.

I'm not going to give an account of all the suspensions and other parts of the Gordon story. Fans know them well.

From 2014 to 2017, he played only 10 games in four seasons. General managers/CEO's from Heckert to Banner to Farmer to Sashi Brown to John Dorsey ended up having press conferences answering questions about why Gordon was absent.

It was almost a rite of passage for the new guy running the Browns football operation.

I was talking to Banner late in the summer of 2018.

"It's too bad they didn't just let me trade Josh," he said. "It would have saved the franchise a lot of grief."

Ten Years Was Enough for Randy Lerner

"If you're the guy who fixed it, it would be so much fun."

I can't confirm this, but I often heard Randy Lerner had promised his mother that he'd keep the Browns for 10 years.

Randy took over as owner when Al Lerner (his father) died of cancer on October 23, 2002. The sale of the Browns to Jimmy Haslam was announced on August 2, 2012.

Pretty close to 10 years.

Furthermore, the sale closed with what former Browns CEO Joe Banner called "unprecedented speed . . . about 40 days."

Banner also was aware of the 10-year rumor, although he didn't know what exactly was behind it.

"Before hardly anyone heard it, I was told Randy wanted to sell the Browns," said Banner. "He didn't want anyone to know. He didn't want to get involved in a long, complicated process. He wanted to quietly do it."

Meet Joe Leccese.

He is chairman of a New York based law firm called Proskauer, "a renowned Sports Law Group," according to its website.

Leccese has been involved in the sale or acquisition of the Buffalo Bills, Jacksonville Jaguars, Houston Astros, New York Jets and Philadelphia Eagles. That's also according to his website.

Leccese is friends with Banner.

"Sometimes, his firm represents the buyer, sometimes the seller," said Banner. "They've helped teams with their stadium deals."

Banner was looking for a new challenge after 18 years with the Philadelphia Eagles. He had spent the last 12 years as team president. But he longed to really be in charge of a franchise. He had helped hire Andy Reid as the Eagles coach in 1999, and that led to the Eagles becoming a power in the NFC.

Leccese had heard Randy was open to selling the team. Part of Leccese's job is knowing who would be viable buyers for NFL teams. Jimmy Haslam had been a minor owner of the Pittsburgh Steelers since 2008. He was very interested in buying his own team. He knew it would not be the Steelers. The Rooney family loved the franchise and planned to keep it.

Leccese was aware of Haslam's desire to own a franchise.

"He called Jimmy and said the Browns could be bought, but they were not officially on the market," said Banner. "The Browns had yet to hire an investment banker. But it seemed Randy really did want to sell. Jimmy said he was interested in Cleveland."

That led to a discussion between Leccese and Haslam about who'd run the franchise. The Haslam family owned Pilot Flying J—a huge chain of truck stops across the country. The corporate headquarters is in Knoxville. Haslam said he didn't want to move to Cleveland. Leccese talked about the need to have someone in Cleveland run the team for him.

Leccese brought up Banner, who was open to leaving the Eagles for the right opportunity.

In June of 2012, the Browns issued a statement denying the team was for sale. Another time that month, team president Mike Holmgren did the same.

Also in June, Banner was meeting in Martha's Vineyard with Jimmy Haslam and his father.

"We had confirmed the Browns were available," said Banner. "We talked about how we'd proceed in acquiring a team. And we talked about how to keep it confidential."

Leccese had brought Banner and Haslam together. Banner and the Haslam family had several meetings.

This is not new.

When the expansion Browns were on the market in the late 1990s, Carmen Policy was introduced to Al Lerner by Dennis Swanson of ABC Sports. Swanson was friends with Al Lerner. Policy's daughter was looking to work in television. A casual conversation about Policy's daughter with Swanson led to Swanson later telling Al Lerner, "If you are serious about getting the Browns, you need to call Carmen Policy."

Policy and Al Lerner combined forces. They emerged as the group that won the bidding war for the Browns in 1999.

The price? It was $530 million.

Keep that in mind as you read this discussion of the sale to Haslam.

*   *   *

Banner was excited about the opportunity to help Haslam buy the Browns. He saw it as a revival of his career, an incredible professional challenge.

"I wanted to go somewhere that had been a total failure," said Banner. "Really, I mean that. I wanted to go to a team that was awful and be the guy who fixed it. The Browns were a huge challenge, but that appealed to me."

In 2012, no NFL team fit that description better than the Browns. They had a 53-100 record since Randy took over as owner in 2002. It was similar to Policy joining an expansion team in 1999. Cleveland was a football-crazed market with so little to cheer for.

Just some success would be greeted with loud ovations for those who could bring it to town.

"Cleveland is a great football market," insisted Banner in 2017. "If you're the guy who fixed it, it would be so much fun. It would be unbelievable."

The Haslam family became very comfortable with Banner serving as CEO.

Jimmy Haslam met with Randy Lerner. The goal was to determine the price Randy had in mind.

"We're wasting our time unless the numbers are going to begin with a 'B,'" Randy Lerner said.

"We had been tipped off," said Banner. "For a billion dollars, he'd sell the team."

Something else was helping the sale along.

Randy Lerner was not interested in bringing in a high-powered investment banker to handle the deal. He was using family lawyers. Keep in mind, the Lerner family was in the banking business.

But the lack of an investment banker was a positive for both sides. Haslam also used his own legal people. Banner said this simplified the process.

"Right away, we realized we could get this deal done," said Banner.

*   *   *

Al Lerner bought the Browns for $530 million, so Randy Lerner would nearly double the investment if he could secure his price of ONE BILLION DOLLARS.

In 1998, the NFL was putting the Browns expansion franchise up for an auction conducted by Goldman Sachs. I was at an NFL owners meeting at the Dallas Airport Hyatt Hotel. I talked to several owners about the Browns situation.

At one point, a few of us in the media chatted with Alex Spanos, owner of the San Diego Chargers, about what should be the price of the expansion team. Remember, the higher the price, the more each team received. It was going to be divided into 30 parts—every team getting a share except Art Modell and the Baltimore Ravens.

"A billion dollars is not unfair," said Spanos. "I know it's worth a billion. I don't know if anyone will pay it."

In 1998, the NFL owners made it clear they were interested in one thing . . . *the most money.*

As Tampa Bay Bucs owner Malcolm Glazer said, "It will go to the highest bidder."

Al Lerner recognized that. As he told us in the media: "The owners will see a number (bid) they like best and decide that person is brilliant."

A few facts from the summer of 1998, when the NFL was seriously trying to build up competition between the various ownership groups bidding on the Browns:

1. In 1993, Carolina and Jacksonville had paid $140 million to become expansion teams. Five years later, the NFL realized that was too cheap.

2. By 1998, each NFL team was to receive about $75 million annually in national TV revenue.

3. Browns fans had bought more than 50,000 season tickets and 90 of 116 available luxury suites for a team with no owner, no coach, no players. And don't forget all those fans also being forced to purchase the dreaded PSL—Personal Seat License. OK, they weren't forced. But if you wanted a season ticket, you also paid extra for a PSL.

4. The main groups bidding on the Browns were Larry and Charles Dolan, Howard Milstein and Al Lerner. Others such as former Tribe owner Dick Jacobs and Bart Wolstein had dropped out or were eliminated by the NFL.

5. In retrospect, Al Lerner was probably the best man bidding. Larry Dolan is an honorable man and a solid owner of the Cleveland Indians. But he was connected to Charles Dolan, whose son James has been a disaster as an owner of the New York Knicks. Charles Dolan would have been the main owner of the Browns.

6. When I was writing *False Start*, Carmen Policy told me that Al Lerner nearly dropped out of the bidding. Lerner was appalled by the raw greed of the other owners, how they seemed to have little interest in what ownership group was best for Cleveland. In the end, Policy convinced Lerner to stay in the bidding, and bid high. Because in a few years, the franchise would be worth more.

7. The bidding became a media event. The winner was Lerner, at $530 million. The Dolan family was second at $525 million. The issue was decided on September 7, 1998. That gave the Browns one year and five days to prepare for the September 12, 1999 season opener.

8. The $530 million price tag became the highest amount paid at that time for any team in professional sports. The highest had been $350 million paid by Rupert Murdoch's Fox Group for the Los Angeles Dodgers in March of 1998. The highest previous price for an NFL team was $250 million for the Minnesota Vikings.

*   *   *

The reason for the history lesson on the sale of the Browns was to say something nice about Randy Lerner. He could have turned the sale of the team into a circus. He could have hired Goldman Sachs to run an auction, as the NFL did for the Browns.

Not only that, when Dick Jacobs sold the Indians to Larry Dolan in 2000, guess who ran the auction? It was Goldman Sachs. My theory was Jacobs paid the NFL the $150,000 fee to bid on the Browns so he could study how best to sell a team for the most profit. He knew he would soon be putting the Indians on the market.

But Randy Lerner did it quietly. He did it quickly.

In most negotiations involving money, the seller wants more—the buyer is interested in paying less.

This was a civil and honorable negotiation in the billion dollar era of sports.

But it still was about ONE BILLION DOLLARS!

Not only was that Randy Lerner's price for the Browns, that's what Jimmy Haslam was willing to pay . . . sort of.

"Even though we thought that was a good price, we wanted to get the best deal we could," said Banner. "We stayed with the price of a billion."

Haslam knew it was important for Lerner to be able to say he sold the Browns for ONE BILLION DOLLARS!

Haslam and Banner stayed with the ONE BILLION DOLLAR price tag. That would be the announced price.

"In the end, we paid only $600 million up front," said Banner. "Instead of negotiating down the price, we negotiated a deferred payment. We'd pay the $600 million up front and then we'd pay the $400 million in four years."

Banner said there would be "no interest, no nothing" paid during the four years before the $400 million was due.

It was a way for the deal to move quickly. Randy Lerner could correctly say he secured ONE BILLION DOLLARS for the Browns.

"Jimmy could own the team for four years with money coming in before having to make the last $400 million balloon payment," said Banner. "That would off-set some of the last $400 million."

That last $400 million was paid by 2016.

"As far as I know, there were no other serious bidders," said Banner. "Randy gave us all the documents we wanted . . . the financials, stadium lease, etc. He was great."

Banner said he had a casual relationship with Randy Lerner for years. Philadelphia Eagles owner Jeffrey Lurie is friends with Randy Lerner.

"I liked Randy," said Banner. "He is a bright guy, not arrogant. I sensed he cared about people and about the Browns fans. His character was good. He showed it in the deal."

Banner said the sale took "less than 40 days to negotiate, that's almost unheard of. For a deal this big, four months is fast."

Banner said during the negotiations, it was obvious Randy Lerner "was absolutely ready to be done with the Browns. He wanted to move on as quickly as possible to the other things in his life."

How Rob Chudzinski Ended Up Coaching the Browns

"He can coach."

It was supposed to be Chip Kelly.

At least, that's what many in the media were reporting when the Browns were searching for a coach after the 2012 season. The Browns supposedly were fixated on Kelly, a hot coaching candidate after turning Oregon into a national college football power.

He met with the Browns for seven hours during a single day.

Then word was Kelly had turned down the Browns.

"We never offered Chip Kelly a contract," said Joe Banner.

Banner was the Browns CEO. Along with owner Jimmy Haslam, he was leading the search for a coach.

"We were very interested in Chip heading into the meeting," said Banner. "But after the meeting, we were not as excited about Chip as we thought we'd be."

Haslam had bought the Browns on August 2, 2012. He named Banner as the CEO. They decided to watch Pat Shurmur coach the team for the season. It was too late to make any changes. Training camp had already opened.

"I knew Pat from when he was an assistant in Philadelphia," said Banner. "He had a lot of the qualities we wanted in a coach in terms of integrity and character. He is a very good person."

But the Browns were looking for something else.

"There are coaches like Pat who are very successful in the NFL," Banner said. "But others are like Bill (Belichick), Andy Reid . . . guys who can be tough and even a jerk at times. We had so much to change in terms of the Browns culture, we thought we needed a stronger leader type. We needed a coach with that strong personality, a dynamic leader to drive the organization, to hold people's feet to the fire."

That was not Shurmur's personality, according to the new Browns front office. Haslam also preferred a more vocal and charismatic coach.

The Browns were 4-12 and 5-11 in Shurmur's two seasons. He also had rosters among the three youngest in the NFL both of those years. The 2012 season was really difficult. Because of the ownership change, the assumption was Shurmur and most of the front office would be fired when the season ended.

That's what happened.

The quest for the "dynamic leader" began with Kelly, who certainly had the powerful personality when he coached at Oregon. Kelly had used a no-huddle, fast tempo offense in college and planned to do the same in the pros. He thought he could revolutionize how the NFL game was played.

I didn't like the idea of Kelly for the Browns because he had zero NFL experience. Not as a player. Not as a coach. He was a pure college guy and he wanted a situation where he had massive control of whatever NFL team would hire him.

*   *   *

Banner didn't want to go deeply into the reasons the Browns decided not to offer Kelly a job, but they never did.

And I believe that's true, because of what Banner said next.

"Our top candidate was Doug Marrone," said Banner.

Marrone had played briefly in the NFL. He was an NFL assistant with the New York Jets and an offensive coordinator for the New Orleans Saints. When the Browns interviewed him in 2013, he had been the head coach at Syracuse University for four seasons. That was his alma mater.

The Browns interviewed Marrone the day after Kelly. They came away even more impressed.

"He's tough, he's smart, he knows analytics and he knows how to put together a coaching staff," said Banner. "He was the strong leader type we were looking for."

Banner said he was "stronger" about Marrone than Haslam, but Haslam was intrigued. They wanted Marrone to come back for a second interview.

"It turned out Doug is friends with Chip," said Banner. "Doug said, 'Why are you bringing me in for a second interview, I know you are offering the job to Chip.' We had to convince him that our minds were open."

Banner said the Browns continued to be impressed with Marrone.

"We offered him the job," said Banner. "We never offered Chip the job. We offered Doug what was the highest contract ever given to a first time NFL head coach."

But there was a problem. The Buffalo Bills also were looking for a coach. They really liked the idea of Marrone, who coached at nearby Syracuse University. The fans of Western New York knew him and liked him.

For Marrone, it came down to Cleveland vs. Buffalo. Two bad teams. One had a new owner in Haslam, a new CEO in Banner. Marrone had no previous relationship with either man. The Bills were owned by Ralph Wilson, a legendary NFL figure and well respected.

Marrone picked the Bills, signing a 4-year, $16 million deal.

In the middle of these talks with Marrone, the Browns received a call from Kelly's agent. The message was: Kelly was not coming to Cleveland, so don't even ask for another interview.

Kelly went to the Eagles.

Banner's story has credibility because his claim that Marrone was their first choice doesn't make the Browns look good. They lost out on a coach . . . to the Buffalo Bills.

*   *   *

Banner said the Browns had two top candidates: Marrone and Kelly.

Then they had a secondary list of names: Ken Whisenhunt, Marc Trestman and Rod Chudzinski.

The Browns were not impressed by Whisenhunt. He had just been fired as head coach of the Arizona Cardinals. In 2008, he teamed up with quarterback Kurt Warner and went to the Super Bowl. But from 2010 to 2012, Whisenhunt had an 18-30 record coaching in Arizona.

There were media reports of a conflict between Banner and Whisenhunt in the interviews. I'm not sure that's true. It could be Whisenhunt's supporters explaining why the Browns didn't offer him the job. From talking to Banner and others with the Browns during this time, I sensed there was little enthusiasm for Whisenhunt.

The Browns then turned to Chudzinski, the offensive coordinator with the Carolina Panthers.

Chudzinski is from Toledo. He grew up a Browns fan. He had been the tight ends coach with the Browns in 2004. He was their offensive coordinator from 2007 to 2008.

"Chud loved the Browns," said Banner. "He is like Pat Shurmur in terms of character and personality. Chud is just a really good guy. He believed deeply in trying to make the Browns a winner."

But there was a problem.

After Marrone, the others on the list—at least those willing to interview—did not fit the profile of a "dynamic leader."

The Browns had to hire someone. Chudzinski was very organized. He was willing to surround himself with experienced coordinators.

Norv Turner would be his offensive coordinator. Turner had been a head coach in Washington, Oakland and San Diego.

Former Arizona Cardinals defensive coordinator Ray Horton was willing to come to Cleveland to run the defense.

Turner and Horton had just been fired, making them available. Having experienced coordinators appealed to the Browns.

But here was yet another problem. Chudzinski was not an enthusiastic choice by the Browns. He was a fallback.

There were wild rumors of the Browns trying to hire Alabama's Nick Saban, Tony Dungy, Jon Gruden and . . . naturally . . . Bill Cowher. None of them were returning to the NFL to Cleveland with a rookie owner and very little talent on the roster.

*   *   *

So what happened to Doug Marrone?

He had a 6-10 record in his first season with Buffalo. In 2014, that record rose to 9-7.

Marrone had a special clause in his 4-year contract. If the team was sold, he was able to opt out to coach elsewhere. The Bills were sold. Marrone had conflicts with some members of the front office and the new ownership.

After the 2014 season, he walked out.

Marrone expected to be offered an NFL head coaching job somewhere for the 2015 season. None came along. He went to Jacksonville as an assistant. In 2017, he was named Jacksonville's head coach. He led his team to the AFC title game.

"Had Doug said yes to the Browns, I really believe he and I would still be in Cleveland," said Banner. "Look how he improved things in Buffalo, and did it without major roster changes or getting a (franchise) quarterback. He did it through leadership and coaching. Then look at what happened in Jacksonville. He can coach."

In Jacksonville, Marrone had long practices with lots of no-huddle work to keep things moving. He is working for Tom Coughlin, a very tough-minded coach in his day.

As Lindsay Jones wrote in an August 2, 2017, article in USA Today: "Afternoons end with several sets of 80-yard sprints for every player. Breaks throughout the day are shorter and the schedule is rigid . . . being on time is considered late, and players are fined for tardiness."

Would it have worked with Marrone in Cleveland? Who knows?

But how Chudzinski ended up with the job almost set him up to be fired quickly.

It Should Have Been a Great Trade

"A rolling ball of butcher knives"

From the moment he took over the Browns, Joe Banner sensed something was wrong with Trent Richardson.

Banner was watching the Browns late in the 2012 season. He had been installed as CEO on October 16, 2012 by new owner Jimmy Haslam. Banner knew Browns fans were pleased with Richardson, who rushed for 950 yards as a rookie. Richardson ran for 11 touchdowns. He also caught 51 passes.

It appeared to be an excellent start to a pro career.

"But he averaged only 3.6 yards per carry," said Banner. "You want a running back to be at least 4.0."

But what about the 950 yards?

"Part of that was simply a product of getting a lot of carries," said Banner. "It's why you have to look beyond the total yards."

Which Banner did.

He discovered Richardson had only two carries of at least 20 yards. The longest was 32 yards.

That was in 267 rushing attempts.

But to be fair to Richardson, he had not one, but TWO knee surgeries after his final season at Alabama.

The second came early in the 2012 training camp. Exactly four weeks after having his knee scoped for a second time in eight months, he started the opening game of the regular season. Given all that, what he accomplished was impressive.

Heading into the 2013 season, the Browns were hoping his surgically repaired knee would be stronger. They put him on an off-season diet and conditioning program. They thought he played 10 to 20 pounds too heavy as a rookie.

But when Richardson reported to training camp in 2013, he was somewhat overweight.

As for his speed, he looked even slower than the year before. It appeared that Jim Brown's prediction that Richardson was "an ordinary" running back would come true.

Banner began to wonder if it would make sense to trade Richardson. Perhaps another team would still place a high value on him. Banner hoped Richardson would show some spark once the 2013 regular season opened.

Instead, he was regressing. In the first two regular season games, Richardson carried the ball 31 times for 105 yards—his longest run was for 10 yards. His 3.6-yard average in 2012 dropped to 3.4 yards.

Banner began to look for a place to trade Richardson—quickly.

During week 2 of the 2013 season, the Indianapolis Colts lost starting running back Vick Ballard to ACL knee surgery. The Colts had Andrew Luck at quarterback. They expected to be a playoff team and perhaps make the Super Bowl.

But they needed a running back.

Banner picked up the phone and called Colts general manager Ryan Grigson with an idea.

"Trent Richardson," said Banner.

Grigson should have been alarmed that Banner was so willing to trade Richardson so soon. But then again, Banner didn't draft Richardson. That pick was made by the Mike Holmgren front office.

Furthermore, Banner already had written off the 2013 season. Just look at his 2013 draft. He traded away the Browns picks in the fifth and fourth rounds of 2013 for higher picks in 2014.

Banner was loading up draft picks and salary cap room for the 2014 season. It made some sense to trade Richardson.

To put it kindly, the two men were highly motivated to make a trade. Perhaps, even desperate.

The Colts absolutely, positively had to secure a running back—right now!

Banner feared the more Richardson played for the Browns, the more his trade value would drop. Something was wrong with Richardson, who showed none of the speed or quick change of direction that he flashed at Alabama.

Banner and Grigson exchanged some ideas. Banner wanted a draft pick and some players from the Colts.

Grigson wanted to keep all his current players. He was in WIN NOW mode. He offered Banner the Colts' first-round pick in 2014.

Banner took it. Deal done.

*   *   *

The national media believed the Colts fleeced the Browns.

"The Colts got the better of the deal," wrote Sports Illustrated's Peter King. "They fortified a need position on a playoff contender with Richardson who is better than he's played in his 17 NFL games."

King made a key point in his comment. The case for Richardson was that he would turn into the same dominant back who was picked No. 3 in 2012.

I can quote a lot of NFL experts, but the consensus was:

1. The Browns probably gave up on Richardson too soon.

2. The Colts were being aggressive and couldn't waste a chance to compete for a Super Bowl by hanging on to a 2014 first round pick.

3. The Colts' pick in 2014 would be near the bottom of the first round because they were destined to win a lot of games in 2013. That made the trade even worse for the Browns.

Meanwhile, in Cleveland, Banner was generally savaged.

I was one of the few who liked the trade. I had been looking at some of the same numbers as Banner, realizing Richardson didn't even look like "an ordinary" starting running back. A few days before the trade, I wrote a column alarmed by Richardson's lack of production.

At the time, I had no idea Banner was looking to trade him.

When the deal was made, my column ran under this headline:

"Cleveland Browns Trading Trent Richardson? It's Painful Now, But I'd Make the Deal."

That turned out to be true.

*   *   *

The Browns' coaching staff was upset.

Banner could talk about stockpiling picks for 2014, but rookie head coach Rob Chudzinski was trying to win games in 2013. He had no natural replacement for Richardson on the roster. To Chudzinski's credit, he never publicly criticized the trade.

But the deal brought out the booming voice of former Browns president Mike Holmgren, who often was heard on Sports Radio 950 in Seattle.

Some of his comments:

"At first, I didn't believe it . . . I really like the young man and I really think he's an outstanding football player . . . He had a really fine first year . . . he played through a lot of pain and injury."

"They started the season 0-2 and couldn't score any points, and I think the trade was a knee-jerk reaction."

"If I'm the coach and someone came in and did that, my response would be fire me or I'm going to quit. Or we're both going into the owner and talk about this and see who is left standing."

"I'd shake hands and walk. I would quit on the spot. If I disagreed with it and couldn't buy into it—I would (quit). I'm not saying I'm right. That's just what I would do."

*   *   *

Naturally, the Colts were overjoyed.

In their press conference, Colts coach Chuck Pagano called Richardson: "A rolling ball of butcher knives. He fits our system to a T."

Pagano said he couldn't believe the Browns would make that trade: "You're kind of like, 'Are you being serious? Are you messing with me on this deal?'"

Many Browns fans felt the same way—only with despair. Richardson was becoming one of the favorite players to a fan base that loves running backs. His No. 33 jersey sold well.

In many ways, it seemed one of those "butcher knives" went right into the heart of the fan base—especially those who bought tickets in the 2013 season expecting to see Richardson play.

Instead, the Browns used a variety of mediocre to poor running backs: Willis McGahee, Chris Ogbonnaya, Fozzy Whittaker and Edwin Baker.

The Browns finished 4-12. Within a few months after the season, the front office and coaching staff were fired.

With Richardson, the Colts finished 11-5. They won their first playoff game, then lost in the second round.

As for Richardson, he rushed for 458 yards in 14 games, a dismal 2.9-yard average. Remember, Andrew Luck was his quarterback and Luck was having an outstanding season throwing the ball. Richardson should have thrived.

When the playoffs came, he fumbled his first post-season carry. In those two playoff games, he carried the ball only four times for one yard.

Something remained very wrong with Richardson.

The 2014 season was even worse.

The Colts set a weight limit for him. According to ESPN's Mike Wells, Richardson missed it 14 times. He sometimes was late for team meetings. He was suspended for the 2014 AFC championship game because he missed a practice.

He would never play an NFL regular season game after 2014. He was cut by the Colts. He later had tryouts with Oakland and Baltimore, but never made those teams.

*   *   *

One theory was too much, too soon.

Richardson signed a 4-year, $20 million contract with the Browns before the 2012 season. He received a $13 million signing bonus.

"Some guys lose something when they get a lot of money," said Phil Savage, a former Browns general manager who was part of the Alabama radio team when Richardson was a star in college.

Savage still marvels at how Richardson played at Alabama: "He could run inside. He could catch the ball. He had lateral quickness.

He was excellent in pass protection. Early in his career, he'd score a touchdown on offense. Then he'd be part of the special teams and he'd run down the field in kickoff coverage and make a tackle. He was a real football player."

Savage credited Nick Saban and his Alabama coaching staff with keeping Richardson focused.

"He had guardrails when he was at Alabama," said Savage. "They kept him on track and provided real guidance. When some guys get to the pros, they think they can handle their own affairs—and they're not ready."

That appeared to be the situation with the Colts when Richardson was out of shape, skipping team meetings, etc.

"But I also think he was never fully healthy after he left Alabama," said Savage.

Richardson did have two knee scopes within eight months between his final year at Alabama and his first regular season game with the Browns. That could explain what happened to his speed.

But it doesn't explain his lack of personal discipline, which never was a problem at Alabama. Richardson made his knee issues worse by piling on the pounds—rather than getting into the best shape of his life.

In the end, Banner was right to make the trade.

As for that 2014 draft pick . . . Banner was not around to use it.

Mike Pettine's Turn

"Don't take that job."

The 2013 season ended with Rob Chudzinski and the Browns losing to Pittsburgh. Then Chudzinski was fired right after the game.

Browns CEO Joe Banner made the decision to fire Chudzinski. He was supported by owner Jimmy Haslam and general manager Mike Lombardi.

A year earlier Chudzinski had not been anyone's first choice to coach the Browns—at least, not anyone who was doing the hiring. Doug Marrone was the initial target, but he picked Buffalo over Cleveland. The Browns had an interest in Oregon coach Chip Kelly, but not nearly as strong as many in the media believed.

Marrone was their guy.

And he had little interest in the job.

Kelly went to Philadelphia, Banner's old team. That was not considered a huge loss by the Browns.

A year later, Marrone was still coaching Buffalo. Kelly was coaching the Eagles.

And the Browns needed a coach.

Here's where the story takes the first of several strange turns.

The San Francisco 49ers have denied this several times, but I was told by several sources there was discussion between the two teams about Jim Harbaugh coaching the Browns—initiated by the 49ers.

At the time, Harbaugh was the 49ers head coach. He had taken

San Francisco to the NFC Conference Championship game in his first three seasons. He had a record of 36-11-1. He led the 49ers to the 2012 Super Bowl.

I remember hearing a rumor about the Browns and Harbaugh. I assumed the Browns had called the 49ers, seeing if they'd be interested in letting Harbaugh out of his contract. Why not make a call?

But I've been told by two sources it was the 49ers who called the Browns. The two sides talked extensively. Draft picks were going to the 49ers. The Browns thought it had a good chance to happen. Harbaugh was having a major personality conflict with 49ers general manager Trent Baalke. Making it worse for Harbaugh, Baalke had influence with ownership.

In the end, Harbaugh had to agree to come to the Browns. He turned them down. I've heard from one source it was a family issue, I'm not sure.

I do know the Browns were prepared to send a second and third round draft pick to San Francisco for Harbaugh—and then sign the coach to a lucrative long term contract.

In the end, no Harbaugh.

* * *

This is where a split between Banner and Lombardi led to both of them being fired.

It's hard to put together all the details, but it seems Lombardi was bringing in his own coaching candidates for Haslam's consideration. Most of those from the Bill Belichick coaching family came through Lombardi.

There was a dance with Josh McDaniels, New England's offensive coordinator. He also had been the head coach at Denver. McDaniels has Northeast Ohio roots, where his father Thom McDaniels was a legendary high school coach. McDaniels played at Canton McKinley High and John Carroll University.

McDaniels was interviewed. First, he was interested in the job. Then he wasn't. Then he wasn't sure. Or something like that.

Banner's favorite candidate was Dan Quinn, who was Seattle's defensive coordinator. Quinn was very lukewarm about the job.

Here's a key to understanding why the Browns so struggle in their coaching searches. Quinn was with a winning team in Seattle. His friends told him to sit tight, a better opportunity would come along. The same with McDaniels in New England.

This was after the 2013 season, when the following had happened to the previous three Browns head coaches:

1. Chudzinski was fired after one season.
2. Pat Shurmur was fired after two seasons.
3. Eric Mangini was fired after two seasons.

Banner could correctly talk about the Browns having 10 picks in the 2014 draft—including two first-rounders—along with a lot of salary cap room. But the Browns' reputation and history of losing made the franchise toxic.

Denver offensive coordinator Adam Gase (a favorite of Banner's) would not even interview, other than on the phone. He wanted to stay with Broncos and try to win a Super Bowl with Peyton Manning during the 2014 season. Gase was close to the superstar quarterback.

But something else happens. Sometimes, the Browns do a very good job of selling the position to various candidates. But after the interview, football people tell the candidates, "Don't take that job."

My guess is that's what happened to Gase, McDaniels and Quinn.

To this day, I have no clue why they bothered to talk to Greg Schiano. He was not liked by his players in his two seasons where he had a 11-21 record with Tampa Bay.

I believe Haslam made the obligatory call to Bill Cowher, who once again turned down the Browns.

They also talked to Ken Whisenhunt for the second time in two years. Banner didn't like Whisenhunt the first time, so it's unclear who decided to interview him again. Whisenhunt also was confused about why the Browns wanted to talk, but he did spend some time with them.

He was not offered the job. Instead, he was hired by Tennessee to be the head coach.

You can see what's happening here.

Banner should have been allowed to lead the coaching search, in conjunction with Haslam. But it seemed Lombardi had his agenda.

And suddenly, it looked like a mess from the outside. Haslam was listening to several different people for advice on coaches.

*   *   *

The search continued.

Banner had three more names:

Ben McAdoo: Green Bay Packers quarterback coach.

Todd Bowles: Arizona Cardinals defensive coordinator.

Mike Pettine: Buffalo Bills defensive coordinator.

At this point, the Browns were being ridiculed for what looked like a very disjointed coaching search.

Pettine was a new name in connection with the Browns. He was a former high school coach who had worked his way up from the film room of the Baltimore Ravens to defensive coordinator under head coach Rex Ryan with the New York Jets from 2009 to 2012. It was Ryan who spotted Pettine putting together scouting videos for the Ravens. Ryan was Baltimore's defensive coordinator. He had iffy computer skills. The Ravens were putting a lot of material on-line. Pettine helped Ryan with the computer, taking care of a lot of detail work.

In the meantime, Pettine was promoted to linebackers coach with the Ravens under Ryan. When Ryan went to the Jets, Pettine followed—now as defensive coordinator. Pettine wanted to become a head coach. He knew he had to climb out of Ryan's shadow for that to happen.

Pryor to the 2013 season, Pettine was hired as the defensive coordinator for the Buffalo Bills. The Bills head coach? Doug Marrone, who had turned down a chance to coach the Browns. With the Bills, it was clear Pettine was in charge of the defense. Marrone's expertise is offense.

"We were looking for a strong leader," said Banner. "No one believes it, but he was on our original list. When you make a coaching list, you have 2-3 guys you really like, then 3-4 more who are interesting."

Harbaugh, Gase and McDaniels were probably at the top.

Pettine was on the next list with Bowles, Quinn and McAdoo.

"If you fast-forward a few years, you see that Quinn, Bowles and McAdoo all became head coaches," said Banner.

Banner liked Quinn . . . a lot.

At the press conference where Pettine was hired, Banner said this about Quinn: "That was a tough decision (between Pettine and Quinn). He's an outstanding guy, an outstanding coach. There's no doubt in our minds he'll be an excellent head coach. So that was the toughest decision. We were very impressed with him in the interview."

While Banner never said it, my guess is Quinn was his first choice, After Banner was fired by the Browns, he became a consultant for the Atlanta Falcons coaching search when they hired Quinn as head coach. Quinn was Seattle's defensive coordinator in 2013-14. In 2015, he became the head coach of the Falcons and led them to the 2016 Super Bowl.

Would anything like that have happened in Cleveland? Quinn has Pro Bowler Matt Ryan as his quarterback in Atlanta. With the Browns, he'd have been handed Brian Hoyer and Johnny Manziel.

But when the Browns were looking for a coach, Bowles, Quinn, McAdoo and Pettine were sort of the same in that none had been a head coach in the NFL before. There was no real track record to examine.

The Browns had gone from possibly having Harbaugh—a proven NFL winner—to looking for a younger coordinator who *might* be able to do the job.

*   *   *

In the end, the owner hires the coach for most teams.

Or the owner has to approve the coach. He interviews the candidates. Just like the front office people leading the search, he checks with friends in the NFL for input on coaching candidates.

Haslam really liked Pettine. The Browns wanted a tough guy "to change the culture." Pettine is a burly man with a shaved head, an angry goatee and a deep voice. He can read the ingredients from a candy bar label and make it sound like a new version of The Ten Commandments.

Pettine looked and sounded like a football coach should look and sound, at least to many with the Browns. One of his nicknames is

Blunt Force Trauma because he is a "straight talker," according to those who worked with him.

That had an appeal to Haslam. His personality was different from the more reserved Chudzinski.

Within 12 years, Pettine went from coaching at North Penn High in Pennsylvania to head coach of the Browns. He also was the son of Mike Pettine Sr., a legendary high school coach who won four state titles. He played quarterback for his father at Central Bucks West High. He also was an assistant under his father and went on to run his own high school program.

Here's a key point: Pettine was hired as the Bills defensive coordinator by new Buffalo coach Doug Marrone. That was in 2013, when Marrone turned down the Browns head coaching job in favor of Buffalo. Marrone's willingness to add Pettine to a key coaching spot caught Banner's attention. And Pettine knew he had to get away from Ryan to develop his own identity—just as Pettine had to leave his father's coaching staff to make his own reputation as a high school coach.

So Pettine had two "football fathers" in Mike Pettine Sr. and Rex Ryan.

I heard the high school background followed by the determined rise in the NFL coaching ranks appealed to Haslam. I also wonder if Haslam could relate to Pettine's background with strong football fathers. Haslam had a powerful father in James Arthur Haslam, who started what is now Pilot Flying J in 1958. He spent $6,000 to buy a four-pump station in Gate City, Va., according to the company's website.

It was Jimmy Haslam who took his father's business and made it boom. Jimmy pushed for the truck stops to become full service convenience stores with lots of food items and other goods for sale. That appealed to about anyone driving along the highway.

The Browns had two different interviews with Pettine. Those talking to Pettine were Haslam, Banner, Lombardi and team president Alec Scheiner.

But they hesitated to offer him the job.

*   *   *

Meanwhile, the national media was having fun ripping the Browns for not being able to find a coach.

McDaniels, Gase and others had pulled out.

It was clear Lombardi had one idea on the direction of the coaching search, Banner had a different one. Both were talking to Haslam. He was interviewing people from both camps.

One of the strange twists was Lombardi suddenly pushing Greg Schiano for the job. He had a dismal two seasons as Tampa Bay's head coach (11-21 record). Schiano had success as a college head coach at Rutgers.

Schiano has friendships with Bill Belichick and Ohio State coach Urban Meyer. They were urging Haslam to talk to Schiano.

And that was a major problem—the ever-growing split between Lombardi and Banner. That's why it appeared the Browns didn't have any plan as they looked for a coach. Banner had his list. But Lombardi was bringing others into the search.

They left the second interview with Pettine without offering him the job. They went to Tampa to interview Schiano. Banner was adamantly against hiring Schiano.

In the end, they settled on Pettine. He was acceptable to Banner. He was intriguing to Haslam.

He signed a 4-year, $14 million deal to coach the Browns for the 2014 season.

* * *

At the press conference where Pettine was announced as the new Browns coach, I wondered, "How am I going to write this?"

I had all the basic information on the 47-year-old coach. He was a Rex Ryan disciple who had never been a head coach anywhere except high school. It was hard to evaluate his performance as a defensive coordinator with the New York Jets because Ryan was the head coach.

In his four years with the Jets, the defense never ranked lower than No. 8. How much was Ryan, how much was Pettine?

In 2013, he took over the Buffalo defense and its ranking rose from No. 22 to No. 10.

He had experience in the AFC North because he was with Baltimore early in his career. He knew the division where the Browns play.

He said things such as the Browns "needing to bloody a nose a bit."
Pettine said his team would be "built on toughness."

He talked about the need to "hang tough when things go bad.
Heads can't drop. It can't be the same old Browns. Teams talk themselves into losing. To me, that culture has to change here."

It's this kind of things coaches say when taking over losing teams.

About taking over the Browns where coaches rarely last more than
two years, he said, "I'll bet on myself . . . I'm not backing away from
a job."

There are only 32 NFL head coaching jobs. About 6-9 come open
each season. Few go to former high school coaches.

The headline over my column was "Cleveland Browns May Be OK
With Mike Pettine as Coach."

I had no clue. Who could even guess what Pettine would do in the
job?

None of us in the press room that day imagined Banner and Lombardi would be fired two weeks later. Banner was telling everyone
about the Browns' "thorough" coaching search.

I wrote, "I'd have preferred the Browns to stay with Chudzinski, but
that ship not only has sailed—it's sunk."

I also wrote, "If the Browns truly were in love with Pettine, they
would have hired him a week after Chudzinski was fired."

And I wrote, "It's impossible to know how Pettine will fare. He'll
obviously need a strong offensive coordinator and the Browns must
find him a quarterback, or he'll have no chance."

No one sitting in that press conference knew three weeks later,
Banner and Lombardi would be gone. Or that Johnny Manziel would
be a Cleveland Brown.

How Johnny Manziel Ended Up with the Browns

*"The day I was fired, Johnny Manziel
was off our draft board."*

It starts with Jimmy Haslam.

That's where any discussion of the Browns and Johnny Manziel must begin.

I'm not saying that simply because Browns owner Haslam is from Tennessee and he's a huge SEC football fan. Manziel was a star at Texas A&M and a favorite of most fans who watched SEC football. The 6-foot Manziel scrambled around, finding receivers open downfield—and fired reckless, daring but often successful passes.

He also ran for touchdowns, putting an exclamation point on these dashes by diving head first into the end zone.

That's the superficial explanation for why the Browns selected Manziel with the 22nd pick in the 2014 draft. The owner wanted him. The marketing and sales department wanted him, especially team president Alec Scheiner. Most fans wanted him.

All of that was true.

But there was more.

So much more.

During the 2013 season, CEO Joe Banner was looking forward to the 2014 draft.

He had 10 picks—including two in the first round thanks to the Trent Richardson trade.

He had about $55 million in salary cap room.

He had hired an outside analytics firm to study the quarterbacks in the 2014 draft. He also had his own analytics people with the Browns doing so. Ray Farmer and other scouts were sent across the country to watch the top college quarterbacks.

"The day I was fired, Johnny Manziel was off our draft board," said Banner.

Banner was determined not to allow the Browns to draft Manziel.

At that point—February 13, 2014—Banner's analytics team and scouts had ranked the top two quarterbacks in the 2014 draft this way:

1. Teddy Bridgewater of Louisville.

2. Derek Carr of Fresno State.

Banner had a lot of disturbing information about Manziel's personal problems at Texas A&M.

As Banner told me, "We knew everything. I mean . . . everything."

Some of it wasn't hard to find out. There was a long Sports Illustrated story about Manziel's drinking and other issues. Basic scouting led to reports of Manziel not working hard in practice, showing up late for meetings, failing to take his job seriously.

The Browns also had reports that Manziel's body was breaking down from all the hard hits he took in college.

"It was hard to believe he was going to hold up physically," said Banner. "We didn't think he looked that smart on the field. We didn't think he looked that accurate when passing. He didn't stay in the pocket very long . . ."

The two analytics reports had different ratings for the other quarterbacks. Some preferred Carr, some Bridgewater. Other names coming up were Blake Bortles and Jimmy Garoppolo. There were some stats about Manziel completing 75 percent of his passes from the pocket.

One problem: Manziel was one of quickest quarterbacks in college football to leave the pocket.

In other words, when he threw from the pocket, he could be effective. But he hated throwing from the pocket because he was afraid of being sacked. He also had trouble seeing over taller linemen.

"My goal was for us to come out of the draft with a quarterback," said Banner. "It was either going to be Bridgewater or Carr. And if you look what happened, when it came time for the Browns to use their second pick in the first round—both were there."

*   *   *

Haslam's first mistake was firing Banner after Banner had helped lead the coaching search and do the draft research.

His next mistake was promoting Farmer, who was not ready to be the general manager. Banner told Haslam that on the day he was fired. Banner stressed he liked Farmer. He had brought Farmer to the Browns from Kansas City, promoting him to assistant general manager.

At some point, Farmer could be ready to be a general manager—but not yet. Banner would have been willing to allow Farmer to replace Lombardi as general manager.

Haslam didn't care. He was sick of Banner, Lombardi and the negative media swirling around his franchise. At the age of 40, Farmer became the NFL's second-youngest general manager when he was promoted by Haslam.

Farmer had been a star at Duke and played three years (32 games) as a linebacker with the Philadelphia Eagles. A major knee injury led to an early retirement.

Farmer worked in the scouting departments for Atlanta and Kansas City from 2005 to 2012 before coming to the Browns in 2013. He was building the right background to eventually become a general manager.

But the odds were stacked outrageously against him by how Haslam flung him into the job and paired him with a rookie coach when both men were strangers to each other.

*   *   *

There's something else about Farmer that led to Manziel becoming the Browns quarterback.

Farmer was an old-style football man. He believed in building teams on the lines—offense and defense. He thought a team with a strong defense and a respectable running game could overcome the lack of a star quarterback.

I had several conversations with Farmer after he became general manager. He wasn't a fool. He knew the Browns needed a franchise-changing quarterback. But he didn't see one in the 2014 draft.

He also didn't believe in drafting wide receivers high, or spending a lot of money in free agency to sign them.

It's unfair to say Farmer considered the quarterback just another position on the field. But he thought many quarterbacks were interchangeable parts. That's an important point.

I was told Farmer scouted Manziel personally. He had major doubts about Manziel's NFL future.

I also was told Farmer liked Teddy Bridgewater. But Bridgewater had a dismal pro day. The coaches and scouts had major concerns about the Louisville quarterback. Farmer began to feel alone in his support for Bridgewater, and even he was shocked by how poorly Bridgewater threw that day.

Now, Farmer was trying to form some type of quarterback consensus. Offensive coordinator Kyle Shanahan liked Jimmy Garoppolo. There was some support for Derek Carr, some for Manziel.

Remember how Farmer viewed most quarterbacks. He believed you could work around their weaknesses by having a team strong in other areas.

After Banner was fired, it was easier for the pro-Manziel voices to become louder. Quarterback coach Dowell Loggains was a Manziel fan. It's unclear where Pettine stood on Manziel. I sense he was a little like Farmer—not willing to stand up to the Manziel tidal wave that was emanating from the owner's suite and elsewhere.

Because Farmer was rooted in very traditional football, he had little interest in analytics. The $100,000 Banner spent on the outside research combined with the Browns' own analytics put a metaphorical BIG RED X through the name of Manziel. That had little influence on Farmer or Haslam.

Farmer was not ready to pound the table and demand any quarterback in the 2014 draft be picked by the Browns. He didn't feel strongly about any of them.

*   *   *

It's fascinating to look at the scouting reports on Manziel from the media "draft experts."

Here's how ESPN's Mel Kiper ranked the top seven quarterbacks on his final "big board" on the eve of the draft:

1. Johnny Manziel.
2. Blake Bortles.
3. Derek Carr.
4. Teddy Bridgewater.
5. Tom Savage.
6. A.J. McCarron.
7. Jimmy Garoppolo.

That's right, the media's biggest names among draft experts rated Manziel the top quarterback in the draft.

Former Dallas Cowboys vice president of player personnel Gil Brandt (1960–89) rated Manziel as his top quarterback. He did that for NFL.com.

NFL.com's Mike Mayock is well known for his draft work in the media. Here were his quarterbacks in order:

1. Manziel.
2. Bortles.
3. Carr.
4. Zach Mettenberger.
5. Bridgewater.

ESPN's Todd McShay also is well known for his draft work. Here is how he rated the quarterbacks:

1. Bortles.
2. Manziel.
3. Bridgewater.
4. Garoppolo.
5. McCarron.
6. Savage.
7. Carr.

Other than Pro Football Weekly's Nolan Nawrocki, it's hard to find a draft expert who was not caught up in the Manziel hype.

Nawrocki wrote Manziel had "suspect intangibles . . . he carries a sense of entitlement and prima-donna arrogance . . . (He) is known to party too much and is drawn to all the trappings of the game."

Some Browns fans will recall how at the draft press conference, Haslam said he ran "into a homeless guy" who told him to draft Manziel.

So there you go—everyone from Mel Kiper to "the homeless guy" was wrong.

But it was the Browns who paid the price.

For what it's worth, I wrote not one but two columns pleading with the Browns not to draft Manziel. Like Banner, I disliked the system he played on the field. It's the chaotic style never taking snaps under center and no significant playbook.

*   *   *

Farmer took an odd approach to the 2014 draft, especially given he was so new to the job.

The general manager skipped the pro days of Manziel, Bridgewater, Bortles and other top prospects. Farmer did watch video tapes of all those workouts. Nor did the Browns interview the highest rated quarterbacks at the scouting combine—where most teams try to do just that.

"A pro day of orchestrated throws, I don't know what that tells you," Farmer told several media people who cover the Browns.

Farmer is right because the quarterback is in shorts and a shirt. The receiver goes out for passes. No one rushes the quarterback or covers the receiver. The point is to display the quarterback's arm strength and accuracy. It's kind of like watching a basketball player practice 3-point shots—alone in the gym.

You can see if the player is moving as if he's healthy. You can talk to some people at the school where the pro day is held. It's the player's school. It's a very small part of the evaluation process.

"It's a piece of it that people blow up into this great thing," Farmer told the media in 2014. "I went to a lot of games and practices. I've seen them throw the ball."

But for Browns fans, it brought up questions. Why isn't Farmer doing the same basic work of most general managers?

Coach Mike Pettine also skipped a lot of those workouts.

Farmer explained the top quarterbacks were coming to the team training complex in Berea to work out and meet with the Browns for private visits.

I remember thinking, "None of this will matter if the Browns have a good draft. But if they don't, it will count against Farmer."

Well, the 2014 draft went badly.

Very badly for the Browns . . . and Farmer.

*   *   *

The Browns went into the 2014 draft with 10 picks, including No. 4 and No. 26 in the first round.

My hope was the Browns would simply take receiver Sammy Watkins at No. 4 and Bridgewater at No. 26. I wrote that before the draft.

Down deep, I had a fear the rumors of the Browns falling in love with Manziel were true.

In another chapter, I described how the Browns talked themselves out of future star linebacker Khalil Mack, ending up trading down— and picking Justin Gilbert.

Can't blame that one on Haslam, unless you believe (as I do) the owner never should have fired Banner. The former Browns CEO had no interest in Gilbert.

Or Manziel.

But Banner was gone.

One person close to Farmer told me that Farmer wanted to trade down. He targeted Notre Dame guard Zack Martin (went No. 16 to Dallas). He also was very intrigued with Oregon State receiver Brandin Cooks (went No. 20 to New Orleans). Cooks has been a good receiver, Martin a very good guard.

That would have looked so much better than Manziel and Gilbert, assuming that information was correct. I certainly can believe Farmer wanted Martin. The former general manager loves linemen.

Remember how Farmer viewed most quarterbacks. They were like most receivers to him—simply not that important in terms of "allocating resources" as Farmer termed his approach to the draft.

Of course, Farmer would never say, "Quarterbacks don't matter." But he took a completely different approach to the 2014 draft than the one planned by Banner. The former CEO made the Trent Richardson-to-Indianapolis trade with the idea of adding another first round pick—possibly for a quarterback. He made trades in the middle rounds of the 2013 draft to add picks for 2014—and a quarterback.

That's why Farmer had 10 picks at the start of the 2014 draft.

But he was thinking defense and bolstering the lines. He had Brian Hoyer coming back from a knee injury, and thought the Cleveland native and veteran backup could do a decent job at quarterback.

When the pressure to take Manziel built in the draft room, Farmer was not about to fight it off. Ownership and others wanted to try Manziel, that was OK. Those around Farmer at the time seemed to think the general manager viewed several quarterbacks about the same.

Quarterback coach Dowell Loggains made things even worse for his new front office after the draft. He gave an interview with radio host Bo Mattingly on Arkansas ESPN.

Loggains said he was texting Manziel during the draft. The quarterback coach was one of the pre-draft supporters of Manziel.

"We were sitting there and they keep showing Johnny on TV," Loggains told Mattingly. "Johnny shoots me a text and says, 'I wish you guys would come get me. Hurry up and draft me because I want to be there. I want to wreck this league together.' When I got that text, I forwarded it to the owner and the head coach."

At that point, it wasn't anything special. Manziel's ego was showing. Loggains was excited. But the quarterback coach wasn't even in the draft room for most of the draft. Loggains was not in the draft room when he sent Manziel's text to Haslam, then followed up with his own text: "Mr. Haslam said, 'Pull the trigger, we're trading up to get this guy.'"

Talking to someone who knows what happened, the Browns had already traded their No. 26 pick (the Trent Richardson draft pick) and a third-round pick to Philadelphia for the No. 22 pick. The Browns were convinced Kansas City, which had the 23rd pick, wanted to draft Manziel.

They called Manziel's name.

And the Loggains interview made it even look worse for Farmer, as if he was absent during the process.

I happen to think Loggains was creating his own scenario so that he could be a part of the process of drafting Manziel. Not sure all his details are accurate. But it made the Browns appear disorganized when he told the story to the radio host, who was his friend.

"It shows you how competitive this kid is," Loggains added in the radio interview. "I got to spend so much time with him leading up to this process. I feel like I know him very well . . . He has a chip on his shoulder and he wants to be a Brown."

Manziel went on the draft-night stage, rubbed his fingers together in the money sign and put on a Browns cap.

Fans and most members of the media were gleeful.

I held my head. I kept thinking, "The Browns have no idea what's coming."

Neither did I, but I knew this was a relationship destined for disaster because Manziel had so many weaknesses as a player and off-the-field.

*   *   *

In the post-draft press conference, Farmer explained the Browns decided to pursue Manziel "in the middle of the draft (first round). We took the opportunity to take players in the order we had them ranked."

I can give you a lot of other quotes from Farmer, but they are just generalities.

But one thing did stand out.

Immediately after Pettine became the head coach, he talked about wanting players "who play like a Brown." He meant they were tough, unselfish and hard-working.

Pettine brought that phrase with him from New York. When he was the defensive coordinator for head coach Rex Ryan, both men talked about wanting guys "who play like a Jet"—as in the New York Jets.

And Manziel?

"We liked his ability to perform and make plays," Farmer said on draft night. "We liked a guy that brought all those things when we talk about 'play like a Brown.' He was passionate. He was relentless. He played fearlessly."

I listened to that and thought, "Manziel is a gutsy player, but this is not a guy who will 'play like a Brown.'"

At Texas A&M, Manziel was known as a poor practice player. He wasn't a quarterback who loved to study scouting reports and video of opponents. An ESPN magazine story had his father saying he worried Manziel was an alcoholic.

There were huge question marks next to Manziel, especially in the "play like a Brown" category that the new regime was selling.

Pettine said "playing like a Brown" was "passion, competitive, being tough mentally and physically . . . being accountable . . . it's a list of intangibles. It's not how high they jump. It's not athletic ability . . . when we say 'He plays like a Brown,' that's the biggest compliment you can give."

Pettine also talked about how Manziel had the "it" factor.

"His 'It' factor is at an extreme level," said the coach. "It's to the point where it's really created 'Johnny Football.' He has all those things to an amazing degree. He's ultra-competitive, ultra-passionate . . . he's just a guy who finds a way."

And that's what Farmer and Pettine found themselves saying about Manziel on draft night.

*　　*　　*

Then came the Haslam/homeless guy story.

That was from ESPN's Sal Paolantonio. He said he spent about 30 minutes with Haslam after Manziel was drafted.

Haslam told Paolantonio: "I can go out to dinner anywhere in Tennessee and nobody bothers me . . . Here in Cleveland, everywhere I go, people know me. I was out to dinner recently and a homeless person was out on the street. He looked up at me and said, 'Draft Manziel.'"

Paolantonio also said: "That convinced him the Cleveland Browns fans wanted Manziel."

Haslam meant it as a funny story. Paolantonio was not claiming

Haslam was taking the advice of anyone on the street when it came to the draft.

But when Manziel flamed out, this was yet another part of the draft night story that looked bad for Haslam and the Browns.

*   *   *

By 2014, the NFL draft covered three days. Only the first round was on the opening night.

By the next day—right before Manziel and Justin Gilbert appeared in Berea for a press conference—ESPN reported Josh Gordon had failed another drug test. It was likely he'd be out for the season.

This was something Banner feared.

In the middle of the 2013 season, he had a deal set up to trade Gordon to San Francisco for a second-round pick. The coaches were adamantly against it. They had already lost Richardson in a trade. Gordon was on his way to a Pro Bowl season. Haslam had no interest in trading him.

The Browns decided to gamble that Gordon would stay clean and pass his tests.

But sometime after the 2013 season, Gordon was tested and failed. The league didn't announce the results, but someone leaked it (bad pun) to ESPN right after the Browns drafted Manziel.

My understanding is the front office was aware of Gordon's failed test before the first round of the 2014 draft. That didn't lead Farmer to change direction and draft a receiver. Remember his philosophy of finding receivers lower in the draft.

In the second and third rounds, Farmer actually picked players who would "play like a Brown."

Or at least, play like a Brown who is worthy of the wonderful fan support the team receives.

In the second round, he picked offensive lineman Joel Bitonio— who'd develop into an excellent guard.

In the third round, he picked linebacker Chris Kirksey, who'd become a starter and eventually one of the team's captains.

In the third round, he also took running back Terrance West. He has had a marginal NFL career.

The Browns picked Pierre Desir in the fourth round.

And then, that was it.

After the fourth round, the Browns were done. They'd traded their picks in the fifth, sixth and seventh rounds for picks in future drafts.

I sat there thinking, "They took 10 picks and turned them into six picks. They stopped drafting after the fourth round as if the team was loaded with talent and didn't need anyone else."

It was yet another strange twist to that draft weekend.

Justin Gilbert . . .

Johnny Manziel . . .

Josh Gordon suspended . . .

The Dowell Loggains text story . . .

The Jimmy Haslam/homeless guy story . . .

Farmer cashing in all his draft picks after the fourth round . . .

Banner watched the draft and couldn't believe what had happened. As he told me years later, "When they drafted Manziel, I nearly fell off the couch."

But Browns fans stood and cheered and bought 1,500 season tickets within 12 hours of Manziel's name being called. Browns jerseys with Manziel's name were quickly produced and sold briskly.

It turned out, this was the highlight of Manziel's two seasons with the Browns.

When It All Fell Apart... Again

"Play like a Brown!"

Why did the Browns ownership eventually turn to Sashi Brown and an analytics approach?

Because of what happened after CEO Joe Banner was fired.

What team had its general manager suspended for the first four games of the season?

The Browns did in 2015 when Ray Farmer had to sit out because of his illegal texting in 2014.

What team had its offensive coordinator quit partly because of Farmer's texting and generally because he wanted out?

The Browns did in 2015 when Kyle Shanahan departed and then moved on to the Atlanta Falcons.

What team had to fire its offensive line coach right before the season because of personal problems?

The Browns did in 2015 when they fired Andy Moeller after police were called to his home for an alcohol-related incident. Moeller had three alcohol-related incidents before the Browns hired him.

What team had its most talented receiver suspended for the entire season before training camp even began?

That Browns did in 2015 when Josh Gordon failed yet another NFL substance test.

What perpetually losing team had a starting quarterback with a 7-6 record and decided not to bring him back?

The Browns did in 2015 when they allowed Brian Hoyer to leave via free agency. Hoyer also wanted out because he was weary of what he later called "a circus" surrounding Johnny Manziel.

What team was set up for disaster as the general manager and coach had to work through some trust issues?

That was the Browns in 2015.

I always wondered when owner Jimmy Haslam first began to realize what a mistake he'd made by throwing coach Mike Pettine and Farmer together.

Before the 2015 season opened, Haslam told the media, "You have to look at the individual's body of work and we're comfortable with Ray's body of work. Very comfortable."

At this point, the Browns had lost the last five games of the 2014 season to finish 7-9. Johnny Manziel and Josh Gordon were suspended for the final game of the year because of their personal problems. Farmer was facing a suspension for texting during games. Haslam knew Farmer's top 2014 draft picks Justin Gilbert and Manziel had major personal problems and underachieved on the field. In fact, Manziel was in a rehabilitation center when Haslam spoke to the media on February 11, 2015.

In one of his stranger comments, Haslam insisted he had no idea what was in the texts sent out by Farmer during games.

"I haven't seen the texts so I don't know," he said.

Quick thoughts:

1. It's a failure of his leadership if he didn't immediately demand to see Farmer's cellphone and texts once the story broke. It's the owner's job to know what was in the texts.

2. Maybe he knew, but he just didn't want to deal with any more questions about the content of the texts.

3. But here was Haslam nearly one year from when he had fired Banner and promoted Farmer, and the owner had two troubled first-round draft picks. He had a general manager being investigated by the NFL and Haslam had to know a suspension was coming.

"Despite public reports, this is a very cohesive organization headed in the same direction where everyone understands their roles," said Haslam. "We think we have the right people in the right places to succeed."

When you go back and read the comments, they sound as if Haslam was doing more than backing his embattled general manager. It appears the owner was trying to reassure himself things would turn out well. But he had to sense trouble looming.

A few weeks later, Farmer talked to the media.

To his credit, he took full blame for breaking the texting rules. He offered no excuses.

"I take full responsibility for myself and my actions," he said. "I know I made a mistake and I'm owning that . . . It's not an excuse, but sometimes your emotions get the best of you at times."

Farmer insisted he needed "no relationship mending" with Pettine. He explained, "We had our conversations, we've worked through what that was . . . and he expressed his disappointment, etc. We had those conversations and we moved on full speed ahead."

All of this sounded good, but it was unrealistic.

Haslam threw Farmer and Pettine together. Then they had a rocky first season, Pettine knew Farmer was second-guessing the team's play calling in texts to quarterback coach Dowell Loggains.

After the 2014 season, Loggains was fired by Pettine.

All the unrest set up an atmosphere of mistrust that continued in the 2015 season.

*   *   *

One name: Dwayne Bowe.

While Farmer also took complete responsibility for drafting Johnny Manziel, it was clear ownership had some influence on that decision.

And while Justin Gilbert was Farmer's pick, it was Pettine who was a strong advocate for Gilbert.

But Bowe was the decision of one man—Ray Farmer.

Farmer had been a member of the Chiefs front office when Bowe had some good seasons as a receiver. In 2015, he was two years removed from the Chiefs—but told me he still had contacts in the organization.

In 2014, Bowe caught 60 passes for a 12.6-yard average. He had zero touchdown receptions. But that was a strange year where no Kansas City wide receiver caught a touchdown pass.

When free agency came, the Chiefs had no interest in keeping Bowe. They believed he was slowing down at the age of 31.

Farmer quickly signed Bowe, convinced the 8-year veteran receiver would fit in with other veterans he'd recently signed.

The deal was $13 million for two years, $9 million guaranteed. There could have been other teams interested, but I was never able to find out if anyone but the Browns made Bowe a firm offer.

Farmer replaced Hoyer with veteran quarterback Josh McCown, who was 35 when signing with the Browns.

He also signed 31-year-old defensive lineman Randy Starks and 32-year-old defensive back Tramon Williams.

Remember that Bowe was 31 when he joined the Browns.

Football common sense and analytics both issued warnings for most free agents over the age of 28. Other than quarterbacks, who tend to play longer, passing 30 is entering a danger zone for most players. It's a blinking yellow light for teams to proceed with extreme caution as the end of their careers is coming soon.

Why did Farmer do it?

Because the Browns had ended 2014 on a five-game losing streak. And because he had a lousy 2014 draft, no matter how he pleaded for more time for the players to mature. He knew Gilbert and Manziel were roaring down the road to ruin.

He did it because of the texting scandal, which hurt his credibility with the coaching staff.

He did it because he knew the history of the Browns. He replaced Joe Banner, who had lasted only one year.

He did it because he needed a quick fix.

*   *   *

Right before the season opened, offensive line coach Andy Moeller was suspended and later resigned when police were called to his home because of an ugly incident with alcohol and a woman.

When the season opened, Farmer was beginning his four-game suspension. The Browns had no offensive line coach.

Coach Mike Pettine grew impatient with Terrance West, and he was traded to Tennessee for a seventh round pick. A third-round pick in 2014, West rushed for 673 yards as a rookie and showed some promise.

Pettine wanted guys "who play like a Brown."

It's a motto he brought from the Jets and Rex Ryan, where they talked about "playing like a Jet."

We heard it over and over: Play like a Brown . . . PLAY LIKE A BROWN!

What was "playing like a Brown" supposed to look like?

"It's being in the huddle and looking at the guy next to you and knowing he knows where to line up," Pettine told me right before the 2015 opener. "It means knowing he'll do the job to the best of his ability. When I'm in the huddle and a guy doesn't do those things, that's extra baggage for me to carry."

That was why he wanted West gone.

It also made Farmer look bad because West was one of his high hopes from the 2014 draft. By the opener of 2015, Farmer was not about to fight his coach about West. Pettine was more popular than the soon-to-be-suspended Farmer, who was just trying to hold on to his job.

I give Pettine a lot of credit for not bashing Farmer, even off-the-record, when I dealt with the coach.

"He played in the league," Pettine said of Farmer. "He's a football guy. I don't want this to be a division between the player personnel department and the coaches."

Pettine was hopeful on the eve of the 2015 season. He talked about how McCown was a "great role model" for younger players, especially quarterbacks. He talked about being with Baltimore, Buffalo and the Jets—teams that found ways to win games without an elite quarterback.

Pettine recalled conversations he had with Hall of Fame coaches Bill Parcells and Jimmy Johnson.

"If you want to change the culture, change the people," Pettine said. "Both Jimmy Johnson and Parcells said that, almost word-for-word."

Of course, all the Browns had been doing since they returned in 1999 was changing the people—from the front office to the coaching staff to the players.

*   *   *

I'm not going to spend a lot of time on the 2015 season.

McCown was injured in the first game when he threw his body into the air trying to score a touchdown. He suffered a shoulder injury. He also sustained rib and back injuries during the year.

Manziel started the second game of the season, and the Browns beat Tennessee 28-14. It was the high point of Manziel's Cleveland career. He connected on touchdown heaves of 60 and 50 yards to Travis Benjamin. He was 8-of-15 passing for 172 yards.

The Browns would win only three games.

Gilbert and Manziel would both have problems on and off the field.

What about Bowe, the big acquisition as a receiver?

He showed up overweight and under-involved. He clearly had taken the cash knowing his heart was not in it.

There were games where Pettine didn't even put Bowe on the active roster. In Haslam's setup, Farmer picked the 53-man roster.

Pettine designated the 46 who'd dress on game day.

Pettine was sending a message about Bowe—and it also reflected poorly on Farmer.

Bowe would catch only five passes all season.

That's right, five catches for $9 million guaranteed.

The Browns were 2-3 after five games, coming off a 33-30 victory over Baltimore.

They would lose 10-of-11 games to end the season.

With a month left, it was obvious Pettine and Farmer were both destined to be fired.

Jimmy Haslam was not only ready to try something new, but completely different.

The Awful, Terrible Browns Draft Pick Barely Mentioned

"We were thrilled to be able to turn the card in."

The 2014 Browns draft will always be about Johnny Manziel and how he was a disaster for the team.

But to be somewhat fair to Manziel, he was not even the Browns' first selection in that draft.

Remember Justin Gilbert?

Few Browns fans do.

It was the defensive back from Oklahoma State who was the Browns' first pick in the 2014 draft—not Manziel.

When the draft opened, the Browns had picks No. 4 and 26 in the first round.

While there were rumors of the Browns being interested in Clemson's Sammy Watkins at No. 4, I know that wasn't true. Ray Farmer was running that draft. He had zero interest in drafting Watkins or any other receiver that high. I had a few private conversations with Farmer during his two years as general manager. I swear, he had memorized the names of every low-round draft pick or undrafted free agent who had become an excellent NFL receiver. Farmer simply didn't believe it was necessary to use prime draft picks on receivers.

It was an interesting road leading to the Browns making Gilbert their initial selection in the 2014 draft. They knew Buffalo wanted Watkins. So they traded their No. 4 pick to the Bills. In exchange, the

Browns received the No. 9 pick in the 2014 draft—and Buffalo's first round pick and a fourth-rounder in 2015.

That was considered fair value when it came to trading down.

But the Browns surrendered the right to take the fourth best player in the draft.

On the day before the draft, veteran ESPN writer and broadcaster Sal Paolantonio reported the Browns were interested in Gilbert. I paid a bit of attention because Paolantonio is well connected. But I also knew front offices tended to float rumors on the eve of the draft just to confuse other teams. The general rule is the closer to the draft, the less you can believe when it comes to speculation about what team favors what player.

Not only did Farmer trade down from No. 4 to No. 9, then he turned around and traded up to No. 8 to pick Gilbert. To do that, he gave up a fifth-round pick to Minnesota.

It's hard to know why Farmer thought the Vikings were going to draft Gilbert. Think about it. If Minnesota had its draft heart set on Gilbert, why only take a fifth-round pick in return?

My guess is the Vikings had no intention of drafting Gilbert. They took advantage of a rookie general manager/head coach combination to pick up an extra draft pick.

Anyway, the Browns traded down . . . then traded up . . . then picked Gilbert.

In the post-draft press conference, Farmer was questioned about not only passing on Watkins—but also skipping Khalil Mack, a linebacker from the University of Buffalo. That was the name I heard attached to the Browns.

I heard wrong.

Paolantonio heard right when it came to Gilbert.

*   *   *

You can't blame this on Jimmy Haslam. The Browns owner had very little knowledge of Gilbert. There was no reason for him to insist on his team drafting a defensive back from Oklahoma State.

I heard Mike Pettine liked Gilbert. The new head coach favored tall, athletic and fast defensive backs. The 6-foot, 200-pound Gilbert ran a 4.37 in the 40-yard dash at the NFL combine. Anything under 4.4 is impressive for a defensive back. At Oklahoma State, he played four years. He ran back six kickoffs for touchdowns.

The Browns did not talk to Gilbert at the NFL Combine. Nor did they attend his pro day at Oklahoma State. Had they done so, they would have discovered Gilbert refused to run back kickoffs and punts. That was strange, considering it was one of his strengths.

Only a few days before the draft did Farmer finally connect with Gilbert for an individual visit.

After the first round, Farmer and Pettine met the media. About 90 percent of the questions were about Manziel.

What about Gilbert?

"He's long, he's fast and he's explosive," said Farmer. "He's going to play relentless. He's going to play on the line of scrimmage and press people."

But what about passing up Watkins and Mack?

"There was a trade opportunity and we were able to secure more resources moving forward with the team and building long term," said Farmer. "We knew there would be interest (from other teams) at No. 4 . . . if there was a player we wanted, we'd select him."

Farmer was all over the place, discussing "resource allocation" and not doing something "that is going to cripple us."

He even refused to say if a player the Browns wanted was selected in the top three.

"It was never just one player that we ever considered in one spot," said Farmer.

I can give you more quotes, but they just go in circles.

Pettine said: "He's an exceptional athlete. He has elite man-cover skills. The shortcomings are things easily corrected through coaching. We were thrilled to be able to turn the card in."

Pettine meant the draft card with Gilbert's name.

Pettine also mentioned how Gilbert was very good in one-on-one, "press-man coverage." The idea was to put another elite cornerback on the opposite side of the field from Joe Haden, who was a Pro Bowl cornerback at the time.

"He clearly was our top corner because he fit our scheme," said Pettine.

The way Pettine discussed Gilbert on draft night and projected the rookie into how the coach liked to play defense was an obvious indicator the Gilbert selection was primarily to please Pettine.

Yet Pettine never spoke to Gilbert before the draft.

*   *   *

What did the draft experts think of Gilbert?

ESPN's Mel Kiper rated Gilbert the top cornerback in the draft— and No. 14 overall.

"Superior athlete with good size," wrote Kiper. "He can allow too much separation (in coverage) at times, but he's fast enough that it rarely matters."

ESPN's Todd McShay wrote: "(Gilbert) can be inconsistent at times when it comes to focus and a little tight when he runs. I don't think he's deserving of an early first-round grade."

Nonetheless, McShay had Gilbert rated No. 20 overall and the No. 3 cornerback in the draft.

NFL.com's Mike Mayock had Gilbert as the No. 3 cornerback and No. 23 overall in the draft: "The prototype cornerback in today's NFL . . . is a bit soft-tempered—not as aggressive or physical in run support as you'd expect . . . at times, coasts on his natural talent and is not immune to mental errors."

The NFL draft experts said Gilbert was a soft tackler. They knew it was somewhat alarming how he went from five interceptions as a sophomore to zero as a junior and then seven as a senior.

Word out of Oklahoma State was Gilbert was a quiet young man, somewhat immature. But his strong senior year indicated he was growing up as a football player.

In a USA Today story, Oklahoma State cornerback coach Van Malone said: "Gilbert is a hard-working player whose film study was central to his seven-interception rebound from a disappointing junior year."

Not a word of what Malone said of Gilbert's work ethic or willingness to watch film applied to his time with the Browns. He displayed neither.

In his four years at Oklahoma State, there were no reports of suspensions or failed drug tests—at least, none made public.

After the Browns picked Gilbert, ESPN's Kiper wrote: "Gilbert is a minor reach at No. 8. But he's a good fit and hit a big need. And again on this theme, you move down and add major pick value (with the Buffalo trade). What's a minor reach, really? You can't always get the perfect slot in terms of value."

None of the reports even hinted of Gilbert having some major personal problems that soon would surface.

*   *   *

Passing on Khalil Mack is what haunts the Browns the most about the Gilbert selection.

The Browns had it right about Mack when they projected him as an impact player. But they decided to make the trade with Buffalo instead. Drafting right behind Buffalo at No. 5, Oakland grabbed Mack.

Mack had a promising rookie season in 2014. From 2015 to 2017, he made three consecutive Pro Bowls. He averaged 12 sacks per season. He made first-team All-Pro. Farmer was a former linebacker. Mack was everything he valued—a driven, old-school style linebacker.

If the Browns had drafted someone besides Gilbert, it would have been easier to digest the move.

For example:

1. Remember how Minnesota traded down one spot with the Browns? The Vikings picked UCLA linebacker Anthony Barr, who made three Pro Bowls in his first four seasons. Their focus was on Barr, never on Gilbert.

2. The New York Giants picked star receiver Odell Beckham at No. 12.

3. The Rams picked star defensive lineman Aaron Donald at No. 13.

4. Baltimore picked Pro Bowl linebacker C.J. Mosley at No. 17.

There are other examples, but the point is clear. There were talented players available for the Browns.

Instead, they drafted a troubled one. Gilbert signed a 4-year contract that included a $7.8 million bonus.

Gilbert was never "relentless," as Farmer called him. He never fit into Pettine's system, or any other system. He was late for meetings. He started only three games in two seasons with the Browns.

In 2016, Gilbert was traded to Pittsburgh for a sixth-round pick in 2018. He played little with the Steelers and was cut after the 2016 season.

In 2017, Gilbert was first suspended for four games for flunking a drug test. He later was suspended for the entire 2017 season because of more failed tests.

After Gilbert's disastrous rookie season, I asked Farmer at a press conference if there were any red flags or warning signs about Gilbert's attitude.

"Like most young kids, did he have some issues during the time he was in college? Absolutely," said Farmer. "But that information also stated he had turned the corner and was moving in the right direction. You do the research . . . there is an inexact science to this thing . . . You would hope and think you could move guys past some of those small issues they had while in college."

They may have been "small" at Oklahoma State, but they loomed large and helped sink the careers of Farmer and Pettine with the Browns.

The Accidental Owner: Randy Lerner

"He woke up one morning with the Browns."

This is not about feeling sorry for Randy Lerner.

But I remember sitting in his office, the walls decorated with abstract modern art.

There was a pattern and theme to the expensive paintings on the wall, I just couldn't figure it out. The more I stared at the paintings, the less I saw that made any sense—at least to me.

Listening to Randy Lerner was a lot like that.

In my few encounters with Lerner, he came across as a nice man. There are no whispers about Lerner ripping into employees or publicly humiliating them. In fact, Lerner hated confrontation. That was one of his failings as an owner.

I remember Randy Lerner telling me about hanging around the Browns training camp when he was kid. He said he helped some of the ballboys. He was in awe of the players. He had the access because his father—Al Lerner—was a close friend of Art Modell. At some point in Modell's ownership, Al Lerner also bought about 10 percent of the old Cleveland Browns.

Randy Lerner insisted he was a Browns fan as a kid and an adult. He desperately wanted them to win.

But no matter how he discussed his association with the Browns as a teenager and then an adult, it was clear he never wanted to own the Browns. He had no part in the family decision to pursue the franchise.

It was his father (Al Lerner) who purchased the expansion Browns in 1998 for $530 million—putting them on the field for the 1999 season. In all the press conferences surrounding the Lerner family buying the Browns, I never remember seeing Randy Lerner in attendance. I don't recall a single word said about Randy Lerner. Nor have I been able to find any mention of him as eventually taking over for his father as owner—or even helping Al Lerner in any way operate the Browns.

CEO Carmen Policy was the man always at the side of Al Lerner at various press conferences.

Randy Lerner was mentioned only as one of Al's two children—the other being his daughter Nancy.

When Al Lerner died on October 23, 2002, at the age of 69 from brain cancer, the team was passed down to Randy Lerner.

At the time, Randy Lerner was 40 years old. He had a law degree from Columbia. He worked in the financial field, just like his father. Al Lerner became a billionaire owning MBNA, which was primarily a credit card company. Al was the Chairman of the Board for MBNA, Randy was a member of the Board of Directors.

Not only did Randy Lerner become the owner of the Browns when his father died, he also became Chairman of the Board of MBNA—making him, his mother and sister worth more than $1 billion.

I'm not going to venture an opinion of how Randy Lerner operated in the world of business. He certainly was well-trained and had extensive experience.

In the business world of sports, he often seemed lost.

*   *   *

Al Lerner was born in Brooklyn, and born rather poor. His parents owned a sandwich shop. In a 1998 interview with Business Week, Lerner said the shop had a soda fountain and six stools. The family lived upstairs. Except for three Jewish holidays, the shop was open every day of year, from 6 a.m. to midnight. They sold cigarettes, cigars and little treats along with sandwiches.

He worked his way through Columbia, spent two years in the Marines and his first full-time job after he left the military service was selling furniture.

Lerner didn't receive much money from his parents. But they instilled the drive of a Jewish/Russian immigrant family to be a success in America. He learned the essence of running a small business from working with his parents in the sandwich shop.

Lerner relentlessly built one business after another. He was especially gifted in the area of finance, where he moved from banking to running MBNA—the nation's second largest credit card company.

He also had massive real estate holdings. He had the strong, confident persona often found in Marines and self-made men. He had little patience with fools, and wasn't very interested in what his critics had to say.

I had a few conversations over the years with Al Lerner and walked away thinking, "When he was younger, I bet he was a very, very tough guy—even a scary opponent in business."

Lerner was 65 years old when he bought the Browns.

He once was livid with me for saying part of the reason he bid for the expansion team was to "get his honor back" after being blamed for helping Modell move the original franchise to Baltimore. I thought he was ready to ask me to step outside so we could duke it out. He'd boxed a bit in the Marines, I was later told.

As time passed, we made up. We had a respectful relationship by the time he died. I found him focused and a straight-shooter when we talked about the team. He wisely relied on Carmen Policy to teach him what he didn't know about running an NFL franchise.

He gave away millions and millions to various charities, including $100 million to Cleveland Clinic.

At first, Lerner was reluctant to appear at press conferences after buying the Browns. But Policy loved the interactions with the media. He'd bring Lerner along, and soon the owner began to enjoy it. His forceful personality was on display, and Lerner gave the impression that he was a wealthy man who was willing to spend to get the Browns winning.

And the fact is the best back-to-back seasons of the expansion era were 2001 and 2002, the final two where Al Lerner was the owner. Had he lived three more months, he would have watched the Browns' only playoff appearance since 1999.

*   *   *

Of the various people who were either coaches or general managers during Randy's 10-year ownership, Phil Savage survived the longest (2005-2008) and knew the owner the best.

"He truly had a desire for the Browns to win," said Savage. "He almost looked at the Browns through child-like eyes, thinking back to when he was a 10-year-old wearing Browns PJs and the team was winning. He desperately wanted to capture that magic again."

Wanting to win is important. So is spending money.

Both of those things were true of Randy Lerner.

"But I don't think he had a sense of the hard part of the game," said Savage. "You're in a competition. People are going to say ugly things. They won't always do things the right way. And because of the expansion situation, it was even harder for the Browns."

It didn't take long for Randy Lerner to clash with Policy.

My theory is the son wanted to prove he could run the Browns—and he didn't need his father's trusted advisor to do it. He'd find his own advisor.

Someone who also knows Randy once told me, "His father's death was a shock to him. He woke up one morning with the Browns in one hand, MBNA in the other. And suddenly it was like, 'Now what do I do?'"

It's easy to play amateur psychologist when looking at Randy Lerner.

His father had the personality of a Marine, the mindset of a driven business man. He didn't feel the need to always be a nice guy.

"Randy is a nice person," said Savage. "He wasn't used to criticism. Part of him wanted his general manager or coach to be his chest protector. I think that's why he was so reluctant to face the media—he worried how it would come across."

At first, Randy thought coach Butch Davis would be the guy who'd shield him—and fix the Browns.

But as I wrote in another chapter, Davis is convinced the death of Al Lerner and the departure of Policy doomed his days with the Browns. Davis believed Randy Lerner was too inexperienced at that point early in his ownership of the team.

Then Randy Lerner turned to Savage, and the Browns had the 10-6 record in 2007.

"Now that I look back at it, I should have become more of a friend to Randy," Savage said. "I should have paid more attention to how Ozzie (Ravens general manager Ozzie Newsome) built his relationship with Art Modell in Baltimore. Ozzie would be in an important meeting. Art would call. The last thing he wanted to do was talk to Art . . . but they'd talk for 45 minutes. He knew if he kept Art happy and really explained things to Art, it would be better for all of us."

*   *   *

Several executives and coaches told me how Randy would green light one big idea as a way to turn the Browns into a winner . . . then back off when it took time for success to come.

That's what Savage meant when he said Randy didn't understand "the hard part."

Al Lerner and Policy both knew there would be times when it seemed public criticism would be all they'd hear. Both also knew that things sometimes went from bad . . . to worse . . . to awful . . . before they suddenly improved.

You have to tough it out.

One executive who worked for Randy Lerner told me, "He was a nice person who recognized he needed help. But at the same time, he had this need to prove he knew more than he actually did."

It was the product of being the son of Al Lerner.

Part of him probably wondered, "How can I handle all this—especially the Browns?"

Part of him probably thought, "I bet people don't think I can handle it."

Part of him probably believed, "I'll show them. I'll make this work."

Instead, the team got worse after his father died.

The Browns were 16-16 in 2001-2002.

In the next four years, here were the records: 5-11, 4-12, 6-10, 4-12.

Then the Browns were 10-6 in 2007. I called it the "Halley's Comet Season" in another chapter.

It was a very short victory lap for Randy as injuries and other things devastated the team in 2008. The Browns were 4-12. Savage was fired.

Then he turned to Eric Mangini as head coach and the strongest voice in the football front office. That lasted a year.

In December 2009, he hired Mike Holmgren as team president. Holmgren was a Hall of Fame caliber coach (1992–2008), but he was supposed to straighten out the front office.

Randy kept looking for a strong personality after firing Savage. It was supposed to be Mangini, who was a Bill Belichick disciple. After a year, it was clear Mangini was best as a head coach, not running the draft and the other responsibilities of the front office.

Next came Holmgren.

Maybe this is a stretch, but I wonder if Holmgren reminded Randy of his dad—at least in a few ways.

Like Al Lerner, Holmgren had the tough-guy, take-over-the-room personality.

Like Al Lerner, Holmgren oozed confidence that could give an insecure owner a sense of hope.

Like Al Lerner, Holmgren allowed Randy to fade even deeper into the background and away from the eye of the public.

By 2010, Randy had been in charge of the team for seven years— and had one winning season. More than a few fans wanted him to sell the team.

He eventually did in 2012, as I explained in another chapter.

*   *   *

In the middle of his tenure owning the Browns, Randy bought the Aston Villa club in the English Premier League. He owned 85 percent of the team and became Chairman of the Board.

We're talking soccer. Big time soccer.

A strong case can be made for the English Premier League being the most popular league of any sport in the world, given the global interest. It was in 2006 when Randy bought the Aston Villa franchise. He fell in love with English soccer while he was a student at Cambridge.

"When Randy bought the team, a lot of people were excited," said Tom Reed. "He even got an Aston Villa tattoo."

In case you're wondering, the tattoo was on his ankle.

Reed has worked for the Akron Beacon Journal, the Cleveland Plain Dealer, the Columbus Dispatch and a new sport website called The Athletic. He absolutely adores soccer. He watches Premier League games on his computer. He has written about the sport for years.

He took a special interest in Randy's soccer venture.

"He was one of the first Americans to buy a team," said Reed. "He came in and immediately spent a lot of money. He hired Martin O'Neill as manager—and he's a very respected soccer coach. He immediately had the team on the cusp of what we'd consider to be the Final Four."

When Lerner bought the team, he said at the press conference that he planned to "compete at the highest level within the Premier League and in Europe."

The Premier League consists of 20 teams. There is no salary cap.

When Aston Villa had three consecutive sixth-place finishes, it was considered tremendous progress for a franchise that had been near the bottom of the league for years.

"At one point, a fan wrote a nice song about Randy Lerner," said Reed. "You can find it on YouTube. It's a guy singing and playing an organ."

Here is the chorus:

"When I was young, I had a dream

"To watch the greatest football team.

"And here I am, the dream is real.

"With Randy Lerner and Martin O'Neill."

In England, "football is soccer."

And for a while, Randy Lerner almost had a team prepared to contend for a title.

The three consecutive sixth-place finishes raised expectations of eventually making the Final Four. Randy kept spending and spending to bring in players to help O'Neill and his team take the next big step.

But Aston Villa was stuck . . .

Stuck in sixth place . . .

Stuck with big financial losses in this league with no salary cap . . .

After four years, Randy decided to make a major cut in his spending. This upset O'Neill, who quit five days before the opening of the 2010–2011 season.

As CNN reported: "Much of Villa's success was aided by Lerner's willingness to invest millions on new players, such as Ashley Young, James Milner and Stewart Downing. However, after ultimately being unable to break into the top four . . . the American began to embark on a cost-cutting program in recent seasons—selling star players to rival clubs."

This followed a pattern for Randy. In 2003, he walked into a meeting with Browns Coach Butch Davis and insisted the payroll be slashed immediately. They were coming off the 2002 playoff season.

Davis and others told me how Randy's moods and plans would quickly shift. He was going to spend . . . then not spend.

"When things started to go bad with Aston Villa, Randy kept hiring and firing coaches," said Reed. "He hired a coach from Birmingham City (Alex McLeish), one of the bitter rivals. The fans couldn't believe it. Randy was tone deaf on that one."

He went through six coaches in six years after O'Neill quit.

"Suddenly, it was clear Randy was way over his head," said Reed. "Early on, he went to games and was very visible. But after a while, it was like with the Browns—Randy was almost invisible."

Media people began to say Aston Villa had become "like the Cleveland Browns on the other side of the pond," according to Reed.

*   *   *

Along with no salary cap, there is another big difference between the English Premier League and the NFL.

No matter how bad an NFL team performs, it stays in the NFL. In 2016–17, the Browns were 1-31.

If they were in the Premier League, they would have been "relegated."

"It would be like the Browns being kicked out of the NFL and sent to the Canadian Football League," said Reed.

That happened after the 2015–16 season. Aston Villa finished with a 3-27-8 Premier League record.

That's right, they won 3-of-38 matches. They scored only 27 goals in those 38 games, allowing 76.

According to a 2016 Forbes Magazine story by Bobby McMahon, Randy bought the franchise for $94 million in 2006, and also assumed $24 million in debt—a total of $118 million.

"Since then, the club has racked up after tax losses of $356 million," wrote McMahon. "That works out to $100,000 per day."

Randy put the franchise up for sale in 2014. He was asking $290 million. It took him more than two years to sell it. During that time, the franchise was heading toward what is considered English soccer's second division.

"Randy waited too long," said Reed. "You want to sell a team when it's still in the Premier League. Not when it has been relegated."

In 2016, Randy finally sold the franchise, for $90 million.

Let's do the math:

1. He bought it in 2006 for $118 million.

2. He lost about $356 million, according to Forbes.

3. He sold it for $90 million.

4. Certainly he lost money in some other areas. Let's round it off finishing about $400 million in the red.

5. According to Reed, Randy turned down an offer of $220 million for the franchise while it was still in the Premier League.

At least Randy made about $500 million on the sale of the Browns to Jimmy Haslam in 2012.

But why did he buy the soccer team in 2006?

Was Randy trying to prove something, reviving a once great franchise in England—away from his critics in Cleveland?

Here is how his Aston Villa team finished each season in the 20-team Premier League:

2006–07: 11th	2009–10: 6th	2012–13: 15th	2015–16: 20th
2007–08: 6th	2010–11: 9th	2013–14: 15th	
2008–09: 6th	2011–12: 16th	2014–15: 17th	

In the end, some fans brought signs to Aston Villa games reading: "IF LERNER STAYS, THEN WE STAY AWAY!"

As a 2016 ESPN story reported: "Aston Villa has done it—going from darlings and European contenders to relegated in seven years. Amazingly, they did it with the seventh-highest wage bill in England this season, but money can't save the embarrassing run."

Forbes reported Randy Lerner's worth dropped from about $1.6 billion to $1 billion in the years he owned Aston Villa. He still walked away from both sports ventures as a billionaire, but without gaining the respect he seems to want so dearly.

Fans Write In . . .

Browns Loyalty

Readers were asked: Why do you still follow the Browns? (Responses were edited for clarity and brevity.)

Some of my earliest memories are sitting in my family room cheering on the Kardiac Kids with my parents and my brother. When things got tense, my mom would hide in the bathroom until the game ended and we could tell her the Browns won.

Sundays always meant family and the Browns. When I got older, I realized I had learned a lot from being a Browns fan—about rooting for the underdog and sticking by your team even when they let you down.

Being a Browns fan taught me how to be an optimist. There is always a silver lining to find, a first down to celebrate even if there isn't a win or a touchdown. Maybe it is about celebrating the small things. Maybe it is about texting my dad about draft picks and game points. We all need something to look forward to.

After 44 years, Sundays still mean family and the Browns and to me, the Browns are family. You don't stop loving your family just because they don't live up to your expectations.

— *Jessica Del Vecchio*

You might as well ask me why I still breathe. Being a Browns fan is in my DNA. My dad and grandfathers and uncles and aunts and cousins are all Browns fans. It's all I've ever known, and I can't imagine anything else. Why would I? Yes, the losing is draining, but the fandom will never, ever go away.

— *John Taylor, Glenville, West Virginia*

Why do I still follow the Browns after two decades of struggling with ineptitude? Because the Browns were something I could share with my family. When I was a kid, my dad liked to wrench on cars and go hunting as his hobbies while I was a bookish nerd who preferred to tinker on the computer and read books. We didn't share much in common, but what we did share was what happened every Sunday during football season—we'd sit down in front of the TV, turn on the game, and throw popcorn at the screen when something went poorly, hooting and hollering until time ran out.

The Browns remind me of home. They remind me of my family, of sitting with my dad (and sometimes my mom and my grandparents) on game day, of my hometown that has struggled as the world has moved on, of my friends who have spread out across the world like autumn leaves on the wind, of apple cider and leaves changing color. It's unlikely I'll ever come back to Ohio for more than a brief visit, but that's OK—a part of my heart never left there in the first place, and that part of me is rooted with the Browns.

— *Kit Smith, Arvada, Colorado*

I identify with the underdog. This is particularly true for us Clevelanders who came from the immigrant working class. We identify with the Browns because we grew up as underdogs ourselves. We immigrants were not destined to win, we did not know the language, did not have the income, lacked the goal guidance and education. But those of us that achieved our American dreams had to fight multiple times harder and our victories are that much more gratifying.

It means so much more when the underdog wins. There are no lower underdogs than my Cleveland Browns, thus there is no greater high than when they win! The gratification of a win is a multiple of how likely the Browns or me were predicted to lose.

—*Bruno Del Vecchio, Twinsburg, Ohio*

I always say that when they finally win that Super Bowl, the first person under the age of 40 wearing a Browns hat, I'm taking it from them. No way do you get to be a fan now without the suffering that we have endured. One thing I know for sure: No matter how bad it gets, I'll never root for anyone else.

— *Drew Ward, Waxhaw, North Carolina*

Growing up in Central Ohio during the '80s meant we'd see the Browns (on TV)—usually. I remember a pot of chili, a roaring fireplace and whoever wanted to show up was there to watch.

Then Dad got a promotion, and he and his buddy Louie went in on season tickets. They were big time, and the legend grew. We'd send them off early Sunday mornings, hoping they'd come back like conquering heroes. Then I got the news. Friends had someone drop out and there was an extra ticket—to the Dawg Pound. The OG version. I just got the call to the big leagues, was 12 years old, and I was going to the show.

Beverage smuggling was in high gear at the time and I earned my stripes. My ski coat had many compartments, and Dad thought they'd never check a kid. I stuffed 13 Miller Lites into the pockets of my jacket and instantly went legend to those guys. Once inside, I saw a dog house that strangely took four guys to carry in and only two to carry out. I smelled new smells, heard new words. Got chills when the Olympic theme played. The crowd thundered to the players taking the field. I had no chance and was immediately hooked for life.

Crazy or not, we are optimistic our loyalty will be rewarded. Someday.

—*Jon Richardson, Medina "by way of Westerville," Ohio*

The easy and sarcastic answer is because we are masochists.

The more difficult and truthful answer is because the love for the Browns was passed down to us by our dads.

My husband and I are both the only children of diehard, religiously fanatical Browns fans. My father-in-law attended the first Browns game in 1946, and my husband made sure they attended the last game in 1995 together when the team left. My father was a Browns season ticket holder for years when I was a kid. Both our dads attended the 1964 championship game (not together).

In our houses, growing up, there was no other option ... you loved the Browns, the Buckeyes and—being raised in Canton—the [McKinley High School] Bulldogs.

We have continued the tradition of Browns' blind love and loyalty with our kids. Every July brings the belief this is the "Year of the Browns." Every Sunday starts with the thought we WILL win this week. We wear our lucky clothes (if we haven't burned or thrown them away due to losses), sit in the right chairs that brought good plays or wins last week or even in the last quarter, and yell at those who don't follow those superstitious rules. We jump up and down in our family room as Joe Schobert is running down the sideline, trying to help him to the goal line and the 1-31 Browns to victory. And then we shake our heads in disbelief a few minutes later and hope we can celebrate next week maybe. They are OUR Browns—for better or worse.

P.S.—I changed my mind after re-reading this before hitting send ... it's an illness! We are insane!

—*Deb and Pat Hogan, Louisville, Ohio*

If I can still be a Browns fan throughout all the losses, I can go through anything in life without giving up or quitting.

— *Tyler Lance, Chagrin Falls, Ohio*

A couple years ago, a plan I had made to transform my orange 2003 Honda Element into a "Brownsmobile" was finally carried out. On went the bold brown and white stripes . . . and voila! I couldn't think of a better way to show what the Browns have always meant to me. And, you know what? I've never heard anyone mock it or say a bad word, even when the team went 0-for-16. In fact, when I pull up to a red light signal, I often hear "woof, woof" and "Go Browns!"

—*Don A. Smeraldi, Murrieta, California*

I am a military child who grew up in and still lives in Germany. My Dad was born in Cleveland in 1953 and grew up on the rugged streets of the East Side. In 1972, he joined the Army. During his deployment in Germany, he met a wonderful German woman who happens to be my mother.

My dad sold lemonade at old Municipal Stadium as a 15-year-old, and he raised his son a diehard Browns fan. I can remember falling asleep in class because I got up to watch those epic battles between the Browns and Oilers on Monday Night Football, which would start here at 2:30 due to the

6-hour time difference. With today's technology we get to at least have a little hometown feeling watching the Browns via GamePass.

The feeling of the Browns being champions is around the corner.

—*Malcolm Sharp, Darmstadt, Germany*

1964 made me a Browns fan for life. I attended training camp in Hiram. One of my most treasured possessions is an autograph sheet with most of the Browns players. I even found Paul Warfield at the gas station in Hiram, and he graciously signed. I remember listening to the NFL championship game on the radio. I thought that would be the first of many in my lifetime.

—*Patrick Finan, Cortland, Ohio*

Mostly I feel like a gambling addict who just keeps doubling down even though he loses constantly. I guess the logic is that victory will be that much sweeter when (or if) it comes. I wouldn't say I'm that same kind of gambling addict anymore, but I do still find myself back at the card table every April for the Browns' version of the Super Bowl.

— *Jason Cocca, Albuquerque, New Mexico*

The reason I've stuck with the Browns is that I've got so much invested in the team. Let's say I decide to give up on them and root for the Philadelphia Eagles. Who started at right tackle for the Eagles in 1964? Beats me. I can tell you, however, that Monte Clark was the Browns right tackle that year. Gene Hickerson was the right guard, John Morrow was the center, John Wooten was left guard and Dick Schafrath was the left tackle. Besides, this might be the year they turn things around.

—*Rick Pastva, Mount Pleasant, South Carolina*

As Sam Rutigliano once said in an NFL clip I remember, "Just one time ... c'mon, one time." And that's all Northeast Ohio needs ... just one time.

—*Fritz Johnson, New Philadelphia, Ohio*

I'm 55. I would never forgive myself if the Browns were good and I gave up. Because I want to experience the joy of June 19, 2016 [the Cavs' NBA championship], on the first Sunday of February as only a vested fan can.

I'm not going to jump on the bandwagon as it's coming into the station. I'm going to earn the joy, the tears, and the bragging rights, one game at a time.

—*Richard Freedman, Mentor, Ohio*

I believe in loyalty. I believe in commitment. I live in Northeast Ohio, which means I am going to be loyal to our teams no matter how bad it gets or how good it is.

People in this area bleed commitment and loyalty. We are not wishy washy. We stay true. This is why we stick with our teams, especially the Browns. We are not going to give up. We are not going to go east or south or north to root for another team. We stay committed to see this through because we believe, because we are committed, because we are loyal, because we love our Browns.

— *Michael Kager Jr., Canal Fulton, Ohio*

The Browns and the Numbers Game

---

*"We had to acquire a lot of draft picks
in a short period of time."*

Late in the 2015 season, Jimmy Haslam knew he had to do something.

It started with replacing general manager Ray Farmer and coach Mike Pettine. Haslam's football shotgun marriage had blown up in the owner's face.

By the end of the 2015 season, the Browns had a 3-13 record. Pettine and Farmer had major doubts about each other. The 2014 first round (Justin Gilbert and Johnny Manziel) was a disaster.

But there was more.

The Browns had the highest-paid defense in the NFL, yet that unit ranked 27th out of 32 teams in 2015.

Haslam bought the franchise in 2012. He replaced the Mike Holmgren front office and coaching staff. It was hard to criticize that move. Holmgren was hired by previous owner Randy Lerner and given incredible power. Most new owners taking over a perpetually losing franchise would want to have their own management team.

Haslam came in with CEO Joe Banner. But Banner and his people were gone in a year.

Then Haslam pasted Pettine and Farmer together. That lasted two seasons, the Browns losing 18 of their last 21 games.

As the losses piled up, Sashi Brown gained influence. He was in charge of the salary cap and some other front office business. He had been brought to Cleveland by former team president Alec Scheiner and Banner. The Harvard-trained lawyer's previous stop was with the Jacksonville Jaguars.

Banner was the first to introduce some serious analytics to the Browns football operation. This wasn't a new concept. New England had been doing it quietly for years with Ernie Adams, while coach Bill Belichick publicly dismissed the analytic approach. No surprise. Belichick didn't want anyone to know even the slightest key to his success.

At least half of the NFL franchises had some type of analytics department.

Farmer was a former NFL linebacker and then an old-school scout. The numbers didn't do much for him.

Haslam talked to owners and front office people from the Philadelphia 76ers, Houston Astros and Chicago Cubs to learn how those franchises dealt with losing and their plans for revival.

Members of the Browns front office were assigned to study how various franchises operate, especially successful ones in markets such as Cleveland. He didn't limit himself to football. Brown talked to several sports executives, including members of the Cleveland Indians and Cleveland Cavaliers.

The Tribe and Cavs have long been analytics driven. The Cavs used the numbers game to determine who were the best players to blend with LeBron James.

Former Cavs general manager David Griffin and current general manager Koby Altman had sets of numbers showing where open shots came on the court when James handled the ball—and who were the best players in the NBA making shots (often 3-pointers) from those spots.

Dating back to the early 1990s with John Hart and Dan O'Dowd, the Cleveland Indians front office engaged in its own approach to Moneyball. It continued with Mark Shapiro and later Chris Antonetti and Mike Chernoff running the franchise.

Griffin once told me the ideal franchise had a smart analytics department that knew numbers weren't everything. The team also needed a strong coach/manager who could lead men—and incorporate stats when making both roster and game-day decisions.

The Indians have been the prime example with their young, bright front office combined with the experienced and open-minded Terry Francona as manager. That marriage consistently helped the Indians to overachieve with one of the lowest payrolls in Major League Baseball, a sport with no salary cap.

Could the Browns do something like that? Furthermore, they would be operating in a league with a tight salary cap designed to take away advantages that large market teams have in baseball.

As the 2015 Browns season came to a close, Haslam was weary of the personality clashes between the front office and coaches. Farmer's texting suspension was just one symptom of the mistrust.

Haslam decided to try something different.

Brown would become vice president of football operations. He'd assemble almost a baseball-type front office with a lot of bright often Ivy League graduates who had been executives. They brought in Paul DePodesta, a former baseball executive with the Indians, A's, Dodgers and Mets. He also was a key figure in the analytics-based Moneyball approach to baseball. DePodesta did play football at Harvard.

Andrew Berry was hired as player personnel director. He played football at Harvard, but grew up in the scouting department of the Indianapolis Colts.

But they'd also retain some old-line scouts.

"We wanted the best of both worlds," Brown told me in 2016.

Then they'd look for their own Terry Francona, a strong leader who would also apply some of the analytic principles. Much of this was Banner's long-term plan, but he was not around long enough to put all of it in place.

Brown later told me, "We needed a coach who could drive the culture, energize our players and maximize their potential, on and off the field."

*   *   *

That coach would become Hue Jackson, a former Cincinnati Bengals offensive coordinator.

Brown and others told Haslam, "We need to focus in rebuilding our pipeline of young players and getting impact players at impact positions."

The Browns had been drafting high. They had two picks in the first rounds of 2012 (Trent Richardson, Brandon Weeden), 2014 (Manziel, Gilbert) and 2015 (Danny Shelton, Cameron Erving).

Starting in 2010, the other first round picks were Joe Haden (2010), Phil Taylor (2011) and Barkevious Mingo (2013).

That added up to nine first-round picks in six years. And four were in the top 10.

But as the Browns projected their 2016 roster, only Haden and Shelton appeared to be certain starters from that group of nine.

I had an exclusive interview with Brown before the 2016 season.

"It would be hard to look at where we were at the end of the (2015) season and say we're on the right track," he said. "Not only were we 3-13, but we didn't have a lot of pieces you need to be successful in the NFL. We didn't want to sugarcoat it or be unrealistically optimistic."

The Browns were not a 3-13 team loaded with young players. They had the 16th oldest roster in 2015—middle of the NFL pack.

The new front office decided not to re-sign Mitchell Schwartz, a second-round pick from 2012 who had played every single snap. He wanted to return to Cleveland. His asking price was not outrageous. He was 27 years old, right in his prime. Allowing Schwartz to depart was a terrible move. He was quickly signed by Kansas City general manager John Dorsey, who would replace Brown in Cleveland.

Free agent receiver Travis Benjamin signed with the Chargers. He was looking for a team with a better quarterback and the Chargers had veteran Philip Rivers. The Browns' interest in keeping Benjamin was lukewarm, at best.

Pro Bowl center Alex Mack left for Atlanta. He had zero interest in playing for the Browns. He tried to leave in 2014 as a restricted free agent, but the Browns matched an offer sheet Mack received from Jacksonville. This time, he was unrestricted—and gone.

They also let safety Tashaun Gipson go to Jacksonville as a free agent.

"We have spent on free agency and it doesn't necessarily drive results," Brown said on the eve of the 2016 season. "Free agency is expensive."

In an interview with Sports Illustrated's Peter King in 2017, DePodesta said: "This was a situation that we felt like we really need to rebuild the foundation of this organization. Its almost like redoing a house. You need to rip down all the walls and get down to the studs. Now, when you do that and you tear out all the walls and floors . . . all you have left are the studs. You look at it and . . . wow . . . this looks terrible."

DePodesta also explained the Browns "never want to go through that again."

But the team was starting over, and no one had an idea how much emotional trauma that would cause the fans or ownership.

* * *

Not long after Sashi Brown took over as vice president of football operations, the Browns compiled a list of seven coaching candidates. When writing a behind-the-scenes story for the Plain Dealer of how Jackson came to coach the Browns, I uncovered a list of candidates.

The names were in no special order.

1. Adam Gase, Chicago Bears offensive coordinator.

2. Doug Marrone, former Buffalo head coach and Jacksonville assistant.

3. Teryl Austin, Detroit defensive coordinator.

4. Matt Patricia, New England defensive coordinator.

5. Sean McDermott, Carolina defensive coordinator.

6. Jerome Henderson, Dallas assistant.

7. Hue Jackson, Cincinnati offensive coordinator.

On the eve of the 2018 season, it's interesting to consider what happened to the names on the list.

1. Gase was the head coach in Miami.

2. Marrone was the head coach in Jacksonville.

3. Patricia was the head coach in Detroit.

4. McDermott was the head coach for the Buffalo Bills.

5. Jackson was the head coach with the Browns.

Several of the candidates didn't have interest in the Browns in 2016. Jackson did, and he quickly moved to the top of the list.

The Browns loved Jackson's infectious personality. He has the ability "to take over a room," as Haslam and others saw and heard Jackson in action. They knew the job would be more than just a big paycheck for him. He wanted to establish himself as a head coach. He opened the 2011 season in Oakland with a 7-4 record, then finished 1-4 to end up at 8-8.

Sashi Brown and the new front office had as much on the line as Jackson. If they failed, it was unlikely any of them would receive another chance to run a franchise. Brown and his front office were met with major skepticism in the NFL.

And there were doubts about Jackson being head coaching material.

When the Browns hired Hue Jackson, he knew the plan. The team would have one of the youngest rosters in the NFL. It would be pain for a few years. They'd build through the draft. Short cuts have been tried and failed in Cleveland.

Jackson also had to accept he was working for a new type of NFL front office.

As the offensive coordinator with the Cincinnati Bengals, his bosses were two old school football men: owner Mike Brown and coach Marvin Lewis. The Bengals had very little interest in the analytic approach to team building.

The same was true of the Oakland Raiders, where he was the head coach in 2011.

When the Browns approached Jackson about being the head coach in 2016, he was a bit scarred after being fired by the Raiders in 2011.

One year as a head coach. A .500 record. Gone.

Jackson gained the reputation for battling with the front office in Oakland. It was a chaotic situation. At one point he was serving as coach and general manager. But something negative stuck to Jackson from the experience.

He received no chances to interview for a head coaching job until 2016. That year, the New York Giants also had an interest in talking to Jackson.

At that point, Jackson was desperate for a chance to be a head coach again. He had been in the NFL since 2001. His college coaching career dated to 1987.

So when the Browns called, he was receptive.

The Browns saw Jackson as the coordinator who revived the career of Cincinnati quarterback Andy Dalton. He also was praised for his work as a quarterback coach in Baltimore, where he worked with a young Joe Flacco.

In games against the Browns, Jackson was a creative play-caller. He knew the AFC North Division because it also was where the Bengals played.

I was excited about the Browns hiring Jackson. So were most members of the media and fans.

An executive from another team warned me, "Hue could be very good, but if things go bad—look out, he likes to play the blame game. He'll try to cover his butt."

Haslam approved the plan to tear down the team and pile up draft picks.

Jackson accepted it because he believed he could improve a 3-13 record with the sheer power of his personality and football experience. Jackson has a big ego, as do most head coaches.

"Hue is uniquely qualified because he knows how to get the most out of players," Brown told me before the 2016 season. "He can change the culture. Hue is a great teacher, a great motivator. That's critical when you have young players."

The Browns opened the 2016 season with 16 rookies and 13 more second-year players on the 53-man roster. Some NFL experts predicted they wouldn't win a game.

"We understand it will be difficult," said Brown. "But we're going to be there with Hue."

Jackson would be on the front-line every day, dealing with the players, media and the losing.

As the 2016 season opened, I was hopeful they'd win at least four games.

They won one game.

*   *   *

Like Jackson, I thought the previous front office/coaching staff relationship was a mess.

At least Brown was hired first, then Jackson was hired.

Haslam still had his business model of Brown and Jackson being on the same level—both reporting directly to the owner.

It's important to remember Jackson heard the vision of the analytic rebuilding approach from Brown and DePodesta.

"We weren't going to be all analytics," said Brown. "Paul DePodesta played football at Harvard. He knew football. But he really knew systems and how to build a championship organization. We wanted to combine the best of traditional football scouting with analytics."

You can like analytics or hate it, but it was hard to defend how drafting was done by some of the previous Browns front offices.

There are a variety of ways analytics are used.

But part of it is common sense.

The Browns were a weak team that had little success signing veteran free agents. Most of those players were paid for what they had done before—not what they could do for the Browns.

And Cleveland became a last paycheck for several of them. Signing with the Browns was a way of enhancing their football 401K retirement plans. More than a few seemed to act as if their career was already over not long after signing with the Browns. Dwayne Bowe was a prime example. He signed a $9 million contract in 2015 and caught five passes.

If you want to build a team through the draft, a good way to do it is with lots of picks.

Belichick believed in it. That's why he often traded down to add more picks.

As Brown told Haslam, "the roster is weak. We have to build through the draft."

So trades were made to keep adding picks and even more picks.

*   *   *

By the start of the 2017 season, only 11 of the 53 players inherited by the Sashi Brown front office remained with the team. They had drafted 14 players in 2016, 10 more in 2017.

"No matter how bad you are, you get only seven draft picks each year," Brown told me on the eve of the 2017 season. "We had to acquire a lot of draft picks in a short period of time. We wanted to have multiple draft picks in high rounds in each season."

I always liked the "Big Volume" approach to the draft. That doesn't always mean trading down. All picks are not created equal. Sashi Brown also studied the Baltimore Ravens. While they have a traditional scouting-driven front office run by Ozzie Newsome, they also were a team that tended to pile up the draft picks. One of their goals was to find value in the lower rounds.

"The reality is no one in the NFL is hitting on all picks in seven rounds," said Brown. "We are going to miss some picks. You need organizational humility about that. You need a firm understanding of how difficult it is to predict what player will flourish in the NFL."

By the start of the 2018 season, the general consensus was nothing done by the Sashi Brown front office was right.

Of course, that's wrong.

The Browns had the top pick in the 2017 draft. They didn't trade it for more picks. They took Myles Garrett, the projected best player in the draft. If he stays healthy, he should be a Pro Bowl player.

In 2016, they took Joe Schobert. He was one of three different picks they had in the fourth round. Schobert became a Pro Bowl linebacker in his second pro season. Another fourth-rounder was safety Derrick Kindred, who started 15 games in two seasons and became a viable NFL player.

Emmanuel Ogbah was the Browns' second-round pick in 2016 and he became a starting defensive end.

You can say, "Hey, they had 14 picks, they were bound to get some players."

That's exactly the point. You try to put the odds of adding talent in your favor with the extra picks.

In a 2016 interview with Pro Football Talk, Atlanta Falcons general manager Tom Dimitroff said about 56 percent of first-rounders become starters in the NFL.

The website Football Outsiders said its research reveals about 30 percent of second-rounders become starters. And the percentage keeps dropping in the lower rounds.

You can get lost in all the numbers, but one last piece of research does underline why a team wants lots of first-round picks—and why some teams devalue lower-round picks.

Patrick Rishe wrote an article for Forbes published on the magazine's website on May 22, 2015. He went back to the 2010 draft, so he was looking at players picked between 2010 and 2014.

He found the following:

1. First rounders became starters 67 percent of the time.

2. Second-and-third rounders were about the same when it came to starting: 34 percent for second rounders, 36 percent for third rounders.

3. More undrafted free agents (14 percent) became starters than players drafted between rounds 4-7 combined (13 percent).

What his research didn't show was how those middle and low round players often become valuable on special teams and as backups.

*   *   *

Football Outsiders does a story each year called, "The NFL Draft, six years later."

If you look at the 2011 draft, five quarterbacks were picked in the top 35. Here is how that list looked heading into the 2018 season:

1. Cam Newton, an excellent player for Carolina.

8. Jake Locker, out of the NFL.

10. Blaine Gabbert, backup with Tennessee.

12. Christian Ponder, out of the NFL.

35. Andy Dalton, starter for Cincinnati.

How about 2012?

1. Andrew Luck, starter in Indianapolis.

2. Robert Griffin, backup in Baltimore.

8. Ryan Tannehill, starter in Miami.

22. Brandon Weeden, backup in Houston.

But some quarterbacks do succeed.

The 2013 draft was considered poor for quarterbacks, but 2014 showed promise:

3. Blake Bortles, starter in Jacksonville.

22. Johnny Manziel, out of NFL.

32. Teddy Bridgewater, backup in New Orleans.

36. Derek Carr, starter in Oakland.

62. Jimmy Garoppolo, starter in San Francisco.

*   *   *

In the draft, quarterbacks can be frustrating—both the ones you draft and the ones you don't draft.

Twice in three years (2012, 2014) the Browns used a No. 22 pick on quarterbacks (Weeden, Manziel). Both failed. So did taking Brady Quinn at No. 22 in 2007.

Yes, all three quarterbacks were the No. 22 pick.

Sometimes, you have to keep drafting quarterbacks.

Players drafted at many other positions can help on special teams. Maybe he can be an extra defensive back in passing situations. Or he can be an extra receiver, a running back.

Other than the offensive line and perhaps the linebacker positions, rarely do players in other positions play every snap. Nearly all come out for a rest.

But a quarterback usually plays every snap—or not at all. A quarterback is all or nothing, in terms of value to a team.

That's why when a team misses on a quarterback, it's a HUGE miss. And that's why teams sometimes hesitate picking quarterbacks high in the draft.

As Sashi Brown told me before the drafts in 2016 and 2017, taking a quarterback high and immediately putting him on the field to start was probably setting him up to fail.

He once told me, "We should have learned something from Tim Couch."

While Couch had some good moments with the Browns, he was physically and emotionally beaten down by his fifth season in the NFL.

The Browns passed on Carson Wentz in 2016 and put the Philadelphia Eagles in position to win the Super Bowl in his second season.

In 2017, the Browns had a chance to draft Deshaun Watson. They traded the No. 12 pick to Houston, who took Watson. The Clemson quarterback was looking like an elite quarterback when he suffered an ACL injury late in his rookie season.

Instead, they traded down and used the picks they received on Jabrill Peppers and Denzel Ward.

When Sashi Brown talked to ownership about this approach, he discussed the pain involved. He tried to convey that to the public.

"The fans have every reason to be cynical and frustrated," Brown told me early in the 2017 season. "It's been more than two decades (of losing). You have to sympathize with that. It's real."

And just like every other front office before his, Brown inherited the mistakes and sins of the previous men who sat in his chair. There has been so much change, so many players who failed for so many different reasons—it's very tempting for fans and media people to moan, "Same old Browns."

That helped lead to Brown's quick exit with four games left in the 2017 season.

Why Didn't the Browns Pick Carson Wentz?

"Four trades involving first-round picks in the last five years . . . Every one has been an abject failure."

If the Browns had to do it over again, they would have drafted Carson Wentz.

That goes for Sashi Brown and the others who were in charge of the 2016 Browns draft.

Brown was not giving interviews after he was fired by the Browns with four weeks left in the 2017 season. But I had several background discussions with Brown while he was the Browns vice president and running the football operations.

The Browns entered the 2016 draft with the No. 2 selection. At that point, they thought they'd have a chance to take their favorite quarterback in the draft: California's Jared Goff.

The analytics people loved Goff. The front office loved Goff. Coach Hue Jackson loved Goff.

The top pick in the draft was owned by Tennessee. The Titans already had Marcus Mariota as their quarterback. He was the No. 2 pick in the 2015 draft.

So the Browns were hoping Tennessee would keep the top pick and select someone besides a quarterback. But the quarterback-starving Rams traded up to grab the top pick.

Suddenly, the Browns were in trouble. The Rams tried to pretend they would take either North Dakota State's Carson Wentz or Goff, but it soon was evident their hearts were set on Goff.

If the Browns wanted a quarterback, Wentz was available to them.

There was no consensus on Wentz. Jackson did like him. Not as much as he did Goff, but the coach was intrigued by Wentz.

The analytics site Pro Football Focus rated Goff as its No. 4 prospect in the draft, the top quarterback.

What about Wentz?

He was No. 14 overall, the No. 2 ranked quarterback.

The website wrote: "There's some projection to Wentz's game, but the raw tools are impressive. His timing isn't always on point in the passing game, but he has the big arm and athleticism to mask that inexperience as he grows."

The Browns front office was struggling with how to evaluate Wentz. He played at the old NCAA Division I-AA level, meaning it was a major step below Division I where Goff played in the PAC-12.

Wentz is 6-foot-5, 240 pounds, and looked the part of an NFL quarterback. Jackson loves big quarterbacks, so that immediately caught the attention of the coach. Wentz also is extremely bright and mature. He had the advantage of playing in a pro-style offense at North Dakota State, meaning he took snaps under center.

Goff and most other top college quarterbacks played in the "Spread Offense," meaning they were always taking long snaps in the shotgun and rarely even working out of a huddle. They just came to the line-of-scrimmage, called a play, then took a long snap. It's a very simplistic style compared to what the vast majority of NFL teams play.

But Wentz was in a pro offense. That counted in his favor.

The level of competition was a concern. So was the fact that he completed 63 percent of his passes in his final season at N.D. State. That was pretty good, but not eye-popping for a guy who was supposed to be an elite NFL quarterback prospect playing at a lower level of college football. He was at the school for five years and was 23 years old entering the draft.

That counts against a player, especially from a smaller school. It could indicate he doesn't have much room to develop physically or on the field.

It was hard to find another top quarterback in the NFL like Wentz—with five years at a school below Division I.

A lot of NFL talent evaluators liked Wentz, not many loved him.

ESPN's Mel Kiper rated Wentz the No. 7 player in the 2016 draft and the No. 2 quarterback.

"The physical talent and intangibles are all here," wrote Kiper. "Wentz has size, well-above-average athletic ability and a power arm to make any throw. He has the upside to be a star but requires seasoning and patience as he deals with a massive leap in competition."

The Browns front office would have taken Goff at No. 2, but even then the front office had major doubts.

As Sashi Brown often said, "One player can't turn a franchise around. No matter who was going to be our quarterback, we needed a talent upgrade to support him."

Philadelphia was the only team to call the Browns with a serious offer for the No. 2 pick. Other teams wanted quarterbacks. Other teams were like the Browns, not quite sure what to make of Wentz. The Eagles had veteran Sam Bradford at quarterback, but were absolutely sold on Wentz.

The Browns kept asking for more picks and the Eagles complied.

Here's what the Browns received for Wentz:

1. The Eagles' first-round picks in 2016 (No. 8) and 2017.

2. The Eagles' third and fourth round picks in 2016.

3. The Eagles' second round pick in 2018.

The moment the deal was made, it signaled the Browns were not about to take a quarterback high in the draft.

Then the Browns traded again, sending the No. 8 and a sixth-rounder to Tennessee for:

1. Tennessee's 2016 first-round pick (No. 15).

2. Tennessee's 2016 third-round pick.

3. Tennessee's second-round pick in 2017.

In the end, the Browns added eight picks—including two in the first round—for the No. 2 pick.

In terms of raw football assets—namely draft picks, the Browns received a huge haul.

But as Sports Illustrated's Peter King wrote before the 2016 draft:

"The Browns have made four trades involving first-round picks in the past five years. Every one has been an abject failure. The deals netted Cleveland Phil Taylor, Johnny Manziel, Justin Gilbert, Brandon Weeden, Owen Marecic, Greg Little and Trent Richardson. That's an amazing run of drafting ineptitude."

King's point was the front office had to prove it could do more than pile up the picks—it had to use them wisely.

After the 2016 draft, Brown told me: "We traded back for young talent. We're going to see a lot of young guys play and grow together. It's the start of a nucleus we need. We need to build the entire roster."

*　　*　　*

This is where it all went wrong for the Browns.

They rated Corey Coleman as the top receiver in the draft, and they believed he'd be available at No. 15.

They were right, the Baylor star was still on the draft board. No receiver was taken in the first 14 picks.

Analytics loved the 5-foot-11 Coleman because of his speed and YAC: Yards After Catch. That means how a receiver picks up yardage after he catches the ball. The coaches also liked Coleman.

None of the receivers were highly rated.

ESPN's Todd McShay and Kiper both ranked Mississippi's Laquon Treadwell as their top receiver in the 2016 draft. Both draft experts had Coleman as the No. 2 receiver in the draft.

The Browns passed on Treadwell, and his first two seasons in Minnesota were a disaster: 21 receptions in 25 games.

The other receiver strongly considered by the Browns in the first round was Josh Doctson of TCU. He was drafted by Washington and suffered a major Achilles injury in 2016, playing two games. In 18 NFL games, he had caught 37 passes heading into the 2018 season.

The Browns also liked Sterling Shepard, a receiver from Oklahoma. He was a second-round pick by the New York Giants and had 124 catches in his first two pro seasons.

After the first two years in the NFL, the best receiver in the 2016 draft was Michael Thomas. The Ohio State product was a second-round pick by New Orleans, and had 196 receptions. Thomas benefited by playing for a veteran team with a future Hall of Fame quarterback in Drew Brees. Would he have been nearly as successful in Cleveland? Hard to say. But the ever-changing group of quarterbacks would not have helped him.

If Coleman had become a Pro Bowl receiver, then the trade would look better—even with Wentz leading the Eagles to the Super Bowl in his second pro season. At least the Browns would have had their own star to show for the deal.

But he had only 56 catches in two years. He played only 19 of a possible 32 games. He broke a hand in each year. He also had some hamstring problems. Jackson and his coaching staff thought Coleman was not a hard-worker.

Right before the 2018 season opened, new general manager John Dorsey traded Coleman to Buffalo for a future seventh-round pick.

*   *   *

Obviously, time could help the Browns. By the time you connect all the dots on all the trades that involved the picks obtained for Wentz, the Browns had the following players:

1. Corey Coleman. Since traded to Buffalo.
2. Cody Kessler. Since traded to Jacksonville.
3. DeShone Kizer. Since traded to Green Bay.
4. Jordan Payton. Cut.

The Browns did add two first-rounders in the deals:

1. Defensive back Denzel Ward was the No. 4 pick in the 2018 draft and a projected starter as a rookie.
2. Jabrill Peppers was the No. 25 pick in the 2017 draft and still in the mix to be a starter in the defensive backfield.

*   *   *

The Browns did pick a quarterback in the 2016 draft.

That was Cody Kessler, a third-round pick from USC.

Analytics followers liked Kessler because he was very experienced—41 starts at a nationally ranked Division I program. He completed 67 percent of his passes. He threw 88 TD passes compared to 19 interceptions. He played for four different offensive coordinators, meaning he had to adapt to different systems. He also played some of the time in a pro system.

But Kessler was only 6-foot-1. He looked even smaller when surrounded by so many of the huge men in the NFL.

On the day Kessler was drafted, Hue Jackson made the "Trust me on this one" comment.

I always wondered about that. Jackson prefers taller and larger quarterbacks with strong arms. Kessler didn't check any of those physical boxes.

Jackson backed the front office on the pick. The front office had signed free agent Robert Griffin III, a quarterback wanted by Jackson. The coach figured he'd support the drafting of Kessler. The rookie was likely to be third-string. The Browns also had veteran Josh McCown on the 2016 roster.

But what often happens to the Browns . . . happened.

Quarterbacks get hurt.

Griffin was injured at the end of the 2016 opener. That was a 29-10 loss in Philadelphia.

It also was the debut of Wentz, who immediately stirred the anger of Browns fans by his impressive performance. Wentz completed 22-of-37 passes for 278 yards and a pair of touchdowns.

For the Browns front office, that was the start of the Wentz nightmare.

McCown was injured in the second game of the season, a loss to Baltimore.

Kessler was not even supposed to play in 2016. Injuries forced him to start the third game of the season.

Kessler had some nice moments in his first two pro starts. Then he began getting hurt. He suffered two concussions during the 2016 season, and never looked the same after that.

Jackson quickly lost faith in Kessler, whose confidence also suffered. Kessler wasn't ready to start so quickly. Perhaps he'll never be an NFL starter for long. But his career was sabotaged by circumstances, injuries and the usual Browns tactic of a rookie quarterback playing before he's ready—and then traumatized by the experience.

Browns fans saw the same thing with DeShone Kizer in 2017,

another rookie quarterback pressed into action too soon. That was Jackson's decision, and Jackson soon became impatient with Kizer. It's been a pattern with Jackson in Cleveland—falling in and out of love with quarterbacks.

* * *

While the Browns have to wait on some of these players before a final verdict on the deal can be delivered, the part that cost Sashi Brown his job is Wentz immediately starting and succeeding.

There was another factor.

Paul DePodesta should have known better when talking quarterbacks with ESPN's Tony Grossi.

He basically said the Browns didn't consider Wentz to be a top 20 NFL quarterback. DePodesta said this before the 2016 season opened.

Here were his exact words to Grossi:

"We have to make judgments on individual players and we're not always going to be right . . . in a given year, there may be 2-3 NFL-ready quarterbacks at the college level. In another year, there literally may be zero. There just may not be anybody in that year who's good enough to be a top 20 quarterback in the NFL. Even though you have a desperate need for one, you have to resist the temptation of taking that guy just because you have a need . . . if you don't believe he's one of those 20 guys at the end of the day . . . that's what we did this year."

Those comments just made the Browns look worse.

There are 32 teams in the NFL, meaning there are 32 starting quarterbacks. DePodesta was saying the Browns thought Wentz would end up in the bottom third of starting quarterbacks.

It would have been wiser for DePodesta to stay away from even remotely talking about Wentz and discussing the need for adding as many young players as possible to find more talent.

But his projection of Wentz was so wildly off-the-mark, it proved to be an embarrassment to the new front office.

I made several requests of the Browns to interview DePodesta. I had met him a few times during his 20-year baseball career. The Browns front office kept telling me that it would happen. It never did.

I would have loved to hear what DePodesta had to say looking back

at the Wentz decision and his explanation. Did the Browns learn anything from it? Why did Wentz have such a low ranking?

But they refused to make DePodesta available to me or most other
members of the media.

In many conversations during his tenure running the team, Brown
never expressed anything close to such a low opinion of Wentz. His
concern was Wentz not being ready to play right away, especially with
a young team such as the Browns.

Obviously, Brown had no clue Wentz would become a star.

There were some other factors, but when Wentz quickly turned
into a franchise-changing quarterback and Coleman failed, that led
to Haslam deciding to fire Brown before the end of the 2017 season.

The Tidal Wave of History and Frustration

"My mother quit watching."

Too much pain.

That's why Jimmy Haslam fired vice president Sashi Brown with four games left in the 2017 season.

Brown was fired when the franchise had a 1-27 record in his tenure.

Ownership was second-guessing the approach.

"It was just way too hard, way too emotional," Dee Haslam told Kevin Kleps of Crain's Cleveland Business.

As time passed in Haslam's ownership, his wife Dee began to give more interviews and take a more active managerial role.

In the Crain's interview on July 12, 2018, she also said: "The way we did it (tearing down the roster), I don't know that I'd repeat it. I don't know that a fan has the stomach to go through what we've been through the last few years. I will tell you this, we (ownership) don't have it."

Dee Haslam admitted it set the team up for having abundant draft picks and salary cap money to use in the next few seasons.

"I know it was hard on our fan base," she said. "And we (ownership) bled every Sunday night, too. It was brutal."

She also admitted, "We made every mistake in the book."

That may be true, but owners are owners. They can out-live nearly all of their mistakes because they don't have to worry about anyone firing them.

As it turned out, the Haslams simply weren't ready for what was coming.

Dee Haslam even said, "My mother quit watching (the games)."

* * *

Brown took the job in 2016 believing he'd have at least three years to put his approach into place. Brown outlined a 4-year plan to build a team that would win the division. The first two years were going to be "extremely painful," Brown told ownership. Winning should come in the third season, then being a title contender in the fourth year. Brown even told ownership not to put him in charge of the front office if they weren't ready for the "pain from losing."

Of course, Joe Banner thought he'd have three years when he took over as the Browns CEO after Haslam bought the team in 2012.

Banner was gone after a year.

Brown lasted 28 games—not quite two full seasons.

Haslam probably won't admit it. Browns fans and most people in the media don't want to hear it. But the general approach first proposed by Banner and then seriously implemented by Brown was the only way for the Browns to truly improve.

That's my opinion. But there also is some common sense attached to that statement.

Banner and Brown both were right when they said the team drafted poorly. And they were right when they said the franchise invested in too many older free agents who primarily came to Cleveland for a paycheck.

Banner and Brown also were right about the need to pile up draft picks and have a lot of salary cap room to be spent at the right time.

Banner was never allowed to implement his plan in 2014. In that draft, his top two quarterbacks were Teddy Bridgewater and Derek Carr. He planned to keep Brian Hoyer and have the St. Ignatius product start while breaking in the rookie quarterback perhaps later in the season.

At the top of the draft, he was enamored with Khalil Mack, who became a Pro Bowl pass rusher. I know this from conversations I had with Banner after he was fired and before the 2014 draft.

Instead, Ray Farmer (his replacement) went with Justin Gilbert and Johnny Manziel in the first round.

I don't know how Banner would have spent the free agent money. But it's doubtful it would have been on the likes of Donte Whitner and Karlos Dansby, both near the end of their careers. Those players were signed by Farmer in 2014.

This is not to say everything Banner did was right. It is to say if he'd remained as CEO for a few more years, the Browns would have escaped some of the pain to come. There would have been no need for the massive franchise teardown in 2016.

*   *   *

When Haslam turned to Sashi Brown, he probably thought the team could not be any worse than the 3-13 record in 2015.

Like every man who took over the Browns football operation, Brown thought he was getting a fresh start. He believed he had at least three drafts to assemble a viable team capable of competing in the AFC North.

Banner thought that. Mike Holmgren thought that. Eric Mangini thought that . . .

You get the point.

The problem is every new Browns general manager inherits the sins and mistakes of ALL the previous regimes that failed.

The fans and media are cynical and quick to lose faith in any man or any plan.

Brown took over in 2016.

The Browns had not had back-to-back winning seasons since 1988–89.

They had not won a playoff game since 1994.

And those things happened with the "Old Browns," who moved to Baltimore in 1996.

The tone for the new Browns was set when coach Chris Palmer (5-27) was fired after the first two years of the expansion franchise.

CEO Carmen Policy lost power in the four years of the franchise after the death of Owner Al Lerner.

No matter who came to town as head of football operations and/or coach, they were weighed down with the huge psychological baggage of past failures.

There also was fear.

The same for the coaches, who generally were fired every two years—or even after one year in the case of Rob Chudzinski.

If it does work in four years, the coach figures he probably won't be around to see it. He will have suffered so some other coach could win in Cleveland.

*   *   *

Sports Illustrated's Albert Breer wrote an interesting column right after Brown was fired.

"Jimmy Haslam's biggest mistake two years ago wasn't making Sashi Brown captain of his personnel department," wrote Breer. "And it wasn't hiring Hue Jackson to be the head coach. We're here today— with Brown out in Cleveland—because he hired them together."

There was truth to that statement.

It didn't take long to figure out Brown and Jackson were a bad match. Jackson and his veteran coaching staff had little faith in the analytics-driven front office. But this can't be stressed enough: Jackson was desperate to become a head coach again. He was willing to agree to almost any setup. He also figured that a 3-13 team couldn't get any worse, regardless of what the front office did.

The front office allowed Jackson to bring in Robert Griffin III as the starting quarterback in 2016. Analytics had no love for this former phenom who was physically and emotionally damaged by a major knee operation and conflicts with the coaching staff in Washington. The front office also kept veteran Josh McCown as the backup. The idea was between Griffin and McCown, the team had enough experience at quarterback to at least win a few games.

But in typical Cleveland fashion where bad luck plays a role, those quarterbacks suffered major injuries in the first two games. That led to rookie Cody Kessler starting—and he was supposed to be the No. 3

quarterback in 2016. Top pick Corey Coleman broke his hand after the first two games. The losses piled up until the final record was 1-15.

In 2017, the Browns went with a quarterback room of DeShone Kizer, Cody Kessler and Kevin Hogan. None had won even a single NFL game. The front office brought in veteran Brock Osweiler, but Jackson didn't believe Osweiler could help.

There was a clash in the front office over Kizer. The front office didn't want to rush him into action. Jackson thought Kizer's raw ability could develop quickly under his coaching. The front office pushed for Osweiler to play early in the season, simply to spare the young quarterbacks (Kessler and Kizer) from being rushed into action.

Jackson also became intrigued by Hogan. That led to Osweiler being cut.

The lack of a veteran quarterback on the roster would come back to haunt Brown—and be considered another of his failures. But Jackson also should receive some blame as he pushed for the young quarterback room where no one had an NFL victory next to his name.

Soon every front office move was scrutinized and criticized. I'm not going to spend a lot of time breaking down what worked and didn't work. Many have already been dealt with in this book.

Losing divides people—especially people who have no history of success with each other.

Haslam's power structure had Brown and Jackson on the same bottom of a pyramid. They both were reporting to him. That was the same situation with Farmer and coach Mike Pettine. It put the coach and general manager on the same level, and it could easily lead to a power struggle.

Jackson was right when he insisted he had the youngest team in the NFL and how was he supposed to win with so many rookies.

But I often wondered how Chris Palmer found a way to win five games in the first two seasons of the new expansion Browns—but Jackson kept his job after winning only one game in two years.

* * *

Jackson had a lot of friends in the media, far more than Brown.

Soon, stories appeared about how the coaches were set up to fail by the front office. Jackson is liked by the players, and they tended to support him.

Brown was vulnerable because of the two quarterbacks available in consecutive drafts—Carson Wentz and Deshaun Watson—who were emerging as stars before both suffered major knee injuries late in the 2017 season.

Paul DePodesta's quote implying Wentz was not a top 20 quarterback was especially harmful to the front office. I don't believe Brown felt that way about Wentz. Brown saw Wentz as a player requiring time to develop while his team needed oodles of draft picks simply to build up the roster.

"We do go back and look at those decisions," Brown said in his final press conference. "What did we miss? What was all the information we had? How did we gather it? How did we analyze the information and put it together to make decisions?"

He talked about how teams missed on Russell Wilson, a Super Bowl quarterback who was drafted in the third round by Seattle. He mentioned Derek Carr, who was drafted in the second round in 2014—after Johnny Manziel.

"There are a lot of teams that passed on them (Wilson and Carr) who know how to evaluate quarterbacks," said Brown.

Brown was speaking on November 6, 2017. He would be fired a month later.

In that press conference, Brown stressed the need for "replenishing talent" by trading down and adding picks used on young players. He stressed that in the 2018 draft, "I promise you, we are very intent on addressing the quarterback situation."

*   *   *

Making it even worse for Brown was a failed deadline trade for quarterback AJ McCarron.

The Browns were 0-8. Jackson was begging for a veteran quarterback. Jackson was the offensive coordinator in Cincinnati when McCarron was the team's backup. The coach was telling Brown and ownership how McCarron could help the Browns.

The front office talked to the Bengals, who put a high price on McCarron. They wanted several draft picks for a player who would be a free agent at the end of the season. McCarron had started only three games, and those were in 2015.

The Bengals are owned by Mike Brown, son of former Browns coach Paul Brown. Mike Brown often acts as his own general manager. He sensed his dad's old team was ready to make a desperate deal. Serious trade talks didn't start until the morning of October 31, 2017. The trade deadline was 4 p.m.

The price tag was a future second and third round pick—outrageously high for a player who could walk away after eight games. And for a quarterback who hadn't started a game for two years.

Ownership wanted to appease Jackson. The front office was pushed to make a deal. At 3:55 p.m., both teams agreed on the second-and-third round picks. But the paperwork wasn't filed in time.

The Browns—specifically Sashi Brown—were blamed for either botching the trade, or intentionally sabotaging it.

This made the coaches angry. To the public, it appeared the front office was inept.

I remember thinking, "These guys have made 18 trades to this point—many of them far more complicated than this. I don't think incompetence was the problem."

Not long after the deal fell apart, people around the NFL told me the Browns started too late on the trade. It was done at the urging of ownership. It was another example of the front office, coaches and ownership not together on a plan.

Something like that did happen.

At the press conference announcing the hiring of general manager John Dorsey, Haslam said the McCarron mess was "Zero . . . zero" factor when it came to the decision to change the front office.

"I place the blame way more on me than Sashi," said Haslam. "We were having a conversation. I probably pushed the question-asking further than I should. I do not blame that on Sashi. I think we decided to push the go button later than we should . . . Sashi got way (too much blame). I want to make it clear, that had nothing to do with the decision."

It did show how Haslam sometimes inserted himself into the details of trades, creating problems for the front office.

As for McCarron, he signed with Buffalo before the 2018 season. He was given the starting job early in training camp. He lost it. He had some injuries. Before the 2018 season opened, Buffalo traded him to Oakland for a fifth-round pick.

So that deal would have been a real loser for he Browns.

*   *   *

Something else was at work, and it became a tidal wave that sank Brown.

It was history.

It was losing year after year after year.

It was the failures of previous regimes.

The fans and media didn't want to hear about patience because they had been patient for decades. They correctly could ask, "When has patience ever paid off for a Browns fan? When have any of these rebuilding plans ever worked?"

And they didn't want to hear how some of the plans could have paid off if only they were given more time.

When Haslam turned to Sashi Brown, most old-line NFL people predicted it would be a disaster. This sport is not like baseball or basketball, where many front offices are run by men such as Sashi Brown.

This is football. Teams are usually controlled by former players, coaches or guys who worked their way up through the ranks of scouting and player personnel. They are "football men."

Brown could have helped himself by having a veteran "football man" near the top of his front office.

His vice president of player personnel was Andrew Berry, who played football at Harvard. He joined the Colts scouting department in 2009 and began to work his way up. He did a lot of pro scouting. Berry was only 28 when Brown hired him. Unfortunately for Berry, his Ivy League background combined with his youth made him seem like another modern analytics-driven executive to the old football guard.

There was yet another factor causing Haslam to feel the pressure to make a change in the front office.

The owner needed some type of victory. Not only was his football team a loser, he had just come through an embarrassing scandal with his Pilot Flying J company. It was raided by the FBI when allegations of criminal business practices emerged.

Haslam was never charged. But 17 former employees were convicted of fraud-related charges. The company paid $92 million in fines to the government.

So Haslam was going through a period where it seemed absolutely nothing was going right. His business was a mess. His football team was a mess. His front office was being publicly ridiculed. His coach was making a strong case that he had no chance to win.

Someone had to go.

Haslam decided to keep Jackson, no matter what. He knew he would be ridiculed for firing a coach and a general manager so soon. The owner also believed more in Jackson than in Brown.

But Haslam believed he had to do something.

So he began looking for a football man to replace Brown about six weeks into the 2017 season. Several conversations with former Kansas City Chiefs general manager John Dorsey made it easy for Haslam to make that decision.

Brown was out, fired on December 6, 2017. Dorsey was hired the next day.

"For five or six weeks, I talked to former general managers because we needed an experienced player personnel man," said Haslam.

The owner talked about Dorsey being a former player for the Green Bay Packers who then went into scouting and worked his way up to being general manager of the Kansas City Chiefs.

"He's spent his entire adult life in the NFL," said Haslam. "He's done everything you can do in scouting and the front office. He has tremendous contacts with college coaches."

Dorsey was a "football man."

Haslam announced Jackson would be back in 2018, no matter what. The team was 0-12 at that point. So even at 0-16, the coach would keep his job.

I questioned that. So did others.

"It's not just Hue's record," said Haslam. "It's on all of us, including ownership. The team keeps playing hard. I want to see what John and Hue can do together. They're both NFL lifers and identical philosophically."

Or at least, that was what Haslam hoped.

They Really Did Play Like a Brown

"We'll start with you."

Joe Thomas came to the Browns expecting to start, the team assuming he'd be headed for a Pro Bowl career.

That's what it's like when a left tackle is the No. 3 pick in the draft. That was where former general manager Phil Savage grabbed Thomas in 2007.

Then there's Phil Dawson.

At the very least, he should be a member of the Browns Hall of Fame. It's called The Legends Club.

Dawson was the Browns' opening day kicker when the expansion franchise was born in 1999.

At that point, Dawson had no idea he'd join Lou Groza as one of the greatest kickers in the history of the franchise.

When Dawson graduated from the University of Texas, he wasn't drafted despite being an All-American. That's not uncommon. Many teams believe drafting a kicker is a "wasted pick" because you can find one through open tryouts.

Dawson received one of those in 1998. From Oakland. He was cut.

He went to New England. He was placed on the practice squad. He never kicked in a game. After the 1998 season, he was cut.

The Browns were a brand new franchise in 1999. Coach Chris Palmer needed a kicker. He brought in three.

Dawson can't remember the other two. But the last week of training camp arrived, and he was the only one left. He thought he had made the team.

Then Palmer brought in Chris Boniol, who had been in the NFL for five seasons. At one point, he kicked 27 consecutive field goals for the Dallas Cowboys.

From 1994 to 1996, Boniol converted 87 percent of his field goal attempts for Dallas. Anything over 85 percent is considered very good. Then he went to Philadelphia as a free agent, receiving one of the highest contracts ever given a kicker—$2.45 million over four years.

From 1997 to 1998, Boniol began to struggle. His confidence was shaky. He made only 69 percent of his kicks.

When he arrived with the Browns for that final week of the 1999 training camp, he was a veteran battling doubt. But he struck fear into Dawson, who is from Texas and had seen Boniol at his best with the Cowboys.

Dawson survived when Palmer let the kicker know he'd made the team.

"We'll start with you," Palmer told Dawson.

Not exactly a warm endorsement.

"We'll start with you," said Dawson. "Those words have always stayed with me. I'm one kick away from losing a job. Down deep, every kicker knows that."

Dawson and I had a long conversation in 2012 about his early days with the Browns. That turned out to be his last season with the team.

"When I came to the Browns, some of the older players told me how this was a special place to play," he said. "It took a while, but then I began to feel it every time I came though that tunnel on Sunday and heard the fans."

*   *   *

The Browns started with Dawson and it only ended when Joe Banner decided Dawson was not worth big money as a kicker. Like most football people, Banner thought you could find good kickers on minimum contracts.

Banner and I had a long debate about Dawson. I wrote not one, but two columns demanding the Browns re-sign Dawson. He had been with the franchise from the beginning when it came back. He had won 15 games with field goals in the fourth quarter or overtime.

Cleveland is a nightmare for most kickers. The wind whirls and changes. The air grows cold, then icy near the end of the season. It's not just kicking in Cleveland. It's kicking in Cleveland on the shores of Lake Erie.

Dick Goddard was Cleveland's most well-known and respected weatherman. I often referred to Dawson as "Dick Goddard in a helmet." He knew the wind currents. He knew how humidity impacted his kicks.

He wasn't just a great kicker, he was a great kicker in Cleveland.

And he was great for a sad-sack of a franchise where often the only special parts of the team were the special teams.

Joshua Cribbs was an elite return man. Chris Gardocki was an excellent punter for the first five years after the franchise returned.

And Dawson was the best of all.

Dawson explained to me how he checks the weather before a game. He decides how far he can make field goals from each direction.

He'd tell the coach, "I'm good from 53 yards."

He did that before the game and then changed his projections at halftime as winds changed.

"Otherwise, I'd say I can make a kick when I know I can't," he said. "That would put my team in a bad position. I have to be brutally honest."

At the end of the game, he'd try kicks out of his range. There was nothing to lose at that point.

But for Dawson, everything was planning, preparation and then poise when it came time to actually kick in a game.

"It's kicking the ball though yellow posts," Dawson said. "It's what I love and what I hate. It's my chance to help the team, and the last thing I want to do is let the team down."

Dawson seldom did that. He improved as his time with the Browns passed.

Banner never understood what Dawson meant to Cleveland.

"He's a kicker," Banner said to me. "There are a lot of kickers."

"There's only one Phil Dawson," I said.

When the Browns didn't offer Dawson a contract for the 2013 season, he signed with San Francisco.

Between 2013 and 2017, the Browns had six different kickers. That's right, SIX in five seasons attempting to find someone to hold the same job Dawson had for 13 years.

*   *   *

"It might not be a sexy pick in April, but it will work in September."

That's what Phil Savage told the media the day he drafted Joe Thomas.

It's now a legendary story, but it's so Joe Thomas—and what made Thomas one of the most beloved players in Browns history. Thomas knew he was going to be a top 10 pick. He was invited to New York to wear a tuxedo and sit in the green room, waiting to appear on national television when his name was called in the 2007 draft.

Instead, Thomas and his father, his future father-in-law and a close friend went fishing on Lake Michigan. He lived in Milwaukee, and they hit the water in Port Washington, Wisconsin.

Rather than wait for a call about being drafted, they sat around waiting for fish to bite. There was an NFL Network camera on the boat. The biggest fish they caught was a brown trout.

And the Browns caught a 290-pound left tackle who would play in 10 consecutive Pro Bowls and 10,363 snaps in a row before a triceps injury in 2017 ended his streak.

I found the transcript of the phone interview with the Cleveland media done by Thomas immediately after the draft. I was in the press room at the time, but I couldn't remember anything notable other than him fishing on draft day.

But looking back to draft day 2007, Thomas indeed said some remarkable things when heard today.

"If you look at the tackle position, it's been the safest pick in the top 10," he said. "You're talking about a good possibility of a top five tackle being a Pro Bowl player. He's going to be a guy who could potentially go to the Hall of Fame."

Let's stop right here.

This is the day Joe Thomas is drafted. He actually knows nothing about playing in the NFL. But he was underlining the goals for his career without saying them directly.

"If you are going to get a Pro Bowl tackle, you have to get him in the top five," said Thomas. "There might have been a couple of guys in the last 5-6 years who didn't pan out, but I think I'm a vastly different person. My attitude and competitiveness will not let me fail."

*   *   *

A few weeks before the 2017 season opened, Thomas and I talked for a long time at training camp.

We had some fun in the beginning when I asked him what he sees during a game.

"I can't see the quarterback," he said. "I can't see the running back. I can't see the receivers. I know it's either a pass or running play. Sometimes, I take a quick peek at the ball right before it's snapped. But I usually don't know what happened until I hear the crowd."

Meaning what?

"If the crowd is really loud, I know something good or bad happened," he said. "But I don't see it happen."

I wondered if he ever wanted to carry the ball.

"NO!" said Thomas.

Why not?

"I didn't want to go running down the field and have some 250-pounder diving at my legs," he said. "That doesn't sound very attractive."

Especially because Thomas had painful knees for much of his career. He said he didn't know how many knee surgeries he endured, but it was at least five.

He said his dream was to one day recover a fumble in the end zone for a touchdown. But it never happened.

"I recovered a few fumbles in the backfield," he said. "But that's usually because a bad thing happened."

Either his quarterback or running back fumbled.

Thomas said he'd sometimes watch the replays on the scoreboard as he walked back to the huddle, "just so I could see what happened."

*   *   *

One day, I was talking to Browns offensive line coach Bob Wylie. He was the last offensive line coach Thomas had with the Browns.

We were talking about what it took to be a great left tackle. Wylie asked me to put out my arm and try to grab his arm.

I did it, and he sort of karate chopped my hand down.

"Do it again," Wylie said.

I did it again.

Chop.

"Again," he said.

I did again.

Chop.

"Joe Thomas would watch tape of the guy he was playing that week," said Wylie. "He'd see exactly how that guy would reach out. Then Joe would practice knocking his hand away. He did it hundreds of times at just the right angle. Each week, it was a slightly different technique, depending on who he was facing."

The 6-foot-3, 312-pound Thomas had the physical gifts to be a great player. He was a star basketball player in high school. His feet were extremely quick, especially moving side-to-side.

But it was the relentless preparation that made him a Hall of Famer.

"I'd spend two hours a day on my own watching tape of the guy I was facing that week," he said. "During the game, I'd watch my man and a few other guys on defense, trying to get a tip of what was coming. It's 1-on-1. You have to have a healthy respect, even a healthy fear. You need to tell yourself that you must be at your best to beat the guy."

Fear?

"When I'd block my man, it was expected," he said. "You're in constant fear of screwing up because that's the only time you'll be noticed."

The best offensive linemen are invisible to the fans. No one does a celebration dance after delivering the proper block.

"You don't look for those exhilarating moments because they aren't there," he said. "It's not like you can do something really good for your team like score a touchdown, catch a pass or make an interception. Your whole purpose is to avoid a negative."

It's why offensive linemen often became very close. They are the only ones who truly understand the pressure that comes with their jobs. They also know that sometimes when a sack happens, it's not their fault.

"You're blocking a guy where the quarterback is not supposed to be, and the quarterback ends up there," said Thomas. "It's a sack. You can't get stuck on the sack, or your brain will freeze. Everybody thinks you screwed up but you didn't."

That's why the offensive linemen hated to play with Johnny Manziel. The quarterback didn't know the playbook very well. He scrambled around, forgetting how the blocking was set up to protect him. He often ran right into sacks.

*   *   *

Thomas played 11 years with the Browns.

He never had a losing season in junior high, high school or college when he came to Cleveland. The Browns were 10-6 in his rookie year.

They never had a winning record again.

The Browns had a 48-119 record in games played by Thomas.

He played for seven general managers . . .

Six head coaches . . .

Eight offensive coordinators . . .

Five offensive line coaches . . .

Two owners . . .

As for quarterbacks, he blocked for 20 different starters.

When a player is a Pro Bowler and the season is coming to an end with no hope of making the playoffs, it's tempting for the star to skip a game as all the injuries begin to wear him down.

But Thomas played through back spasms, high ankle sprains, pain in both knees and a sore back.

"The team counts on you," said Thomas. "If you're a defensive lineman and you don't go all out on a rush, no one gets hurt. But if I don't block my man, the quarterback can get hurt. I'd think about that. It motivated me."

It's why he refused to miss games until he needed triceps surgery after the seventh game of the 2017 season.

"Once, they tried to take me out," said Thomas. "I can't remember what year, but we were beating the Steelers. Are you kidding me? I was not coming out of that game."

A substitute came into the game to replace him, but Thomas sent the player back to the bench.

In another game, he tore the LCL in his knee.

"I heard a pop," he said. "It didn't feel good. The doctor checked me out and I still had stability in the knee. It was the last game of the year and I finished it. For me, it goes back to the pride thing. I never wanted to let my teammates down. If I'm better than the backup, I wanted to be out there."

Thomas was out there, until he had nothing more to give. While the triceps surgery ended his 2017 season, it was the brittle knees that screamed it was time to retire.

"I always wanted to retire with the Browns," he said. "I had people tell me that they wouldn't begrudge me if I wanted to leave. I never wanted to leave. When I first got to Cleveland, I understood the history of the Browns. My mission was to be there when the turn-around happened. I wanted to be part of the solution."

He never wanted out?

"Never," said Thomas. "I was tired. I was discouraged. But I never wanted to leave the Browns."

Can They Finally Get It Right?

"Any personnel man worth his weight would want this job."

Part of the reason John Dorsey was so excited about the chance to become the Browns general manager in 2018 was the treasure chest of draft picks and salary cap room inherited from Sashi Brown.

"Any personnel man worth his weight would want this job," Dorsey said the day he was hired. "Not many personnel guys in my position would pass this up. Sashi did a great job creating some draft picks and salary cap space."

Dorsey was handed two first round picks in the top four of the 2018 draft, and five picks among the first 64 choices. The team also had about $100 million in salary cap space.

That's why he was willing to agree to Haslam's prerequisite of keeping Jackson as head coach.

Yes, it was another shotgun football marriage officiated by Haslam. They barely knew each other when Dorsey was hired. In some ways, it was like Haslam pairing Ray Farmer with Mike Pettine in 2014. The big difference was Dorsey had far more experience and a winning track record as an executive.

Dorsey grew up in an old-school scouting system under Ron Wolf with the Green Bay Packers. He had spent much of his adult life in a film room, looking at video of prospects.

He also knew analytics had become a dirty word to most in the Cleveland media and to Browns fans.

He went right to work.

Dorsey preferred trading for big name players rather than trying to sign them as free agents.

On the eve of free agency, Dorsey did something I've never seen from a Browns executive—he made two huge trades. He shipped a third-round pick to Buffalo for quarterback Tyrod Taylor. And he traded fourth- and seventh-round picks to Miami for receiver Jarvis Landry.

Both players had one year and $16 million left on their contracts. Both of their teams were looking to shed those salaries.

Landry was a Pro Bowl receiver who never missed a game in his first four pro seasons and only 25 years old when joining the Browns.

As Dorsey told me, it signaled "the Browns were open for business . . . and very serious about getting better."

*   *   *

Dorsey knew he planned to draft quarterback Baker Mayfield. He wanted the rookie to be in a quarterback room with veterans who knew how to win games—and do the right things in the NFL. So Dorsey added 34-year-old Drew Stanton as a backup. Stanton had an 11-6 record as a spot starter in the NFL heading into the 2018 season.

It's a good bet Sashi Brown would have drafted Baker Mayfield. Analytics loved the Oklahoma quarterback. He rarely threw interceptions. He was very accurate and had a stronger arm than many thought—because he's only 6-foot.

The analytics site Pro Football Focus swooned over Mayfield, insisting he was the best college quarterback prospect in several years.

Even after being fired by the Kansas City Chiefs, Dorsey kept acting like a general manager and scout. He watched a lot of video of quarterbacks. He scouted Mayfield six times in person.

His scout's eye was watching what the numbers revealed: This was a poised quarterback who started 39 games for one of the premier college football programs. Playing for Oklahoma is like being in the

NFL because the Sooners are the biggest story in that state, where there is no pro team.

Mayfield also had seven starts as a freshman at Texas Tech, giving him 46 for his college career. He completed 68 percent of his passes with 131 touchdowns compared to only 30 interceptions.

*   *   *

Listening to Dorsey and watching his moves, it was clear he was embracing a sizable portion of the data brought to him by Paul DePodesta and the others doing analytics for the Browns.

He was blending old and new school, hoping for a quick turn-around in Cleveland.

The plan made sense. A lot of things could go wrong—quarterback changes, coaching changes, other changes . . . After all, these are the Browns. But at the start of the 2018 season it seemed possible the 4-44 record from 2015 to 2017 could produce something good in the future.

*   *   *

That's right, the Browns were once again starting a new season on a hopeful note.

And if you're a Browns fan, part of you really wants to believe.

Acknowledgments

Thanks to Roberta, my wife of 41 years, who is the first read on all my projects. She also transcribed tapes of interviews. This is my 32nd book, and she has been a huge part of all of them. Too bad the Browns didn't find, recruit, and draft someone like you—the franchise would play for the Super Bowl every year! I married on a huge upgrade.

Thanks to Larry Pantages, my outstanding researcher and friend —and former sports editor at the *Akron Beacon Journal*. If only the Browns had found a quarterback like Larry back in 1999. He did a tremendous job in editing my stuff and going through all the emails from fans.

Thanks to John Luttermoser, a wonderful copy editor and fact-checker. I'm grateful to have had his help on this project.

Thanks to David Gray, my long-time publisher and friend. You have been a tremendous support all these years.

OTHER BOOKS OF INTEREST . . .

Things I've Learned from Watching the Browns
Terry Pluto

Veteran sports writer Terry Pluto asks Cleveland Browns fans: Why, after four decades of heartbreak, teasing, and futility, do you still stick with this team? Their stories, coupled with Pluto's own insight and analysis, deliver the answers. Like any intense relationship, it's complicated. But these fans just won't give up.

"For dedicated Browns fans [the book is] like leafing through an old family photo album." – BlogCritics.com

Browns Town 1964
The Cleveland Browns and the 1964 Championship
Terry Pluto

A nostalgic look back at the upstart AFC Cleveland Browns' surprising 1964 championship victory over the hugely favored Baltimore Colts. Profiles the colorful players who made that season memorable, including Jim Brown, Paul Warfield, Frank Ryan. Recreates an era and a team for which pride was not just a slogan.

"Pluto movingly reveals the substance of a mythic bond between men and a game, a team and a city—and thus lays bare how present-day pro football has surrendered its soul." – Kirkus Reviews

False Start
How the New Browns Were Set Up to Fail
Terry Pluto

A hard look at the unhappy beginnings of the post-1999 Cleveland Browns franchise, this book chronicles the backroom deals, big-money power plays, poor decisions, and plain bad luck that dogged the venerable franchise after Art Modell skipped town in 1995. How long should fans have to wait for a winner? A book the NFL does not want you to read.

"[A book] NFL fans in general and Browns' fans in particular will definitely want to read . . . a fascinating, behind-the-scenes look at how the new Browns were created and what's kept them from making the progress everyone expected." – Houston Chronicle

Read samples at **www.grayco.com**

OTHER BOOKS OF INTEREST . . .

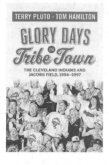

Glory Days in Tribe Town
The Cleveland Indians and Jacobs Field 1994–1997

Terry Pluto, Tom Hamilton

Relive the most thrilling seasons of Indians baseball in recent memory! Cleveland's top sportswriter teams up with the Tribe's veteran radio announcer and fans to share favorite stories from the first years of Jacobs Field, when a star-studded roster (Belle, Thome, Vizquel, Ramirez, Alomar, Nagy) and a sparkling ballpark captivated an entire city.

Our Tribe
A Baseball Memoir

Terry Pluto

A son, a father, a baseball team. Sportswriter Terry Pluto's memoir tells about growing up and learning to understand a difficult father through their shared love of an often awful baseball team. Baseball can be an important bridge across generations, sometimes the only common ground. This story celebrates the connection.

"A beautiful, absolutely unforgettable memoir." – Booklist

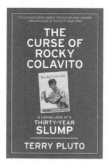

The Curse of Rocky Colavito
A Loving Look at a Thirty-Year Slump

Terry Pluto

A baseball classic. No sports fans suffered more miserable teams for more seasons than Indians fans of the 1960s, '70s, and '80s. Here's a fond and often humorous look back at "the bad old days" of the Tribe. The definitive book about the Indians of that generation, and a great piece of sports history writing.

"The year's funniest and most insightful baseball book." – Chicago Tribune

Read samples at **www.grayco.com**

OTHER BOOKS OF INTEREST . . .

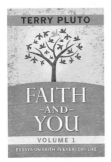

Faith and You Vol. 1
Essays on Faith in Everyday Life

Terry Pluto

Thoughtful essays on faith in everyday life from award-winning sportswriter Terry Pluto, who has also earned a reputation—and a growing audience—for his down-to-earth musings on spiritual subjects. Topics include choosing a church, lending money to friends, dealing with jerks, sharing your faith, visiting the sick, even planning a funeral.

Faith and You Vol. 2
More Essays on Faith in Everyday Life

Terry Pluto

More thoughtful essays by Terry Pluto ("the sportswriter who writes about faith"), based on his popular Plain Dealer column "Faith and You." These plain and personal musings discuss topics we all face in everday life: insults and what they really mean, prayers delayed or unanswered, sibling rivalry, relating to our fathers, losing a pet, and more.

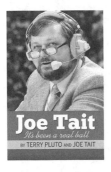

Joe Tait: It's Been a Real Ball
Stories from a Hall-of-Fame Sports Broadcasting Career

Terry Pluto, Joe Tait

Legendary broadcaster Joe Tait is like an old family friend to three generations of Cleveland sports fans. This book celebrates the inspiring career of "the Voice of the Cleveland Cavaliers" with stories from Joe and dozens of fans, colleagues, and players. Hits the highlights of a long career and also uncovers some touching personal details.

"An easy, fun book to read and will surely bring back good memories for Cleveland sports fans who listened to Tait's trademark calls since 1970."
– 20SecondTimeout.com

OTHER BOOKS OF INTEREST . . .

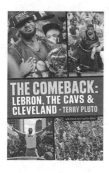

The Comeback: LeBron, the Cavs & Cleveland
How LeBron James Came Home and Brought a Championship to Cleveland

Terry Pluto

One of the greatest Cleveland sports stories ever! In this epic homecoming tale, LeBron James and the Cavaliers take fans on a roller coaster ride from despair to hope and, finally, to glory as the 2016 NBA champions. Terry Pluto tells how it all happened, with insightful analysis and behind-the-scenes details.

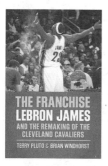

The Franchise
LeBron James and the Remaking of the Cleveland Cavaliers

Terry Pluto, Brian Windhorst

An in-depth look at how a team and a city were rebuilt around LeBron James. Two award-winning sports journalists tell the converging stories of a struggling franchise and a hometown teenage phenom. Will fascinate basketball fans who want the inside story of a young superstar shouldering the weight of an entire NBA franchise.

"Not your typical sports biography . . . Take[s] the reader behind the scenes in the Cavaliers' front office, revealing how championship contenders are built" – Library Journal

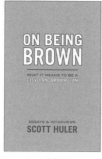

On Being Brown
What it Means to Be a Cleveland Browns Fan

Scott Huler

What makes Browns fans so . . . different? These 33 essays explain: It's about pride. It's about desire, tempered by crushing disappointment. It's about tradition, rivalry, and electrifying victory. It's about longing. It's about heart. Includes interviews with Jim Brown, Lou Groza, Paul Warfield, Ozzie Newsome, and other legends.

Read samples at **www.grayco.com**